Cyber Security on Azure

An IT Professional's Guide
to Microsoft Azure Security

Second Edition

Marshall Copeland
Matthew Jacobs

Apress®

Cyber Security on Azure: An IT Professional's Guide to Microsoft Azure Security

Marshall Copeland
Austin, TX, USA

Matthew Jacobs
Nashville, TN, USA

ISBN-13 (pbk): 978-1-4842-6530-7
https://doi.org/10.1007/978-1-4842-6531-4

ISBN-13 (electronic): 978-1-4842-6531-4

Managing Director, Apress Media LLC: Welmoed Spahr
Acquisitions Editor: Smriti Srivastava
Development Editor: Laura Berendson
Coordinating Editor: Shrikant Vishwakarma

Cover designed by eStudioCalamar

Cover image designed by Pexels

Distributed to the book trade worldwide by Springer Science+Business Media LLC, 1 New York Plaza, Suite 4600, New York, NY 10004. Phone 1-800-SPRINGER, fax (201) 348-4505, e-mail orders-ny@springer-sbm.com, or visit www.springeronline.com. Apress Media, LLC is a California LLC and the sole member (owner) is Springer Science + Business Media Finance Inc (SSBM Finance Inc). SSBM Finance Inc is a **Delaware** corporation.

For information on translations, please e-mail booktranslations@springernature.com; for reprint, paperback, or audio rights, please e-mail bookpermissions@springernature.com.

Apress titles may be purchased in bulk for academic, corporate, or promotional use. eBook versions and licenses are also available for most titles. For more information, reference our Print and eBook Bulk Sales web page at http://www.apress.com/bulk-sales.

Any source code or other supplementary material referenced by the author in this book is available to readers on GitHub via the book's product page, located at www.apress.com/978-1-4842-6530-7. For more detailed information, please visit http://www.apress.com/source-code.

Printed on acid-free paper

Thank you Angela Copeland for your love and support on this "one more book." Thank you Mark Hilley for saving lives as a Firefighter EMT First Responder. Thank you Matthew Jacobs for giving up weekends and providing cloud security insight; you have a future as a cyber security "blue team" leader. A very special thank you to life-long friends and family, Tara Larson, Anthony Puca, Julian Soh, Keith Olinger, Mark Ghazai, Eric Schwindt, and Jaime Segura.

—Marshall Copeland

For my wonderfully supportive wife Elizabeth Jacobs, who has always pushed me to go further than I have ever imagined. I am forever grateful. To my mother Anita Hale, thank you for all you have done to make this possible. Thank you to my mentors and friends, Cayce Borden, Brent Reynolds, Andy Bullington, Zach Hoover, Jay Sundberg, Jeff Prouse, Sharon Asmus, Vern Hall, Rusty Martin, David Joseph, Andrew Scott, Maher Aldineh, and Ben Moss.

—Matthew Jacobs

Table of Contents

About the Authors

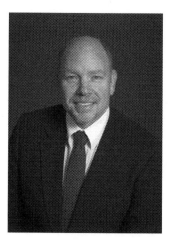

Marshall Copeland is a cloud security architect focused on helping customers "shift left" with cloud security defenses in Azure public cloud using cloud-native services and third-party network security appliances. He uses Infrastructure as Code (IaC) with ARM templates or Terraform HCL to build cloud infrastructure and disaster recovery solutions. Marshall's Azure security design skills include Azure Sentinel, Security Center, Policy, Firewall, and ACL networking and a few open source solutions such as ELK stack, Wireshark, and Snort. He partners with security operations to guide cloud investigations to enhance "blue team hunting" efficiencies.

Matthew Jacobs is a system engineer focused on cloud architecture technologies needed to support identity management, security, and collaboration toolsets for small and medium businesses, including enterprise organizations. His work has focused on digital transformation, including on-premises only, hybrid cloud networks, and complete public cloud-only deployment. Matthew brings a hands-on cloud architecture approach for Identity and Access Management (IAM) and enhanced engineering to enable business agility that secures and supports a global remote workforce. His current work in the Nashville, Tennessee, area includes Fortune 500 media, entertainment, and hospitality companies, and his work history extends into public cloud federal compliance requirements for the banking and healthcare industries.

About the Technical Reviewer

Vidya Vrat Agarwal is a software architect, author, blogger, Microsoft MVP, C# Corner MVP, speaker, and a mentor. He is a TOGAF Certified Architect and a Certified Scrum Master (CSM). He is currently working as a Principal Architect at T-Mobile Inc., USA. He started working on Microsoft .NET with its first beta release. Vidya is passionate about people, process, and technology and loves to contribute to the .NET community. He lives in Redmond, WA, United States, with his wife Rupali, two daughters Pearly and Arshika, and a female puppy Angel.

Acknowledgments

Special acknowledgment to Shrikant Vishwakarma, Smriti Srivastava, and the Apress team; we are so thankful for your guidance, support, and expert advice on this publication. Thank you to Vidya Vrat Agarwal for his professional technical resources; we are very fortunate to have your expert skills for this publication. The Apress team is a fantastic company to help technical people share their knowledge at a global level.

Introduction

The first edition of this book in 2017 placed cyber security front and center to teams of IT professionals who may not have focused on cyber security. This second edition is completely rewritten and updated, with more than 70% of the book containing brand-new Azure cloud security topics. Business relies more on subject matter experts (SME), the professional resources, as they continue to secure applications and data in the cloud. This second edition goes deeper on Azure security features that did not exist a few years ago. This publication is an ambitious resource to provide readers a strong foundation to learn and deploy Azure security best practices.

This book comes from several years of lessons learned and late nights of trying to understand the what, how, and why. Having worked with several customers and organizations moving to cloud-focused technologies, this book will aid in choosing the right path for planning and moving forward with a cloud strategy. It will also empower organizations to start taking their first steps toward cloud adoption, cloud migration, and creating governance around an ever-changing technology and toolset.

This book was written for the following types of IT/cloud professionals:

- IT subject-matter experts (SMEs)

- IT professionals looking to expand their knowledge of cloud technologies

- Cyber security teams

This second edition does not repeat guidance to review current cyber security reports; that should now be part of your security practice. You expand beyond Azure Security Center and learn to use new and updated Azure native security services like Azure Sentinel, Privileged Identity Management, Azure Firewalls, and SQL Advanced Threat Protection and how best to protect Azure Kubernetes Services. Open this book and begin the deep dive into Microsoft Azure Security.

PART I

Zero Trust Cloud Security

In Part 1, the focus is on the configuration of Azure cloud-native security solutions to support a Zero Trust model. Let us first understand the that cloud native are security solutions created by Microsoft Azure for consumption in your Azure Tenant and subscriptions. You need to consider what supports the Azure Tenant, which more closely is tied to the identity layer, and what native solutions support the subscription layer.

The subscription layer has machines, which are tied directly to identity and customer data. The data is what every "bad actor" is attempting to copy, augment, or damage.

The cyber security challenges are used to classify Azure cloud security needs to better focus on improving your security posture in the cloud. Traditional on-premises have been enabling security in different verticals, networks, identities, users, systems, applications, and data.

In every chapter, security tools and techniques are introduced and real-world examples of how attacks were achieved, and each example trains the Azure Security operations teams using the cyber kill chain as their "north star." Blue teams in the cloud need to learn how to disrupt the kill chain at every link. The reader is introduced to the most current command and control (C&C or C2) information framework to support examples. The tool is used to identify hacker techniques based on their past attacks and forensics. Examples will expand on different attack techniques with exercises to upskill their Azure cloud security knowledge from these community-supported tools (https://attack.mitre.org/ and www.thec2matrix.com/matrix).

CHAPTER 1

Reduce Cyber Security Vulnerabilities: Identity Layer

Navigating the shifting landscape of security can be a daunting task, especially when making the jump to cloud services or after reading about the latest breach that happened to "Company Z." It can be confusing learning a new technology as both the threats and the platforms we use evolve every day. By understanding and implementing some of the concepts and technologies outlined in this chapter, you will stay on the forefront of the emerging trends in cyber security.

In this chapter, we will explain some of the mechanisms to create layers of protection around your Azure Tenant; how to manage Azure users and groups, utilizing Azure Active Directory (AAD) as your Identity Management solution with OAuth, SAML, or AD Connect; and how to set up Privileged Identity Management.

Note The topics and guidelines in this chapter represent how to take your first steps to managing your identity in Azure. We cover a baseline that can be tailored to fit your specific organizational needs.

© Marshall Copeland and Matthew Jacobs 2021
M. Copeland and M. Jacobs, *Cyber Security on Azure*, https://doi.org/10.1007/978-1-4842-6531-4_1

Azure Cloud Relations: Tenant, Subscription, Resources

As organizations start their journey toward migrating to full cloud with Azure or by expanding their environment to include Azure in normal operations, we have to beware of a new attack vector in our security posture. Tenant security, which encompasses our subscription, resources, and our Azure AD are all now in play for potential exploitation. In this section, we will outline where the responsibility falls for Tenant security based on your service model and create some controls around your subscription, resources, and APIs.

Azure Tenant Security

Tenant security can seem like one of the most daunting tasks to tackle. Since Microsoft Azure is a public tenant, there is a certain level of responsibility that is shared between Microsoft and the consumer. Your organization's use of Azure for Infrastructure as a Service (IaaS), Platform as a Service (PaaS), or Software as a Service (SaaS) will drive the amount of effort needed to implement security controls.

We can break down the responsibility into three parts: Microsoft, shared, and consumer. No matter which scenario, governance around the physical data centers that Azure resides is Microsoft's responsibility. Microsoft will manage the availability, security controls, and vulnerability for the base on which the Azure platform resides. The consumer is always responsible for the users, data, and level of access within the platform. The shared responsibilities are mixed between the three service models. IaaS commands more responsibility on the consumer side, PaaS is generally 50/50, and SaaS puts more responsibility on Microsoft (Figure 1-1).

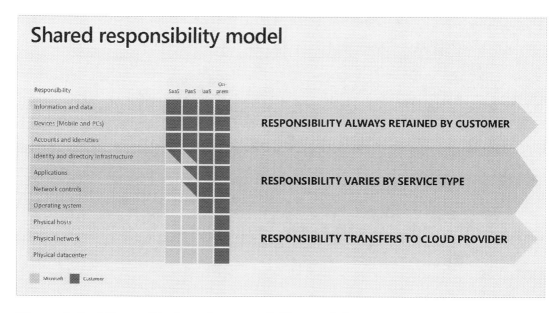

Figure 1-1. *Microsoft's shared responsibility model*

Even through all of these different responsibilities and configurations, Microsoft provides a basic toolset. Activity logs, alerting, and metrics are all configurable to your custom criteria. Take advantage of the work Azure does behind the scenes populating the toolset.

Azure Subscription Security

At first glance, it may seem inconsequential to talk about subscription security. You may be asking, "What kind of data can be stolen from my subscriptions?" Some attackers are not always out for financial gain or to harvest data, but to cause disruption of service. There is also an internal threat from your daily administrators and end users. An end user or administrator may accidently navigate to a section of the Azure portal and inadvertently cause harm. Due to Azure being primarily an operational expenditure, the quickest way to sour an organization's experience with Azure is an extreme increase in cost. The easiest control put in place is an Azure Management Group.

Azure Management Groups are used for access control, policy, and compliance for subscriptions across the tenant. You can deploy an Azure Management Group through the Azure portal, PowerShell, or Azure CLI. Similar to NTFS permissions where you can apply different actionable items to a user or group, the same concept applies to a management group. Owners have the ability to do everything, Contributors can do everything but assign access, and Readers can read. For tighter controls, we can also apply the roles of MG Reader or MG Contributor, which only allow for actions within the management scope. Refer to Figure 1-2 for a detail of roles and actions.

Azure Role Name	Create	Rename	Move**	Delete	Assign Access	Assign Policy	Read
Owner	X	X	X	X	X	X	X
Contributor	X	X	X	X			X
MG Contributor*	X	X	X	X			X
Reader							X
MG Reader*							X
Resource Policy Contributor						X	
User Access Administrator					X	X	

*: MG Contributor and MG Reader only allow users to do those actions on the management group scope.

**: Role Assignments on the Root management group aren't required to move a subscription or management group to and from it.

Figure 1-2. *Microsoft Azure Role-Based Access Control (RBAC) table*

Azure API Security

An application programming interface (API) is one of the mechanisms by which we can deliver requests of information from a single service or multiple services at the same time. At its simplest form, we use an API by sending a request containing information we would like to receive to a given service. The service will review our request, run through a predefined process, and return information back for use. Azure allows organizations to enable a centralized location for the management of APIs within your tenant. API management is broken down into three main parts: API Gateways, the Azure portal, and the developer portal. An API Gateway serves as the external facing entry for access. The Azure portal is where you can administer your policies, create security metrics, and manage access. The developer portal is where you can manage your API documentation and allow web developers the access for integration with your APIs.

According to the Microsoft documentation (`https://docs.microsoft.com/en-us/azure/api-management/security-baseline`): "Azure provides a solid foundation in which to host and manage your organizations APIs but there is a baseline of security practices that should be followed to enhance the security within the platform. Some of the best practices recommended from Microsoft are to Deploy your API Management inside of your Virtual Network in Azure, Monitor the traffic to and from your APIs by using Network Security Groups with flow logs, Create detailed documentation around network traffic rules, Configure a Central Log Management with Azure Sentinel, Perform Regular Audits of accounts access."

Azure Resource Locks

Azure resource locks are a mechanism built into Azure that will allow you to freeze an object from being deleted or being changed. Implementing a resource lock allows for greater safeguards to protect your mission-critical objects inside of Azure. Whether you are creating a barrier for someone who has infiltrated your tenant or the passing administrator that makes an accidental click, it is important to understand the different levels and how they apply. Resource locks can be initiated at three different levels: subscription, resource groups, and the resource. When applying a resource lock, you can set the properties to either CanNotDelete or ReadOnly. Once applied, a resource lock will negate any Role-Based Access Control inherited from a group or subscription, and it will require a conscious administrative override to remove.

In this example, we will create a lock on a resource group.

1. Log in to your Azure Tenant with an account that has an ownership or a user access administrator role.

2. Navigate to the resource group you want to enable the lock on and select it.

3. In the left-hand column, select the Locks option.

4. Enter a description for the lock name and select delete.

5. Add some notes for why you are enabling the lock.

6. Click Okay.

Accomplish this in PowerShell by running New-AzResourceLock:

```
New-AzResourceLock -LockName LockOnCriticalResource -LockLevel CanNotDelete
-ResourceGropuName myResourceGroup
```

> **Note**   Be careful when applying resource locks in certain areas of the Azure tenant as they will block some of the basic functionality of automation such as Azure Resource Manager or Azure Backup service.

Managing Azure Active Directory: Users and Groups

Azure Active Directory (Azure AD) becomes your centralized Identity Management platform for your users to access applications in the cloud and in your on-premises environment. Azure AD uses the same concepts and objects that you are used to in a traditional on-premises Active Directory. Azure AD allows for the creation of users and groups either directly from the tenant or by syncing them from an existing Active Directory deployment using Azure Active Directory Connect, which is discussed in a later section. For organizations that are hybrid cloud or federated with Azure, your on-premises Active Directory will act as your source of truth for any accounts and groups that are replicated to the cloud.

Azure Users

Azure introduces a new flexible option when it comes to managing end user access with the ability to have internal and guest user accounts. In a traditional Active Directory, the entirety of your user base exists completely in your on-premises environment under a set of policies. Adding an external user's access to your tenant provides the flexibility to work with consultants and contract workers without needing to provide access to all of your consumable resources and on-premises resources. For example, when a guest user is added, it will take one license seat in Azure, but it will negate the need to provision the user for email and productivity applications. In the same regard, adding guest users to the tenant instead of syncing them from on-premises provides an air gap between them and your local resources. You will still be about to enforce Multi-Factor and Conditional Access Policies, discussed in a later section, for your guest users.

Azure Groups

Azure groups allow us to combine users together into one object that we can reuse multiple times. In Azure, we have two different group types: security groups and Office365 groups. An Office365 group is used when you are creating a group that is intended for collaboration with email, SharePoint, and teams. When creating an Office365 group, you will set an email address associated with the group that will serve as a distribution list in Exchange and will create a teams/SharePoint site. This type of group is ideal when setting up whole departments such as HR. It should be used to include everyone rather than being granular. For more granularity, we use a security group which has two different configuration types: direct and dynamic. A security group in Azure that has direct membership is similar to a security group in an on-premises Active Directory Group. A dynamic group in Azure reuses the concept of an Exchange dynamic distribution group and affords us some more automation of managing our security group. Dynamic groups can be used to target devices or users.

CREATING A DYNAMIC USER GROUP

1. Log in to your Azure Tenant using an account with global administrator access.

2. Select Azure Active Directory.

3. Click Groups.

4. Click New Group.

5. Leave the Group type Security.

6. Enter the name of the group.

7. Select Membership type as Dynamic User.

    a. Notice the Create button is grayed out until we set a query.

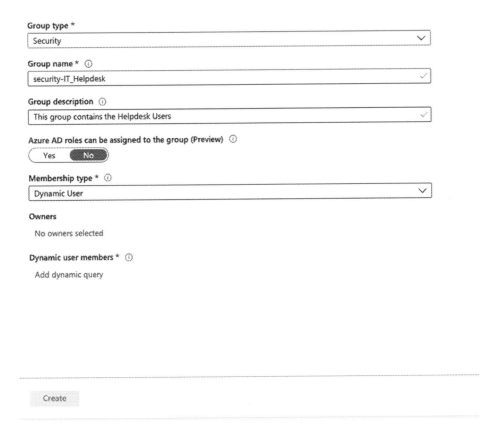

8. Click Add dynamic query.

9. Add the attributes needed to populate the group.

Dynamic membership rules   ✕

🖫 Save   ✕ Discard | ♡ Got feedback?

Configure Rules   Validate Rules (Preview)

You can use the rule builder or rule syntax text box to create or edit a dynamic membership rule. ⓘ Learn more

And/Or	Property	Operator	Value	
	department	Equals	Information Technology .	🗑
And ⌄	jobTitle ⌄	Contains ⌄	Helpdesk	🗑

╀ Add expression ╀ Get custom extension properties ⓘ

Rule syntax   ✎ Edit

(user.department -eq "Information Technology") and (user.jobTitle -contains "Helpdesk")

10. To validate your results, click Validate Rules.

11. Add a user or users to test your syntax.

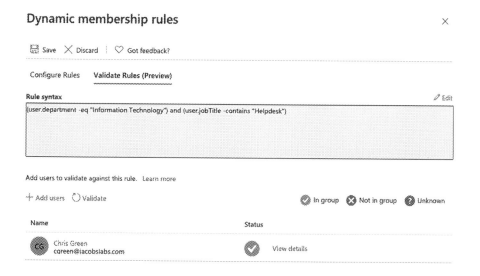

12. Edit your syntax as needed by clicking Edit or Configure Rules.

13. Once you see the results you expect, click Save.

14. You will be taken back to the original New Group create page, and the Create button is no longer grayed out. Click Create.

Your membership may not be populated immediately as the rules will take time to process (Figure 1-3). Once completed, you will see your members added to the group (Figure 1-4).

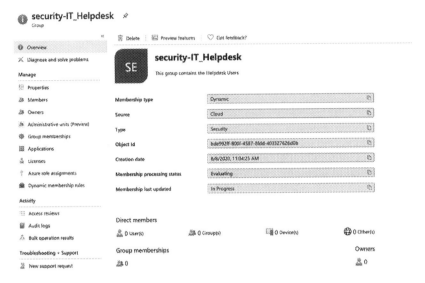

Figure 1-3. *Processing a dynamic membership*

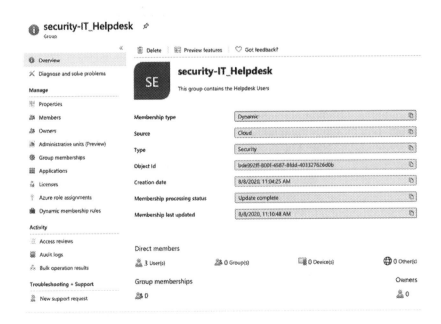

Figure 1-4. *Dynamic membership complete*

REAL-WORLD USE

Company A creates dynamic groups to assign licensing based on the role of an end user. Subscribing to different licensing plans for collaboration, the company can leverage a dynamic group to assign licensing for its customer-facing workers who need a Microsoft E1 plan and its corporate workers who need an E5 plan. By searching for the department, job title, and office location, we set up the licensing to automatically be assigned once the user was created in Azure or replicated from Active Directory.

Azure Active Directory: OAuth, SAML, AD Connect

The days of needing to remember a username and password for every application are in the past. The concept of identity has evolved to encapsulate Single Sign-On (SSO), Multi-Factor Authentication (MFA), and the trust between an Identity Provider (IdP) and a Service Provider (SP). Similar to how Active Directory Federation Services (ADFS) provide a trust between internal applications and third-party resources, Azure Active Directory has the ability to become your organization's IdP and create the same level of federation or trust. There are multiple ways in which Azure AD can provide a trust to your organization's internal, external, and third-party applications.

OAuth

Open Authorization (OAuth) allows for applications and services to interface with a user's Identity Provider by establishing a trust between the provider's server and the service provider's application. When a user or administrator grants access to the requesting application, a token is generated and distributed to the client. The token contains the scope of access and the IdP information for which the application can trust a valid authentication.

It is important to understand that when you accept an OAuth connection, you may not be accepting it for the entire organization. The scope of the request is dictated based on the access level of the user granting permissions. When accepting an OAuth request, be sure to provide the correct level of administrative access to your tenant. Most applications will have an option to "Consent on behalf of the Organization," allowing for an administrator to authorize for the whole tenant.

For Example: Application "A" is Requesting Access to your Organization

- Administrators
  - Grant for me and only me
  - Grant on behalf of my organization
- Users
  - Grant for me and only me

OAuth connections will specify what user attributes are being requested from the application. These values are coded in the application by the application's development team. While it is possible to modify the attributes and access tokens that have been generated for your tenant, doing so may cause unexpected behavior to your production environment.

Note   Read all the documentation when integrating an application to gain a better understanding of the appropriate access needed and information being requested.

SAML

Security Assertion Markup Language or SAML uses Extensible Markup Language (XML) to provide a trust relationship for authentication. At its core, SAML is very similar to Active Directory Federation Services (ADFS). In both technologies, there are three main components: the user, the Identity Provider (IdP), and the Service Provider (SP). SAML requests are done via a web browser such as Microsoft Edge but can be initiated when a program has an internally built web browser that can be used for initiated SAML requests such as Cisco AnyConnect Mobility Client.

When setting up an application or a service to use SAML for SSO, there are some key components to enable between the IdP and the SP. The SP will need access to the IdP's application's SAML metadata, a signed certificate from the IdP, and the login or access URL of the application for where to send the SAML requests. The IdP will need to be configured with the namespace or Uniform Resource Identifier (URI) and the reply

Uniform Resource Locator (URL). The URI or namespace is generally a unique identifier that maps your users to your instance of the application. The reply URL is where your IdP will send the validated token back to the application, acknowledging a valid user, and the attributes associated with that user.

The following are the basic steps involved in the SSO with SAML sign-on process. To illustrate how this works, refer to Figure 1-5.

1. The end user client navigates to the SP.

2. The SP initiates a redirect (Redirect 1) to the IdP for authentication.

3. The end user client redirects (Redirect 2) to the IdP.

4. The IdP receives the request and asks for authentication from the end user.

5. The IdP creates a SAML assertion and replies to Redirect 2.

6. Now that Redirect 2 is complete, the client replies to Redirect 1.

7. The SP receives the SAML assertion and sends the session back to the client.

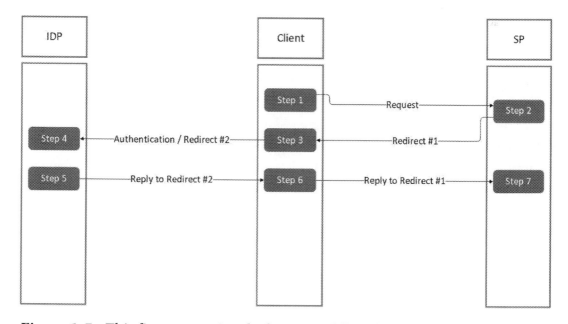

Figure 1-5. *This figure contains the basic workflow for how SSO is achieved using SAML*

AD Connect

Azure Active Directory Connect, also referred to as Azure AD Connect, is a powerful tool that allows you to join your on-premises Active Directory to Azure Active Directory (AAD). This tool can be deployed with different configurations to provide you with the most flexibility, depending upon your organization's needs. Having a clear direction of how your organization will use Azure is critical before taking the first steps in setting up Azure AD Connect. There are two distinct scenarios to understand when navigating through the Azure AD Connect setup: federation with on-premises Active Directory Federation Services (ADFS) and non-federation. In each scenario, you should deploy the use of Password Hash Synchronization (PHS). PHS creates a hash file or checksum that is stored in the cloud that will be used to validate a user's password when attempting to log in. As an added benefit, Microsoft will use these hashes to find credentials that have been leaked and that can potentially be used for exploitation.

As mentioned, it is extremely important to develop a technological road map for how you will deploy, migrate, and integrate your Azure AD Connect deployment. Federation and non-federation provide two completely different topologies and user experiences. It is not advisable to start down either path before having organizational and stakeholder buy-in. Without proper planning, you may find yourself caught managing two Identity Providers, creating an overcomplicated topology, and frustrating yourself, your organization, and end users.

Federation with ADFS

Federation with ADFS allows you to change your tenant from acting as the primary IdP to acting as the Service Provider (SP). By federating your tenant with an on-premises ADFS deployment, all users will be redirected to your on-premises domain for authentication. This scenario is ideal for organizations that are heavily integrated with ADFS for Single Sign-On (SSO) with limited options to move to cloud or are looking to extend their presence into the cloud without switching to a full cloud model for Identity Management. A basic illustration of this is represented in Figure 1-6.

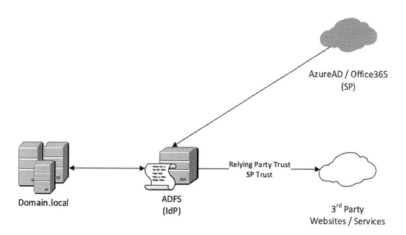

Figure 1-6. *This is a simple example of federation with ADFS as the IdP*

When choosing to federate your Azure AD, be sure to enable Password Hash Synchronization and have an adequate level of redundancy built into your on-premises environment. If you lose connectivity to your local ADFS deployment through Internet Service Provider outages, hardware failures, or local configuration changes, you can rely on Password Hash Synchronization as a backup method for authentication instead of needing to reference ADFS. One precaution is the longer amount of disconnect between your domain, the less up to date your Password Hashes, causing a potential influx of password mismatches when service is restored.

Non-federation

Choosing not to federate extends your Identity Management from local Active Directory to your Azure Tenant. Unlike federation, Azure AD becomes your IdP, and all other applications that are deployed in Azure or integrated with Azure will act as Service Providers. When deploying Azure AD Connect with Password Hash Synchronization, you also enable your on-premises Active Directory to become your source of truth for accounts that exist locally and in the cloud. A basic illustration of this is represented in Figure 1-7.

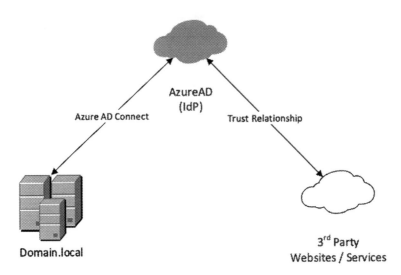

Figure 1-7. *This is a simple example of non-federation with Azure as the IdP*

When setting up your Azure AD Connect using a non-federation model, you have two different options for how your accounts authenticate: Password Hash Synchronization (PHS) and Pass-Through Authentication (PTA). PTA is similar to the ADFS model, but instead of redirecting to an ADFS farm, Azure AD Connect will validate the credentials directly to your on-premises domain controllers. While each method has robust security around the transport and storage for credentials, an ideal scenario is to set up PHS and enable password writeback. Enabling password writeback allows for users to change their password without the need to directly contact a domain controller. When the user changes their password through the Azure tenant, the password will be validated against the password requirements of the local domain. You will also need to have password writeback enabled to perform Self-Service Password Reset (SSPR), outlined in a later section.

Security Measures

Now that we have gone over the Identity Provider scenarios, mechanisms we use to access our identity, and high-level management concepts, we need to look at how we create security measures within our tenant. Security measures are the ways in which we minimize the ability for bad actors to gain access to our resources. We will touch on Azure application permission scopes, provide an in-depth guide on enabling Multi-Factor Authentication for our tenant, set up Conditional Access Policies, and provide a high-level overview of Privileged Identity Management.

Azure Application Permission Scopes

Continuing from our discussion in the "OAuth" section, Azure integrates its tenant applications based on the OAuth protocol. We can break these permissions or scopes down into two categories: delegated permissions and application permissions. An application permission allows for something to be run in the background without the need to sign in. A delegated permission is run while the user is signed in and allows for resource calls to be made during the active session.

OPEN WEB APPLICATION SECURITY PROGRAM (OWASP)

You should adopt the OWASP Top 10 program as part of your web application development program. The OWASP community maintains web application security awareness top 10 list and free articles, methodologies, and tools to help improve DevOps security. You should promote this free online community with your company to help create effective security practices to create more secure applications.

https://owasp.org/www-project-top-ten/

Top 10 web application security risks:

1. Injection: There are many injection flaws, such as SQL, NoSQL, OS, and LDAP injections. Injections of commands or code execution can occur when untrusted data is sent as input to an application.

2. Broken authentication: When an application incorrectly implements authentication and session management, it may lead to attackers compromising passwords, keys, session tokens, or user identities.

3. Sensitive data exposure: Some Internet applications expose APIs that may not protect critical corporate data. Encryption at rest or in transit helps protect data.

4. XML external entities (XXE): Poorly, often older configured XML processors evaluate external entity references within XML documents, which can lead to the exposure of internal files using the file URI handler.

5. Broken access control: Security of least privileged is not always followed, so authenticated users are sometimes allowed to unrestricted access to data or account access.

6. Security misconfiguration: Manual or untested configuration can result in insecure patterns, incomplete settings, Internet access to the cloud storage, or verbose error messages containing sensitive information.

7. Cross-site scripting (XSS): When web applications include untrusted data in a new web page or object without proper validation or escaping, attackers execute scripts in the victim's browser which can hijack user sessions.

8. Insecure deserialization: Insecure deserialization often leads to remote code execution. Even if deserialization flaws do not result in remote code execution, they can be used to perform attacks, including replay attacks, injection attacks, and privilege escalation attacks.

9. Using components with known vulnerabilities: Many thousands of open source repositories have been abandoned with libraries, frameworks, and other software modules, containing a known vulnerability for years but never patched.

10. Insufficient logging and monitoring: Ineffective monitoring or inadequate incident response alerting security measure can aid attackers to gain access, maintain persistent access, and extract or compromise data.

Most breach studies show the time to detect a breach is over 200 days, typically detected by external parties rather than internal processes or monitoring.

Configure Multi-Factor Authentication

Multi-Factor Authentication (MFA) adds a second-level protection to your end users and creates second layer of authenticity to your user accounts. The concept of MFA has been around for several years, and the general public has been using it whether or not they are aware. Banking ATMs use a form of MFA where the customer enters their credentials by inserting their debit card. The ATM prompts the customer for their PIN. The second authentication method in MFA can be categorized into three categories: knowledge, physical, and personal. Knowledge is something that can be remembered like a PIN or passphrase. Physical is a device like a hardware token or cell phone that can travel with a user. Personal is unique to the user such as fingerprint or facial features. Azure MFA supports a physical device.

Enabling Security Defaults

Configuring your tenant's basic Multi-Factor Authentication (MFA) options is pretty straightforward. The options available for configuration expand based on the Azure licensing you purchase. The Azure AD free subscription will offer MFA using the Microsoft Authenticator app to end users and MFA via the app, text, and phone call to administrator accounts. To enable MFA using the Azure AD free subscription, you must turn on security defaults. After enrolling in MFA, your users will be prompted to reauthenticate every 14 days from known devices and sessions, and your accounts that hold an administrative role will be prompted for MFA every time they access the tenant.

ENABLING SECURITY DEFAULTS

---

1. Log in to your Azure Tenant using an account with global administrator access.

2. Select Azure Active Directory.

3. Select Properties.

4. Under the "Access management for Azure resources" section, click Manage Security defaults.

5. Enable security defaults.

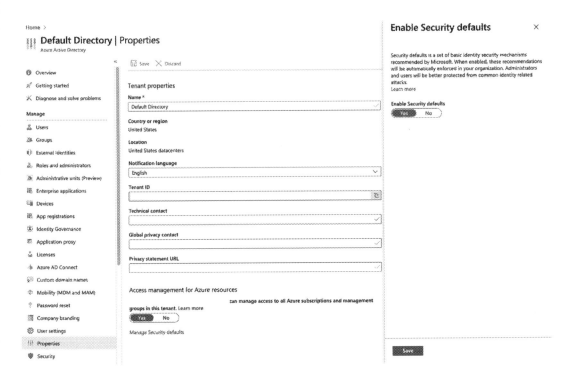

For organizations that subscribe to an Azure Active Directory Premium P1 license or Azure Active Directory Premium P2 license, we can provide more flexibility to our end users by allowing several different options to be used for our MFA method. The most common option is to enable a push notification using Microsoft's Authenticator app; however, you may also want to enable phone calls or text messages to facilitate users that may not have smart phones or simply don't want to put an application on their personal phone.

SETTING UP MULTI-FACTOR OPTIONS FOR YOUR TENANT

1. Using an account that has global administrative privileges, log in to your Azure Tenant.

2. Open Azure Active Directory.

3. Select Users.

4. Select Multi-factor Authentication.

5. Select service settings.

6. Under verification options, select the different options you would like to make available:

    a. Call to phone

    b. Text message to phone

    c. Notification through mobile app

    d. Verification code from mobile app or hardware token

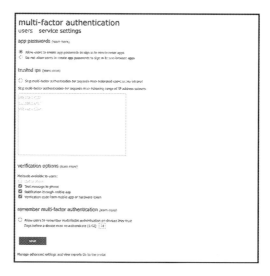

Configure any other settings needed and click Save.

Self-Service Password Reset

Self-Service Password Reset (SSPR) is also available with an Azure Active Directory Premium P1 license and above. SSPR allows your organization to offload the most common tier 1 helpdesk responses by enabling a 24/7 location for users to reset and unlock their accounts. By enabling SSPR, it takes the security burden away from your internal helpdesk and cuts down on workloads to drive efficiency by reducing time and effort needed for end users. As an added benefit, it helps to combat social engineering attacks. A social engineering attack is when an attacker will use industry terms, coupled with persuasion, to bypass the human element of security. Enabling MFA is a requirement to setting up the Self-Service Password Reset (SSPR) option within your tenant.

CONFIGURING SELF-SERVICE PASSWORD RESET

1. Using an account with global administrative privileges, log in to your Azure Tenant.

2. Select Azure Active Directory.

3. On the left-hand side, select Password Reset.

4. Select Properties.

   a. You can enable SSPR for selected users or all users.

   b. Click Save.

5. Select Authentication Methods.

   a. Select the authentication methods to match your selections for your MFA authentication methods.

6. Select On-Premises Integration.

   a. Make sure the option to write back to on-premises Active Directory is enabled (if you are using Azure AD Sync).

   b. If you do not enable this, even if you have password writeback enabled, the password will not be replicated.

Configure any other settings as needed such as notifications, customization, or registration.

Conditional Access Policies

When subscribing to an Azure P1 license or above, Conditional Access Policies behave similarly to Access Control Lists (ACLs). These policies give us more granular control to manage our tenant than a simple on or off unlike security defaults. Conditional Access

Policies can be scoped to apply to different areas such as the whole tenant, a specific application, or how a user accesses an application. Policies can also be applied based on users, groups, tenant roles, and geolocations.

Using Conditional Access Policies also takes advantage of some of the inherent security features that Azure monitors. With an Azure P2 license, we can enable a Conditional Access Policy that will review the IP address, typical behavior, or impossible travel conditions before allowing a user to log in. Conceptually, this adds a third level of authentication to ensure the security of our user's accounts and data.

For example, we have enabled a Conditional Access Policy that enforces MFA and looks for risky activities. Elizabeth, our VP of Information Technology, typically signs in within the United States. Azure has a historical knowledge of her sign-ins and creates an associated pattern. If someone attempts to log in using her credentials outside of the United States, Azure will block the sign-in because this is considered an atypical behavior for this account.

In this exercise, we will enable a Conditional Access Policy for our helpdesk group, which we created in our dynamic group exercise, to enforce MFA for access to the tenant.

CONFIGURING CONDITIONAL ACCESS POLICIES

1. Using an account with global administrative privileges, log in to your Azure Tenant.

2. In the search bar, type "Azure AD Conditional Access" and open the module.

3. Click New Policy.

4. Enter a descriptive name.

5. Under Assignments, click Users and groups.

   a. Under the Include section, check "Users and groups."

   b. Select your user groups or individual users.

   c. Click Select.

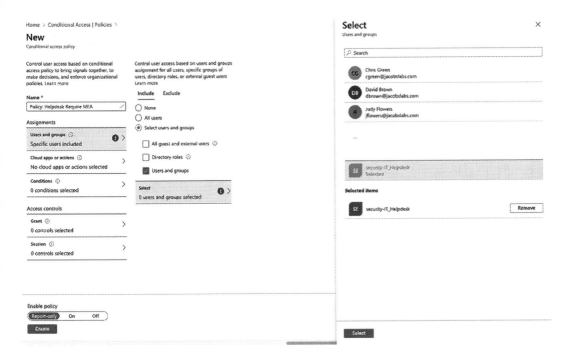

6. Click Cloud Apps or Actions.

7. Select All cloud apps.

    a. You will receive a helpful warning about potentially locking yourself out.

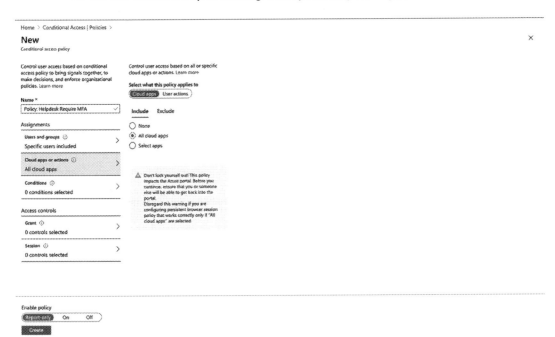

8. Click Conditions.

9. Select Client apps.

    a. Select Yes under Configure.

    b. Check Browser.

    c. Check Mobile apps and desktop clients.

    d. Click Done.

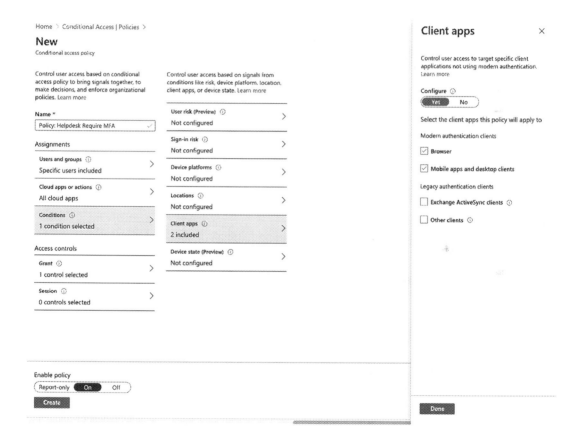

10. Under Access controls, select Grant.

11. Check the box for Require multi-factor authentication.

    a. Click Select.

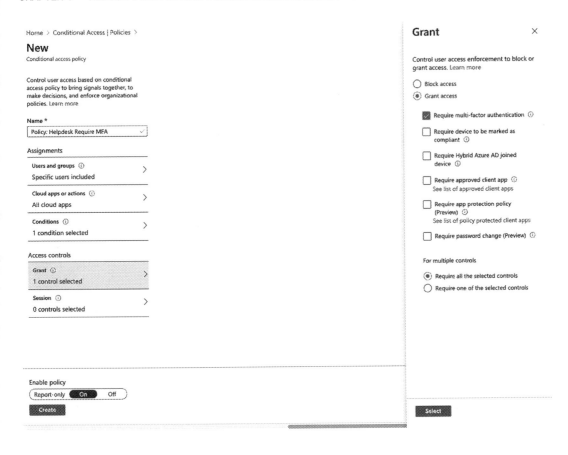

12. Click "On" under Enable policy.

    a. Click Create.

Azure AD Privileged Identity Management

Privileged accounts are still the most sought-after resource when hackers plan for an attack. They typically provide access to crucial behind-the-scenes data and can span across multiple servers and platforms. They are the definition of "keys to the castle." As organizations evolve and make their transition into the cloud and hybrid environments, they are accustomed to implementing a separation of power by using a privileged account and a nonprivileged account for their administrators. Your administrative account would be tied to the "domain admins" group or equivalent access in Active Directory, and your other account would be used for daily functions such as logging in to your computer or checking email. The attack vector of our privileged accounts greatly increases when we start adopting cloud resources due to the always-on and highly available nature of cloud technologies. While keeping a separation of power via administrative accounts is still an effective security strategy, we have the option to configure Azure Privileged Identity Management (PIM) to enhance the security of our critical tenant roles. In order to use PIM, you must maintain an adequate number of Azure Active Directory Premium P2 licenses for your administrative accounts. When setting up PIM, there are two different scenarios that can be used. We can retain the same concept of using an administrative account, or we can transition to elevating our daily nonadministrative accounts when administrative privileges are needed. The direction you take in applying your PIM policies will greatly depend upon your organization's security policies and industry standards and the size of your organization.

The power of Azure PIM can leverage some cost reduction by allowing us to remove the need of licensing extra accounts for administration. By changing your security posture and allowing Just-in-Time provisioning with PIM, it will reduce the amount of accounts needed to secure, monitor, and terminate for your administrators. Also, using the same account for administration creates more efficiencies in your daily operations by negating the need to switch back and forth between accounts. This also drives more focus and awareness of when administration is happening.

In either scenario, the best practice is to reduce the amount of privileged accounts that are active at any given time. To accomplish this with Azure, we can set timeouts on the built-in and any custom roles created in the tenant, require MFA for administrative roles to be activated, require approvals before roles can be activated, and enforce a justification for why a role is needed. Even in the organizations that still prefer the use of separate accounts for administration, by enabling PIM, we safeguard ourselves by forcing elevated roles to expire after a certain amount of time, thereby not leaving multiple accounts with global administrative privileges active. This allows for organizations to automatically clean up privileges on a daily or hourly basis.

SETTING PIM ON THE GLOBAL ADMINISTRATOR ROLE

1. Using an account with global administrative privileges, log in to your Azure Tenant.

2. In the search bar, type Azure AD Privileged Identity Management and select it.

3. Select Manage under the "Manage access" column.

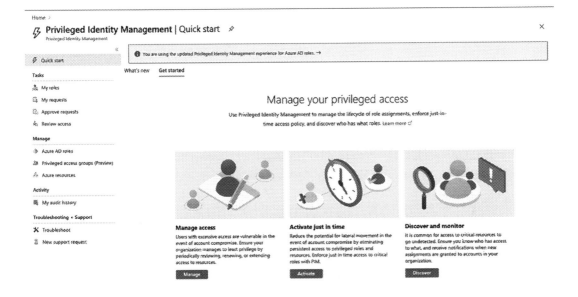

4. Select the Global Administrator role.

5. Click Settings.

6.   Click Edit.

Home > Privileged Identity Management | Quick start > Default Directory | Roles > Global Administrator | Assignments >

Role setting details - Global Administrator
Privileged Identity Management | Azure AD roles

✎ Edit

Activation

Setting	State
Activation maximum duration (hours)	8 hour(s)
Require justification on activation	Yes
Require ticket information on activation	No
On activation, require Azure MFA	Yes
Require approval to activate	No
Approvers	None

Assignment

Setting	State
Allow permanent eligible assignment	Yes
Expire eligible assignments after	-
Allow permanent active assignment	Yes
Expire active assignments after	-
Require Azure Multi-Factor Authentication on active assignment	No
Require justification on active assignment	Yes

7.   Adjust the maximum duration of the role.

8.   Enable or disable requiring MFA when the role is activated.

9.   Configure the options for requiring justification, ticket information, and approval.

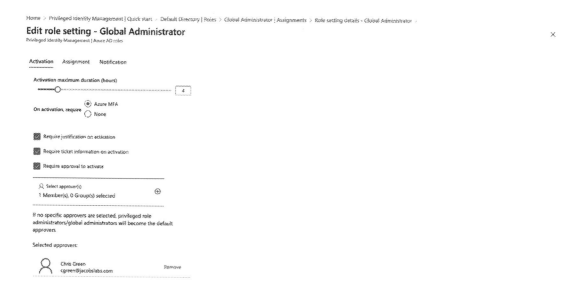

31

10. At the bottom of the page, click "Next: Assignment".

11. Select how long an account can be eligible for the role.

    a. You can allow accounts to be permanently eligible or for a certain amount of time.

    b. You can enable accounts to be permanently active.

    c. You can enable active assignments to expire after a certain amount of time.

12. Configure other settings as needed.

    a. Allowing permanent eligibility will enable the roles to always be assigned for elevation until manually removed.

    b. By unchecking Allow permanent eligibility, we can remove an account from being eligible after a certain period of time.

    c. Allowing permanent active assignment will enable accounts to be always assigned for this role.

    d. By unchecking Allow permanent active assignment, we can remove an account from being actively assigned after a certain period of time.

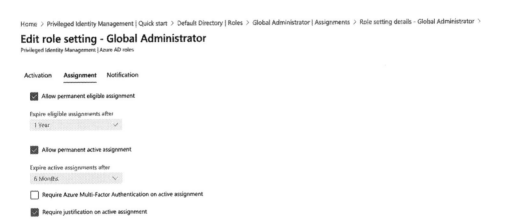

13. At the bottom of the page, click "Next: Notification".

14. Change any notifications needed.

    a. You have multiple options of who gets notified based on which event.

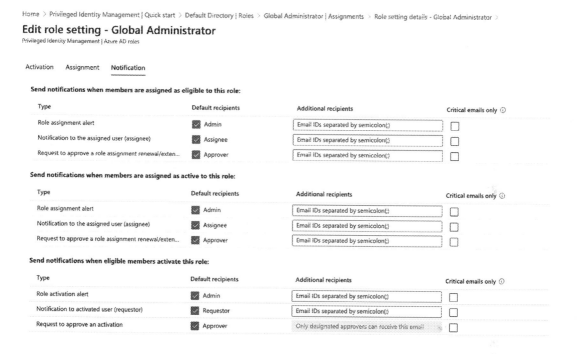

15. At the bottom of the page, click Update.

16. When you return to the Global Administrator Assignments page, select Add assignments.

17. Select the members that need to be assigned to the role.

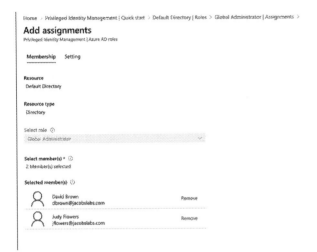

18. At the bottom of the page, click Next.

19. Select their assignment type.

    a. Eligible enables Just-in-Time provisioning that will expire based on the time we set in step 7.

    b. Active will enable them to be permanently active. This will abide by the rules set in step 12.

20. Select if they are permanently eligible or if the eligibility expires.

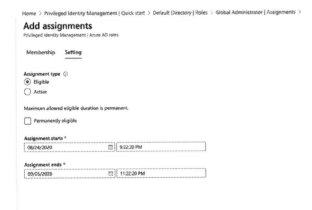

21.   At the bottom of the page, select Assign.

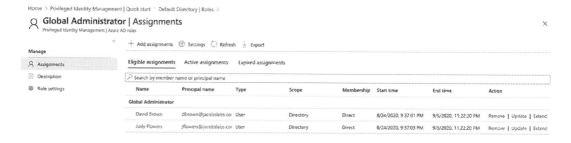

Once the roles have been assigned, you will be able to see who is eligible and until what time. You can also select Active assignments to see who is actively using the role.

Summary

Throughout this chapter, we have touched on some of the principles by which we can manage and secure our Azure tenant subscriptions, resources, and users. We furthered our understanding of SSO technologies using SAML, OAuth, and the built-in power of Azure AD Connect. Finally, we went over some of the baseline security measures by understanding application scopes, MFA, Self-Service Password Reset, and Conditional Access Policies. We also enabled a basic Privileged Identity Management policy on our global administrator role.

CHAPTER 2

Azure Network Security Configuration

Azure Virtual Network (VNet) is the software-defined network inside the Microsoft Azure. Azure continues to add many new features which turn into benefits for customers that rely on built-in security and automation features, like artificial intelligence (AI) with Azure Sentinel and machine learning (ML). These investments and improving over 200 services promote Microsoft Azure as the "intelligent cloud." There are many networking security–related Azure services in cloud native and available through third-party providers.

The services for networking support both Infrastructure as a Service (IaaS) and Platform as a Service (PaaS). The software-defined network is a foundational service, so in this chapter, we present information from an intermediate to advanced level. You learn what the network features are and how they support your infrastructure and hybrid deployment. You learn how VNets and their configuration could be vulnerable to external and internal attacks and how best to secure the VNet services.

In this chapter, you will learn about additional Azure network services including

- Virtual network overview

- Use of VNets

- Network Security Groups

- Azure Virtual Hub

- Network peering

- Azure Front Door services

- Remote access security

- Bastion hosts

© Marshall Copeland and Matthew Jacobs 2021
M. Copeland and M. Jacobs, *Cyber Security on Azure*, https://doi.org/10.1007/978-1-4842-6531-4_2

This chapter is foundational to improve your Azure security posture with a deeper insight into automation and deployment of Azure VNets. First, you gain an overview of the software-defined network and how to best use the network security that is built-in to allow or deny IP traffic. Next, you are introduced to new networking features like the Azure Virtual Hub and how to leverage virtual network peering across Azure regions and other public clouds. You learn about the benefits of Azure Front Door services and how to configure a global website.

You quickly learn how a software-defined network complexity can create security vulnerabilities and how to mitigate risks with the use of remote access security features. Finally, as you read through the chapter and use the examples, you'll learn how to proactively identify security risks and the best methods to reduce risk exposure and create a better security posture.

Note Frictionless Security in Azure   I like the phrase and want to use it.

Virtual Network Overview

Cyber security professionals should enable security controls after they understand how Microsoft Azure supports network services. The Microsoft Azure Virtual Network is specifically labeled Azure VNet, and this section expects you to know how to use and configure it in Azure through the Azure portal or command-line tools like PowerShell or CLI. VNet is an abbreviation used for virtual network throughout this book and the Azure documentation. The challenge for security teams is to know when IP traffic flows on the Azure network backbone and when it relies on Internet connectivity. The VNet security design focuses on TCP/IP packet management and data flow through virtual machines (VMs) or through Azure Endpoint services.

Azure Virtual Network is a foundational software component, and the Microsoft documentation may reference VNet as a key part of the Microsoft Cloud Adoption Framework, previously the Azure enterprise scaffold. A VNet is a programmatically defined network, also known as software-defined network. The VNet enables the communication between virtual systems in Azure and VMs or physical systems outside of Azure across the Internet and in a hybrid design that includes on-premises. The IP traffic flow is enabled between IP subnets in the same VNet by default and denied between another IP subnet in a different VNet.

Virtual networks are how virtual machines (VMs) communicate using IP traffic flow, and the security challenge is how to allow or deny the IP traffic flow based on the business requirements. To address the challenge, one method is to use cloud-native security services, like Network Security Groups and Azure Firewalls. Another method is to use third-party virtual security appliances to control the IP traffic. In many VNet deployments, both cloud-native and virtual appliances are used to provide layers of security. VNets are considered a trust model and isolated from each other by default; as stated earlier, the IP subnets inside the VNet are not isolated from each other, and Azure automatically configures IP routing using Azure DNS and internal private IP address routing.

The early planning considerations for software-defined network architecture include the need for TCP/IP address subnets to support the business services in Azure. You need to plan for a sufficient address space to support the virtual networks and division into smaller IP subnets for applications, devices, and machine management. The security management services should allow maintenance access and still support continued isolation. The overall goal is to securely allow the necessary communication between authorized systems.

Please refer to Figure 2-1 to gain a visual understanding of some of the many Azure networking components and how they are currently designed to create an end-to-end solution as the services work together. Review the Azure virtual services in the figure from left to right starting with the public IP address for Internet access to the business applications. The Application Gateway supports the deployment for the traffic load balance with a Web Application Firewall (WAF) to support application layer routing.

Note   Azure Application Gateway supports OSI layer 7 with URL routing, while traditional local balancers function at the OSI layer 4 for UDP and TCP.

Azure IP subnetting is supported with different VNet address ranges and Azure tagging for better business identification. VNets have added to the layers of security with Network Security Groups (NSG) to allow or deny traffic flow for the VNets. Virtual machines can be deployed to support running applications. Internal load balancers can be deployed to provide traffic loads to provide a responsive solution for an end user request.

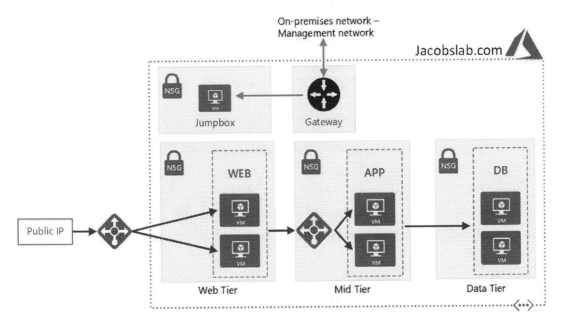

Figure 2-1. *Azure Virtual Network services architected for a complete solution*

The VNet space helps to define the separation of VMs or applications and the deployment across Azure Availability Zones that are needed to support high availability (HA) as shown in Figure 2-2.

Azure VNets operate at OSI layer 3 and simulate OSI layer 2 functionality from layer 3 limitations, and that is why traditional layer 2 protocols are not supported. The question you may have is why aren't VLANs (virtual LANs) supported in Azure since they are layer 3? On-premises VLANs operate at the OSI model data link layer, layer 2. The misperception is that VLANs are mapped to the IP subnet which gives the appearance of operating at OSI layer 3, the network layer.

In Chapter 1, you learned about the cloud service, organization starting with the Microsoft Azure Tenant, the highest level of ownership and configuration. You now know that a single Azure Tenant can include at least one and often many Azure subscriptions. Azure Virtual Networks are deployed at the subscription level, so naturally a VNet can only exist in one specific subscription. In addition, a VNet is deployed in a single Azure region (a geographic location), and so the same VNet cannot be created in two different regions. However, different virtual networks can be connected using a process called Azure Virtual Network peering. Additionally, IP subnets in Azure can span Azure Availability Zones that are part of your subscription. The connectivity of VNets in a single subscription or multiple subscriptions requires cyber security controls to reduce the security risks at the TCP/IP layer.

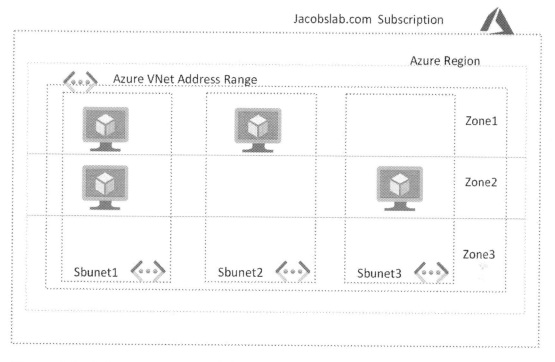

Figure 2-2. *Subnets, VNet, Availability Zones, regions, subscriptions*

Security considerations for the IP traffic properties supported in a VNet are similar to TCP/IP network designs that are enabled in your on-premises data center networks. The key difference being services preconfigured: defined, created, and managed service created from software. One or more virtual network interface cards (NICs) supported through the software can be bound to an Azure VM. The TCP/IP communication from the NIC flows through the Azure VNet that allows communication to other virtual NICs. If we continue this thought process and dig a little deeper, the TCP or UDP ports are also supported with Azure VNet attributes to allow or deny systems to communicate with each other. The rules from traditional IP subnets in a physical data center to manage, deploy, update, and protect against unauthorized access apply to Microsoft Azure Virtual Networks.

Azure VNets support features that enable benefits for cloud operations and the business. Communication from one Azure VNet to another VNet is not allowed by default; each individual VNet created is isolated. This default design is so you can control the routed IP traffic. All virtual machines (VMs) created in Azure are assigned a private IP address using the standard RFC 1918 IP address that is nonroutable on the Internet. Azure allows connectivity to the Internet from virtual networks and virtual machines only if they are assigned an external IP address. Azure network architects choose to leverage the correct VNet design to support the need for a dynamic scale of services, based on the demand and plan for high availability (HA).

Azure regions would be a top priority when you begin the design of an Azure architect. The requirement is to scope the overall size of the virtual network to include the number of subnets to support the business services. Subnets could include many "tiers" such as frontend tier, business tier, and data tier VNets. The production business should be architected for high availability so the use of Azure network regions close to the business services should be included. A single Azure region generally includes several Azure data centers, which means there are several physical buildings. These data centers are physically designed and connected to reduce network latency using a dedicated Azure network. This dedicated Azure network is referred to as the Azure backbone network. The overall Azure global network is connected by this private network backbone.

The connection to your Azure VNets supports connection in the same Azure region using a virtual network peering software configuration. And virtual networks can be created across different Azure regions using a global virtual network peering software configuration. You see the term software configuration to remind you that all of these options can be configured programmatically, using PowerShell, Azure CLI, ARM templates, or HashiCorp Terraform.

If a VM has a public IP, then Source Network Address Translation (SNAT) is used to provide external Internet access. If a VM is behind a public load balancer, then SNAT and Port Address Translation (PAT) are used to hide the private IP address and reduce security risks during Internet access. The Network Virtual Appliance (NVA) uses a public IP address to route IP traffic in and out of the NVA attached to the virtual NIC that has Internet access. The best practice is to limit the type of traffic such as HTTP/HTTPS to pass through the NVA.

Another option to consider using might be an Internet load balancer, Azure Application Gateway with a built-in Web Application Firewall (WAF). The Application Gateway and WAF are a managed service with security features based on the Open Web Application Security Project (OWASP) core rule set. The combination of Application Gateway and WAF is designed to prevent attacks from SQL injection, cross-site scripting, and more.

If you have multiple virtual networks, you can create the site-to-site (S2S) VPN to connect each VNet. Scale sets, managed SQL DB instances, and containers are just a few Azure services that can be shared across the Azure VNets. If you choose Azure VNet peering, the Microsoft network backbone is used. There is a cost for egress and ingress changes for peering, but VNets can be in different Azure subscriptions and even in different Azure Tenants.

If you have a hub and spoke deployment, then you need to set up the user-defined routing (UDR) with a next hop from the Hub to each of the two spokes, shown in Figure 2-3. UDR can also force IP traffic through the Azure Firewall for greater security.

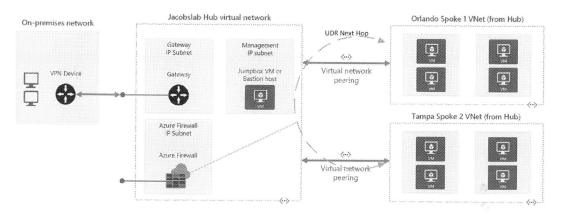

Figure 2-3. *Hub and spoke design supporting Azure network peering*

VNets

Azure VNets are used as an isolation boundary to limit the TCP/IP communication of other VNets or other Azure resources to the same VNet. VMs in one VNet cannot connect and pass data to VMs in another VNet without specifically allowing access and name resolution. Azure supports automatic IP routing and user-defined routing (UDR). A user-defined route would be used to purposely alter some of the default Azure routing. With the use of other networking services like Azure Gateway from a VNet, you can enable Azure forced tunneling. Forced tunneling is a software method used to alter, or force, IP traffic to an on-premises network.

You need to prevent cyber security exploitable misconfigurations in the Azure network. The first thing needed is to understand how Azure routes IP traffic automatically and how users with proper identity permissions can change the default routes.

The deployment of Azure networks starts by selecting an Azure region that supports the compliance features and resiliency features the business requires. From the selected region, the Azure address space is created. The address space (IP address scope) is a virtual network that is composed of one or more IP address spaces with a large address range (a large number used to leverage potential subnet isolation), to support all the IP addresses needed by the business. There is also the ability to create additional address spaces, as shown in Figure 2-4. The address space or address range can be increased to support additional networks for Azure VNets the network expansion may require.

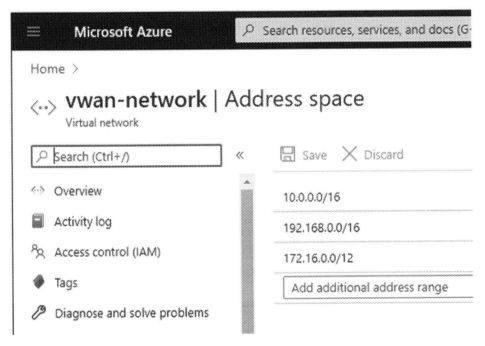

Figure 2-4. *Multiple Azure VNet spaces added for IP subnet segmentation*

You can learn how IP address supports the use of IP subnets and routing of the subnets in the Azure cloud network by having a greater understanding of routing with Classless Internet Domain Routing (CIDR). The defined Azure network space can include multiple network ranges. As an example, shown in Figure 2-4, many CIDR addresses identify the individual network IP addresses. This example used in Figure 2-4 is the address space 192.168.0.0/16 (the /16 provides the 65565 IP address). The IP subnets are calculated using binary math and the AND function as shown in Figure 2-5.

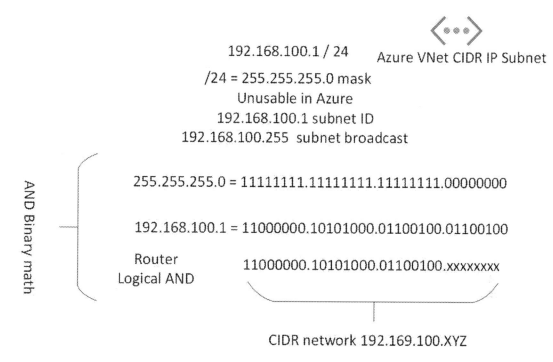

Figure 2-5. *CIDR subnet notation with router binary AND math example*

The Azure address space has a few additional requirements that need to be followed to successfully use the VNet services. If you are a cloud-only business, or have an on-premises data center using a VPN Gateway, then the IP address range should be managed so that each Azure region used is unique. The address space should not overlap the IP address range in other Azure regions. Also, the Azure Virtual Network space or individual subnet IP addresses used in a hybrid network deployment cannot overlap with the IP address from your on-premises data center. Azure network services support any IP range with a few exceptions; you cannot use the following IP ranges:

- Loop back: 127.0.0.0/8

- Broadcast: 255.255.255.255/32

- Multicast: 244.0.0.0/4

- Azure-provided DNS: 168.63.129.16/32

Azure routing (automated routing for the entire network) automatically provides IP traffic routes for each different subnet created; this is called a system default route. Default routes allow Azure to manage any outbound traffic from a subnet, based on the default route tables and UDR updates to route tables. As a Microsoft Azure customer, you cannot create or remove system routes. The Azure default routes can be overridden when a user-defined route is enabled for a specific route. A UDR is manually created from the Azure portal or code.

Azure system routing also provides automatic Internet access from the VM even when a public IP address is not selected as an option. You can create a Windows OS Azure VM without a public IP address and connected by a Remote Desktop Protocol (RDP) to the VM using the Azure bastion host. From that RDP session, you can open a browser and surf the Internet.

Azure networking allows site-to-site network peering between different Azure regions, subscriptions, and tenants. Azure routing supports the creation of a Virtual Private Network (VPN) from Azure to on-premises through the use of a gateway using Virtual Private Networking called an Azure VPN Gateway. When Azure VNets are connected to an on-premises data center, using site-to-site or ExpressRoute, the term hybrid network is used.

Azure provides support for user-defined routes (UDR) by defining the route tables and rules of the desired route. First, you create an Azure route table as a container to list or manage each UDR as they are defined in your Azure address space. Once the route table is created, you simply select the option to add a new route (new UDR). The parameters needed to add a UDR, refer to Figure 2-6, are shown in the image from the Azure portal. These parameters are needed to allow defined routes to be created and used rather than use the internal Azure routes. The properties supported include the name, address CIDR prefix, and next hop type. Options for the hop type are virtual network, virtual network gateway, Internet, virtual appliance, and none. If you select the Azure Network Virtual Appliance (NVA), the additional option required is to add the IP address of the NVA. There may be a future business requirement to use an option to route traffic to the NONE destination. This route option allows the IP traffic to be "dropped," again for specific traffic security reasons.

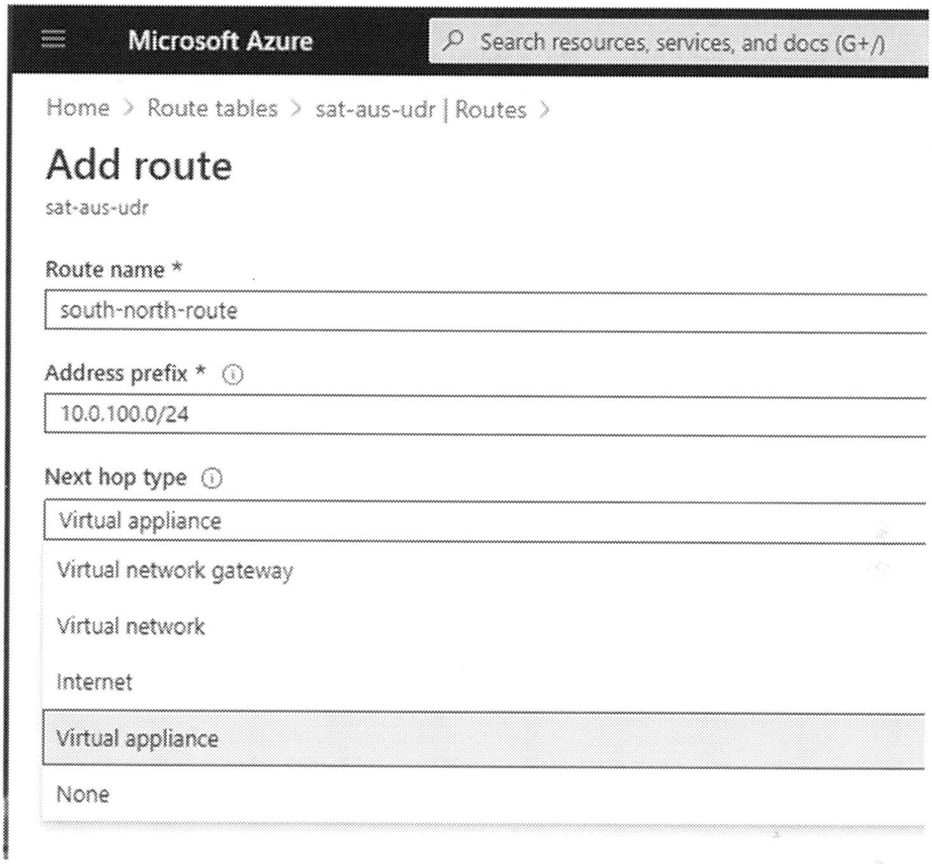

≡   Microsoft Azure   🔍 Search resources, services, and docs (G+/)

Home > Route tables > sat-aus-udr | Routes >

Add route
sat-aus-udr

Route name *

south-north-route

Address prefix * ⓘ

10.0.100.0/24

Next hop type ⓘ

Virtual appliance

Virtual network gateway

Virtual network

Internet

Virtual appliance

None

Figure 2-6. *View of the Azure portal to add a user-defined route (UDR)*

IP subnets are created out of the total Azure Virtual Network address space (or address range). An IP subnet is also identified as a VNet and is used to organize and manage similar resources like VMs. You can secure traffic to a subnet using Network Security Groups (NSGs). Each NSG is a cloud-native service (software-defined security object) used to control IP packets flowing in and out of the subnet.

Azure network teams need to understand the individual IP address available for subnets in the Azure network space. The total usable IP address size of the subnet is decreased by five IP addresses because the networking services allow the first usable IP address is the fourth (4th) on each network.

An example to help you understand the available IP subnets would be helpful for this topic. In this example, the IP subnet addresses used are

- 10.0.1.0/24 (256 IP addresses)

- 10.0.1.4 (first IP address available)

However, using the Azure network limitations, the subnet rules do not allow the use of the address network 10.0.1.0, and you cannot use the broadcast network address 10.0.1.255. TCP/IP networking on-premises identifies both the network and the broadcast address. With Microsoft Azure, you can resize a subnet only if there are no VMs in that subnet.

Please refer to Figure 2-7 to gain a visual representation of subnet sizes and available IP for VMs with this Azure VNet subnet example image.

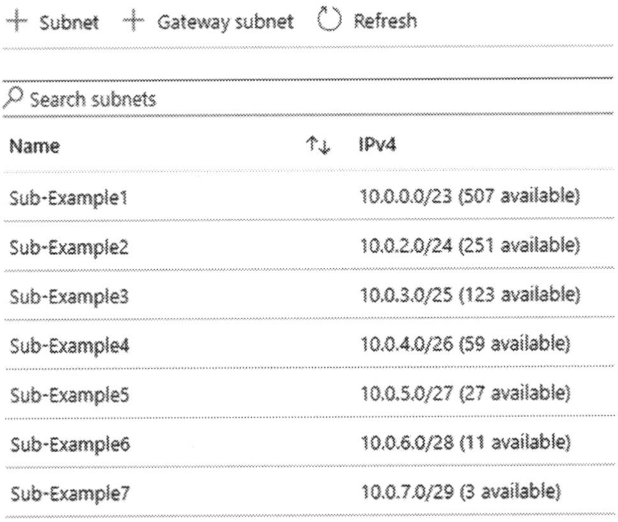

Name	↑↓	IPv4
+ Subnet + Gateway subnet ↻ Refresh		
Search subnets		
Sub-Example1		10.0.0.0/23 (507 available)
Sub-Example2		10.0.2.0/24 (251 available)
Sub-Example3		10.0.3.0/25 (123 available)
Sub-Example4		10.0.4.0/26 (59 available)
Sub-Example5		10.0.5.0/27 (27 available)
Sub-Example6		10.0.6.0/28 (11 available)
Sub-Example7		10.0.7.0/29 (3 available)

Figure 2-7. *Azure VNet range for IPv4*

Your first VNet creation may have been enabled through the virtual network journey using the Azure portal. As your skills mature and multiple VNets are used, you can leverage Infrastructure as Code (IaC). IaC is a deployment framework like Azure Resource Manager (ARM) templates or HashiCorp Terraform Azure cloud providers. Infrastructure as Code at the foundation can be defined, for our Azure discussion purposes, as a software method to deploy the Azure infrastructure design.

Note   If you would like to learn more about using Infrastructure as Code (IaC), please review *Microsoft Azure: Planning, Deploying, and Managing the Cloud*, ISBN 978-1-4842-5958-0, which can be found at `www.apress.com/us/book/9781484259573`.

Cyber security teams need to understand Azure Domain Name Service (DNS). This is another service for name to IP resolution that is included (i.e., cloud native) to support Azure networking. DNS supports routing IP traffic by names, and that is why it is included in this section.

As more subnets are added, the DNS updates the naming service by default and does not require configuration; it just works. From a cyber security perspective, the built-in DNS resolution across Azure VNets is more secure but can be augmented. As an example of DNS additions, let us consider the problem of VNets used in multiple Azure regions. IP traffic to name resolution creates at least two network engineering issues:

- Cross-VNet name resolution.

- DNS suffix cannot be customized (for a domain).

One way to solve the DNS cross-VNet name resolution is with the configuration of a site-to-site VPN connection from Azure to your on-premises data center. Once the VPN is created, you can add a custom DNS server IP address into each VM in the VNet. Each VM will register with your customized DNS server and support name to IP address resolution. If you do not have a VPN connection from Azure to on-premises, you can create a VM and install DNS from inside an Azure VNet. This works well for cloud-only businesses or projects, and you can enable DNS forwarding to other DNS servers with the correct ports open in the Azure Network Security Group (NSG).

Another way to solve name resolution across VNet isolation is to use Azure DNS. With Azure, you can host public DNS domains as a service instead of the DNS management of creating your own DNS servers in a VNet. The Azure DNS service is a geo-distributed name service fabric. You can create a VM and enable a custom DNS server to support multiple VNet name resolution.

Azure DNS has both private DNS and Azure Fabric DNS that support public geo-distributed name resolution. You can also use private DNS zones that do not route the names publicly. Create a private DNS zone and create a registration VNet and allow the VMs to register as each server is created. You are also able to configure a resolution VNet that would support cross registrations. Azure supports the VNet to directly route the individual subnet to an Azure platform service.

The last topic for cyber security teams to be aware of is the use of service endpoints and subnet delegation as they can be used to support IP traffic in an Azure VNet. When you create a virtual network, from code or the portal, please refer to Figure 2-8, both service endpoints and subnet delegation can be selected.

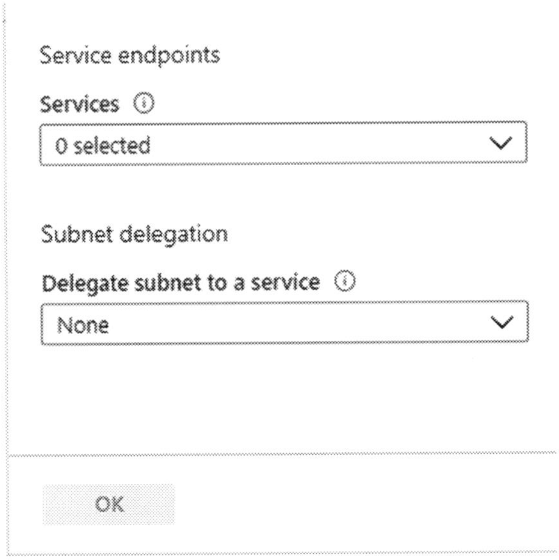

Figure 2-8. *Azure portal view of subnet service endpoints and subnet delegation*

Let's focus on the first of the two final VNet configuration options with Azure service endpoints. You can select endpoints to allow specific Azure services to directly connect over the Azure backbone network. Service endpoints enable the private IP addresses from the VNets you created to reach the Azure service without a public IP address. This process provides a private secure connection by extending the VNet identity. The list of supported services continues to expand, so listed here are some examples of Azure services:

- Azure Storage

- SQL database

- Database for MySQL

- Database for MariaDB

- Azure Key Vault

When service endpoints are used with VNets, they allow Azure to automatically optimize IP traffic from your VNet to the Azure service over the fast and secure Azure backbone network. This change in routing reduces the need for another public IP address since only private IP addresses are used which reduce the outbound Internet IP traffic that is currently monitored and audited by the security team. The VNet service endpoint connection that connects directly to an Azure service does not use Network Address Translation (NAT) or a gateway device.

The subnet delegation feature should be considered when your Azure architecture identifies Azure Platform as a Service (PaaS) when IP traffic needs to be injected in a specific VNet. Subnet delegation allows the Azure customer to deploy the instances into the subnet. The designation from a VNet to a PaaS service enables automatic rules for your VNet subnet that helps Azure to stabilize the connection. The use of subnet delegation allows the NSG filtering of traffic and user-defined routes. Once the option is selected, Azure configures a Network Intent Policy that supports the VNet integration stability with the use of preconditions that are defined when the delegation is selected. Azure then deploys the Azure PaaS service instance into the VNet for easier utilization. The services are delegated through code or from the portal (review Figure 2-9 to see a short list of resources when the Azure portal is used).

Figure 2-9. *Subnet delegation for Azure-managed service example*

Network Security Group

The software-defined security control for TCP/IP traffic is a cloud-native service that can easily be deployed to manage IP traffic between networks and between hosts in the subnet. You have learned that in Azure, software-defined networks are called VNets, and each VNet supports a security control to manage traffic flow through a Network Security Group (NSG). Network traffic control implementing an NSG supports management by allowing or denying IP traffic and reducing the security risk.

An NSG operates at lower layers of the OSI, layer 4 specifically to support TCP and UDP protocols and layer 3 to support the Internet Control Message Protocol (ICMP). With each Azure subscription, you can create 1000 VNets and 3000 subnets for each virtual network. The limit of Network Security Groups is 5000 in total for the entire subscription so security planning is critical for Azure VNet management.

The configuration of a single NSG security control to manage the flow of a single network traffic is simplistic. The security network architecture can grow to a complicated design when the number of rules for each NSG increases. Each Network Security Group can contain up to 1000 individual network rules, which allow or deny traffic based on five attributes (5-tuple):

- Source IP address

- Source port

- Destination IP address

- Destination port

- Protocol

You can decrease the network management time needed if you plan to use Azure IP Groups as a way to become more effective when managing an enterprise network deployment. Azure supports creating an IP Group = "any-text-name" and adding VNet subnets to the group.

NSG reporting on current configuration is a challenge. Understanding firewall capabilities in Microsoft Azure is a critical security area that both cloud architects and cloud operations teams need to consider in providing the best reduction of security risk. Azure Firewall supports routing all "Internet" traffic.

Microsoft has a managed service for use to improve network security, the Azure Firewall. There are many security features supported including

- OSI layer 3–7 (through firewall) policy

- Threat intelligence, known malicious IPS and FQDS

- Threat intelligence NAT traffic filtering rules

- Allow DNS rule Protocol = TCP and UDP

- Application rules work at OSI layer 7 (FQDN tags) external services

- Outbound call to the PowerShell gallery (Allow-pass, gallery http, https, and *.powershellgallery.com)

UDR uses the next hop address so all egress traffic goes through the firewall. The default route for all routing is used to force all traffic to the virtual appliance or Azure Firewall (in this case). You need to add the Route name = default route, address prefix = 0.0.0.0/0 (all IP addresses) go through to the Next Hop Type Virtual Appliance, Next Hop address = Azure Firewall Private IP address (10.30.1.4). Azure Firewall enables IP forwarding on the VNet however if you set the Next Hop for a VNet.

The Azure Firewall subnet, according to the documentation, uses a /28; however, you could select a /30. Create the VNets first. Make sure the Azure Firewall is in the correct availability zone. The Firewall must terminate to the Internet, using the standard SKU with static assignment. The threat intelligence configuration can be turned off, alert, or alert and deny.

The Allow/Deny rules are network aware and application aware. The Azure PaaS solution supports the ability to multiselect, so one rule supports many Azure services. The Network Security Groups (NSG) support Allow/Deny rules at the IP subnet that you have included as part of your virtual network. The Application Security Group supports the microsegmentation of the dynamic workloads. As an example of using the named monikers and groups, refer to Figure 2-10. This removes the need to update IP subnets when you use the Azure service named monikers.

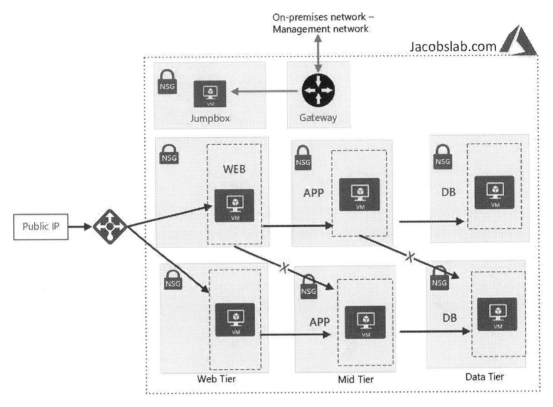

Figure 2-10. *Network Security Groups and Application Security Groups placeholder*

Troubleshooting the network logging and NSG flow logs for traffic monitoring is made easier with the interaction of Network Watcher. The Network Watcher service supports monitoring performance and health issues for your VNet subnets. The diagnostics can allow you to capture packets on a VM to validate the IP flow. With this data, you can validate if the traffic follow your needed rules to allow or deny access.

Note   NIST 800-41 Version 1 provides a deeper insight and is a guideline for firewalls and firewall policy considerations. You can find it at `https://nvlpubs.nist.gov/nistpubs/Legacy/SP/nistspecialpublication800-41r1.pdf`.

VNet Security Best Practices

These security best practices reduce cyber security risks and list some of the details related to security that benefit IaaS and PaaS deployments. You will also have insights into the characteristics of Azure Virtual Networks that help you better understand how Microsoft enables connectivity in Azure software-defined networks.

A best practice is to not expose an Azure workload to the public Internet without using one or more security methods described throughout this book. You could use a Network Virtual Appliance (NVA) from the Azure Marketplace that can be configured to securely filter Internet traffic. You may choose a site-to-site VPN from on-premises to Azure and connect to the private IP address or a point-to-site VPN and connect to a jump-box management server. Also, you may choose to enable Just-in-Time administration that enables limited access from a "specific" IP address for an allocated time window as part of Azure Security Center.

Create IP subnet ranges based on workloads to allow servers with the same workload to leverage the VNet subnet–level security. As an example, if the VNet supports a business tier set of VMs for applications, they are all in the same IP subnet address space.

VNet management at a larger scale is an architectural consideration. The first few Azure subnets may have been created using the Azure portal; however, scripting IP subnets using PowerShell or the Azure CLI allows for a lower resource cost for management.

Bind and manage the virtual machine NIC at the VNet level. Azure does support binding VMs to the VNet or the virtual NIC attached to the server, but this becomes a resource bottleneck for troubleshooting and managing systems at scale at this level. As an example, if you move a VM from one VNet to another, binding at the NIC level is another touchpoint for the relocation to be successful. In addition, the network binding can only be enabled for a single IP range if your virtual machine has multiple virtual NICs. Azure does not support network binding to different IP ranges for two or more NICs.

User-defined routes may be an option to consider.

Use a Network Security Group (NSG) to secure the VNet to allow specific VNet traffic in and out of the VMs in each VNet. In addition, you can reduce security risks with limited IP address ranges, and you can also limit specific protocols to add another level of security. The protocols supported by NSGs include the feature to allow or deny

- TCP

- UDP

- ICMP

- ANY

The NSG also supports the feature to deny outbound traffic to one or multiple IP subnets and specific TCP/IP protocols. Please review the OSI/TCP model section later in this chapter as a refresher for security risk considerations.

Leverage the current skill set from your on-premises security team by reviewing the capabilities of the same vendor system available as a Network Virtual Appliance (NVA) that can be purchased from the Azure Marketplace. Don't let the term virtual appliance create confusion; the NVA is a product that may be running a virtual machine image and preconfigured for testing in your Azure deployment. You need to schedule time with the current security team that allows them the opportunity to share their expertise with the cloud security team. If they include the same security team members, cloud and on-premises, then time is needed to update corporate security policies and deployment guidelines because the virtual applications may be configured differently.

Note   The Azure Marketplace supports vendors selling a product by quickly downloading (size) a preconfigured application (features). This NVA is not a recommended implementation for performance testing, often a smaller VM with limited CPU and NIC configuration.

Consider implementing site-to-site (S2S) or point-to-site (P2S) tunnels for VPN to connect your on-premises systems. Site to site is often considered for a permanent connection from Azure to an on-premises data center. With a site-to-site VPN in place, then user-defined routes may be implemented to better control network traffic. A point-to-site connection is considered if occasionally systems need to connect from a remote location into your Azure subscription.

Additionally, user-defined routes (UDR) may reduce security risks with the configuration for edge network routing. An example is the network configuration for a perimeter network (referred to as a DMZ, demilitarized zone). If you design your DMZ (refer to Figure 2-11) at the edge network without a VM in the VNet, security posture is improved, because there are no trusted VMs or applications placed in the DMZ and using Azure UDR can better secure data to direct traffic effectively.

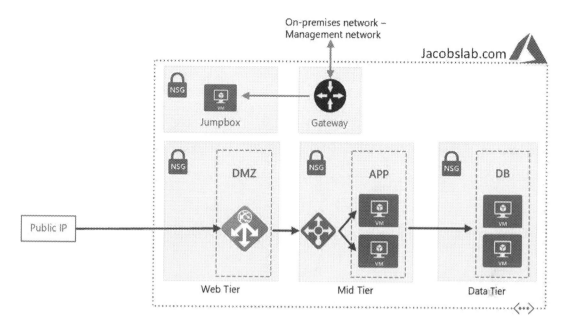

Figure 2-11. *Azure-defined VNets using UDR, DMZ, and trusted VM example*

Network Peering

You can use Azure network peering to enable a network connection for IP traffic across different Azure Virtual Networks. The peering is connected in both directions (please refer to Figure 2-12), from VNet A to VNet B and from VNet B back to VNet A. Once peered, the virtual networks appear as one, from a traditional IP traffic packet flow. As you have learned earlier in this chapter, Azure VNets support the individual IP subnets routing to the private IP address because the traffic is routed across the Azure backbone network. Once the network peering is configured, that IP traffic is also routed over the Azure backbone network. The cyber security risk is reduced because your Azure subscription traffic is never exposed to the Internet.

There are two types of peering to consider for both peering considerations and traffic cost:

- Default VNet peering in the same Azure region

- Global VNet peering across Azure regions

You should be aware of some of the benefits of VNet peering like we presented earlier; the network traffic between peered virtual networks is private, so the IP traffic from VMs remains private since the public Internet is not used. No IP traffic on the

Internet is important to consider if you have encryption configured needed for Internet gateways or if encryption is required in the communication between the global Azure regions. Traffic between the virtual networks (refer to Figure 2-12) remains on the Microsoft backbone network, so saving resources on encrypting products may be a consideration. Additionally, with peering traffic on the Azure network backbone, it is a low-latency, high-bandwidth connection between resources in different virtual networks.

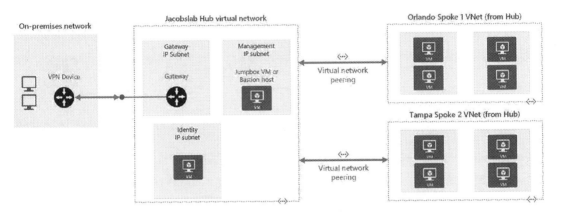

Figure 2-12. *Placeholder of simple network peering visual representation*

Just a reminder, the address space in each of the virtual networks you are peering must not overlap. This can be challenging for organizations to maintain and share the IP address space entirely including IP subnets. In the individual IP subnets, you can edit the IP ranges by adding to or deleting from the VNet space. However, after the peering is completed, no editing can be completed.

Note   VNet creation does not incur a charge. The cost is the data IP traffic in Azure regions and out of the VNet, called "egress" traffic. Charges vary between local country regions and global regions.

The recommendation for deployment across more than two Azure regions is to follow the Hub and Spoke model. If you refer to Figure 2-12, Subscription A with VNet A and VNet B would be designated as the Hub, while Subscription B with VNet C would be a spoke.

Workloads deployed in different environments, such as DevOps, test, preproduction, and production, may require shared services such as DNS and Microsoft Active Directory Domain Services (AD DS). Shared services are placed in the hub VNet, while each environment is deployed to a spoke VNet to maintain the separation of business units or R&D. Peering with the Hub and Spoke model supports resources under different spokes to communicate with each other, if they are peered with the Hub VNet. All Spoke VNet should be peered with the Hub VNet for all shared services to flow between the Hub and each Spoke.

Azure supports a cloud-native virtual wide area network (vWAN) that can be used for global VNet peering. As an example, the connection of two VNets in different regions using a virtual WAN supports network connections to connect VNets to virtual hubs. The user does not need to set up global VNet peering explicitly. VNets connected to a virtual hub in the same region incur VNet peering charges. VNets connected to a virtual hub in a different region incur global VNet peering charges.

Figure 2-13. *Azure virtual WAN (vWAN) enabled from the Azure portal*

Azure virtual WAN (vWAN) is a networking service that combines IP traffic flow, cyber security features, and IP routing in a single view; refer to Figure 2-13. The features support a customer's branch connectivity that may be using Azure site-to-site VPN connectivity or a remote user with Azure point-to-site VPN. Private connectivity with ExpressRoute is supported using the vWAN as the HUB. Security features such as the Azure Firewall are supported. You can enable the vWAN from the portal, as referenced in Figure 2-14, and add additional network connections to SPOKE regions as needed.

The virtual WAN architecture is a hub and spoke architecture with scale and performance built-in for branches. Features include

- VPN/SD-WAN devices

- Azure VPN/OpenVPN/IKEv2 clients

- Virtual networks

Azure vWAN enables more efficient administration processes to support a global transit network architecture; please refer to Figure 2-14 – it is a vWAN diagram. The cloud-hosted network "hub" enables transitive connectivity between endpoints that may be distributed across different types of Azure regions or spokes. The Azure regions are those you want your network architecture to connect with. All hubs are connected in full mesh in a standard virtual WAN making it fast and efficient for clients because of the use of the Microsoft backbone for any spoke connection.

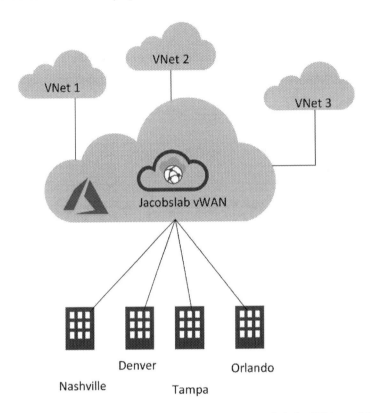

Figure 2-14. *Azure vWAN logical view supporting multiple VNet address spaces*

Application Security Groups

An Application Security Group helps to manage the security of the Azure virtual machines by grouping them according to the applications that run on each group . This service is a feature that allows the application-centric use of security by extending it to the defined application groups using the Azure network. Network Security Groups (refer to Figure 2-15) support a software-defined network change by supporting a security policy between web tier and middle tier systems without updating IP subnets.

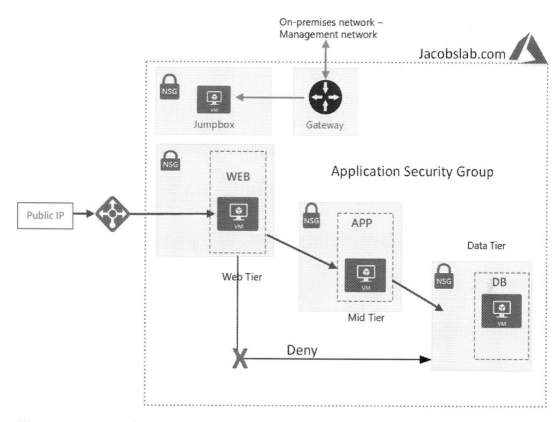

Figure 2-15. *Application Security Group deny access from the web tier to the database tier*

We have an example subnet that contains web servers and database servers. The configured Application Security Group access rules of the subnet's Network Security Group allow http, https, and database access to those servers.

OSI AND TCP/IP MODELS

The Open Systems Interconnection (OSI) model is a standard that supports computing system communication. The goal is to identify layers of services that support standard protocols. The lowest layer, layer 1, serves the layer above, layer 2, and so on. This support continues until reaching layer 7 which supports the software application. A detailed example of the OSI model is shown in Table 2-1.

Table 2-1. *OSI model – seven layers of communication for TCP/IP networking*

OSI Layer #	OSI Layer Name	OSI Layer Description and Protocols
7	Application layer	User applications: Protocols = HTTP, HTTPS, FTP, SMTP (web traffic: Azure Firewall, Application Gateway) Data type = User data
6	Presentation layer	Data translation, compression, and encryption applied. Protocols = TLS (SSL), MIME (email) Data type = Encoded user data
5	Session layer	Establishes the session communication, management, and termination: Protocols = RPC, sockets, named pipes Data type = Session
4	Transport layer	Process-level addressing: multiplexing/demultiplexing, retransmissions. Protocols = TCP/UDP Data type = Datagram and packets
3	Network layer	Logical-level addressing: routing, datagram encapsulation, error handling. Protocols = IP, IPv6, IP NAT, IPsec, ICMP, DLC. Routing protocols = RIP and BGP Data type = Datagram and packets
2	Datalink layer	Logical link control: media access control (MAC) addressing, error detection. Protocols = Ethernet, Token Ring, 802.11 wireless, SLIP, PPP Data type = Frames
1	Physical layer	Encoding and physical data transmission hardware. Protocols = physical connections Data type = BITS

The TCP/IP model reduces the number of layers to four. However, the reduced number of layers must still support the individual work, at that level from the OSI model. Notice in Figure 2-16 that layer 5 and 6 functionalities are still being accomplished, but they are identified in the TCP/IP model at layer 7. Notice in Figure 2-16 also that layer 1, physical layer, is removed and replaced by any hardware.

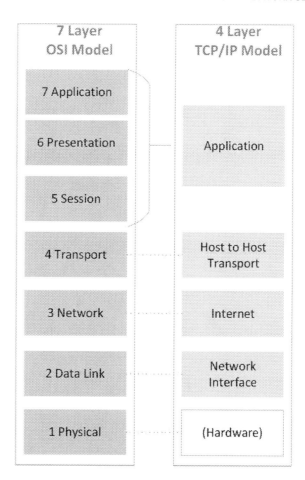

Figure 2-16. *OSI model and TCP/IP model consolidation*

Many Azure security deployment or configuration considerations need to be made based on how Microsoft supports both OSI and TCP models. The application layer sends and receives IP traffic that includes Domain Name System (DNS), Hypertext Transfer Protocol (HTTP), and Simple Mail Transfer Protocol (SMTP). The transport layer, layer 3, is the connection-oriented transporting application like the Transmission Control Protocol (TCP), which includes replacing lost packets of data with overhead resources. It is also used by the User Datagram Protocol (UDP) and has no retransmission of lost packets, for example, the following list:

- Ingress layer considerations

- Load balancers, layer 7, TCP, and UDP

- PIP-UDR switch, active pass

- PIP-UDR without SNAT, all traffic, not limited on port rules

The OSI and TCP/IP models are a foundation for understanding under the covers how transmission from the end user at the web server level uses the interaction based on defined protocols (i.e., TCP/UDP) as shown in Figure 2-17.

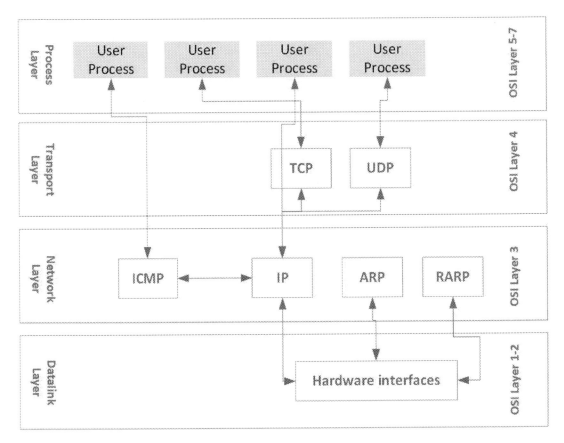

Figure 2-17. *Protocols support each layer for OSI and TCP models*

You need to understand the protocols and the layers they are enabled to gain a better understanding as they relate to the support from Azure security cloud-native services and the support for OSI layers 7, 4, and 3.

TCP/IP Port Vulnerability

The communication in Microsoft Azure between servers using software is supported using the TCP/IP model (please refer to the Open Systems Interconnection (OSI) and TCP/IP model sidebar for an in-depth understanding). The easiest way to gain a clear understanding of TCP/IP ports and how they are used requires you to realize that each virtual machine (VM) is assigned an IP address. As a simplified example, let's use the following:

VM-Server1 is assigned the IP address of 192.168.1.1

With the use of that single IP address, the server can support more than a single TCP/IP service.

If you look at a small office location that has a device configured for Internet connectivity, you can discover many services enabled to send and receive from a single IP address (i.e., 192.168.1.1). The services communicate on different port addresses using TCP or UDP. The address can span from 1 to 65,535. Figure 2-18 provides the result of a default scan that is configured to allow use of the Internet of a small office appliance. (Note the default configuration should be hardened to reduce any security breach.)

```
Initiating SYN Stealth Scan at 14:17
Scanning ▮▮▮▮▮▮▮▮▮▮▮▮▮▮▮▮ (192.168.1.1) [65535 ports]
Discovered open port 53/tcp on 192.168.1.1
Discovered open port 8080/tcp on 192.168.1.1
Discovered open port 443/tcp on 192.168.1.1
Discovered open port 80/tcp on 192.168.1.1
Discovered open port 6048/tcp on 192.168.1.1
Discovered open port 6060/tcp on 192.168.1.1
Discovered open port 1883/tcp on 192.168.1.1
Discovered open port 10000/tcp on 192.168.1.1
Discovered open port 10080/tcp on 192.168.1.1
Discovered open port 49153/tcp on 192.168.1.1
Discovered open port 6049/tcp on 192.168.1.1
Discovered open port 5003/tcp on 192.168.1.1
Discovered open port 49152/tcp on 192.168.1.1
Completed SYN Stealth Scan at 14:17, 12.86s elapsed (65535 total ports)
```

Figure 2-18. *TCP/IP scan of a single IP address with many servers enabled*

Notice in Figure 2-18 the term "open port" from the scanned server. Any Internet connection or network connection service requires specific ports to be in an open state for cross-communication. The communication can be initialized from the client like a web browser or email client. These legitimate services can be exploited by software code that uses the open port, but the software code that was developed for the server OS has a vulnerability. If you install an operating system, it may have open ports by default; however, no software is currently installed that requires the TCP/IP port to be open. The best security practice is to disable unused ports; this shuts the door on cyber attackers. This is one measure to "harden" the server OS and make the server less vulnerable to network scanning or attacks.

If we look at another example, you could install a web server, IIS or NGINX, on a web server which communicates using TCP/IP on port 80 by default. You are a cyber security professional, so you enable Transport Layer Security (TLS) so all web server communication is encrypted on a tunnel running on port 443. Both ports 80 and 443 allow a two-way communication with the client. A single port can send data and receive data on the same port or a two-way dynamically generated conversation is negotiated between the client and server on a single port.

You should create a security process that supports scanning for open ports and closing ports that have no required application or that have a needed software access that requires Internet traffic in or out of the server on that specific open TCP/IP port. The Azure Security Center regularly scans your network for open Internet TCP/IP ports that do and do not have a Network Security Group configured. You could create a policy that mandates only public addresses from an Azure virtual machine must be supported by the Azure Just-in-Time (JIT) administration. Please find the JIT guidance in the "Remote Access Management" section of this chapter.

Azure Front Door Service

An Azure Front Door service is a cloud-native and global solution that provides a method to optimize application performance and failover for high availability; refer to Figure 2-19. In this chapter, you have learned more about the TCP/IP model and how applications operate at specific layers. A Front Door service is a cloud-native application that relies on layer 7 (refer to OSI and TCP/IP models in this chapter) as the delivery network. When you review the sidebar information, you notice that protocols at the application layer, layer 7, include HTTP (port 80)/HTTPs (port 443) and Domain Name Services (DNS port 53).

Some of the underlying network configurations used by the Front Door service includes the use of a routing protocol called anycast. To build on what you have learned in this chapter about Azure networks, anycast is a network addressing and is also a request routing technique in which incoming requests can be routed in different Azure regions. You may remember that Azure supports a content delivery network (CDN), which the anycast address service can leverage to route incoming traffic to the nearest Azure regions (i.e., data center), allowing for faster delivery of the request. Taking into account the Azure network backbone, the global network provides DDoS protection from a variety of attacker skill sets that range from "script kitties" to nation states. An additional feature of the Azure Front Door includes supports for high traffic volume, network congestion, which translates into high availability (HA) using the Azure network backbone.

Front Door services support web and mobile apps, cloud services, and virtual machines. Also, you can include on-premises services in your Front Door architecture for hybrid deployments or migration strategies to the Azure cloud. If you currently do not have a Front Door service, follow the exercise to create the servers for testing.

To complete the Front Door exercise, you should have two Azure web apps or websites to enable the service. If you would like an Azure exercise to create two web apps in two different Azure regions, follow the exercise at "https://ShortenedURLMarshallCopeland/cyberlanguage".

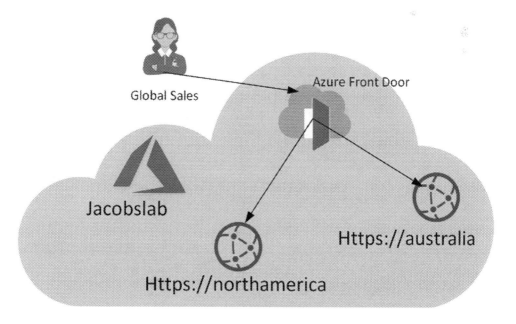

Figure 2-19. *Azure Front Door service features supporting global sales for jacobslab.com*

CREATE A FRONT DOOR SERVICE

1. In this exercise, we will deploy an Azure Front Door service and place these web apps behind it.

2. From the Home view of your Azure portal, select create a resource, enter Front Door, and select Create.

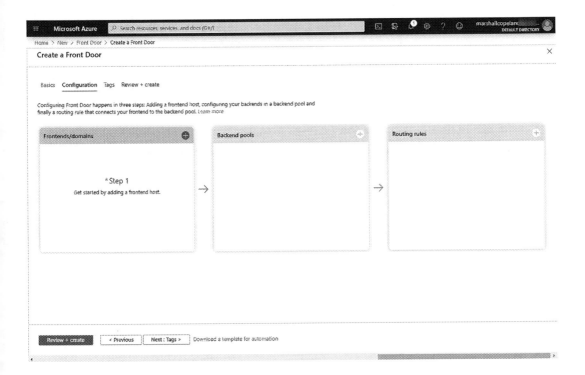

3. On the Basic journey tab, enter a new Resource Group and Location; click Next: Configuration. Your screen should be similar.

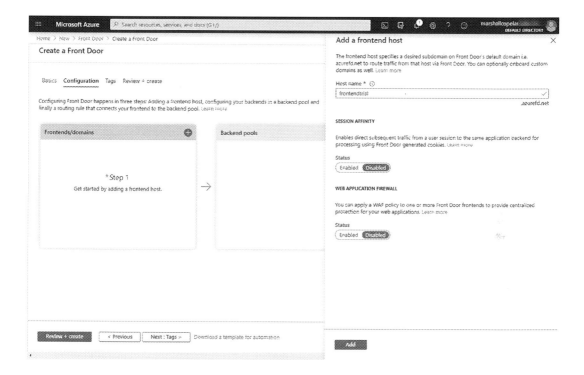

4. In the Step 1 square, click the + sign to enter the frontend host name, similar to the screen. Notice you have the option to enable session affinity, that is, sticky connections (leave disabled for this exercise). Also, there is an option to enable Web Application Firewall (leave disabled for this exercise). Click the Add button.

5. The next step is to add the backend pools. From the Step 2 square, click the + sign in the top right and enter a unique name for the backend pool similar to the screen.

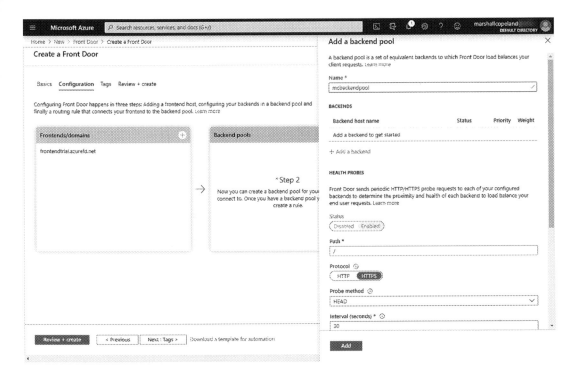

6. Click the + Add a backend label to add the first web apps from the earlier
    steps. The screen should be similar.

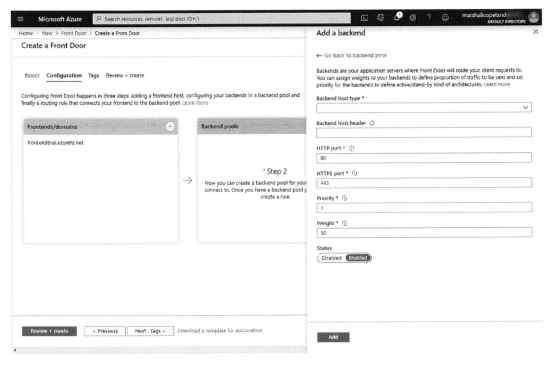

7. Select the first option from the drop-down (App service), and the backend host name is filled in automatically. The screen should be similar. Click Add.

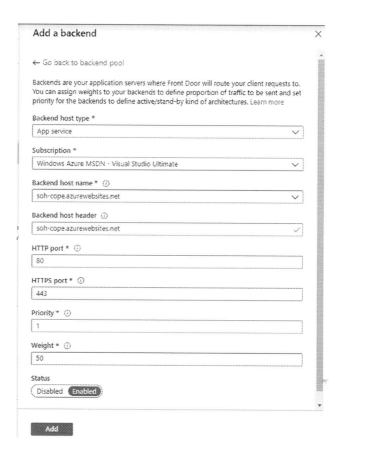

8. You need to add the second web app from West Europe; click + Add a backend and then select the drop-down for the backend host name and select the other web app. Your screen should look similar. Click Add.

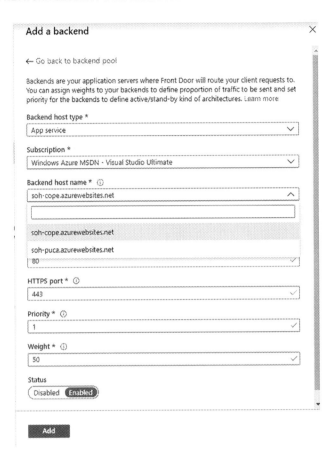

9.   With both web apps configured for the backend pool, select the Add label to
     configure the routing rules. Click the Add button.

10. Enter a unique routing rule name. This process connects the frontend request
     to forward to the backend pool. Leave the other features at their default for this
     exercise. Click Add.

11. Your screen should have the frontend, backend, and routing rules configured.
     Click the Next: Tags label.

12. Use the drop-down to select the Front Door App and location, then click Next:
     Review create. Select the Create label.

13. The Azure portal will change to indicate your Front Door deployment is
     underway. Wait for the completion and select the "Go to resource label" to view
     the Front Door service.

14. The screenshot should look similar to the Front Door view.

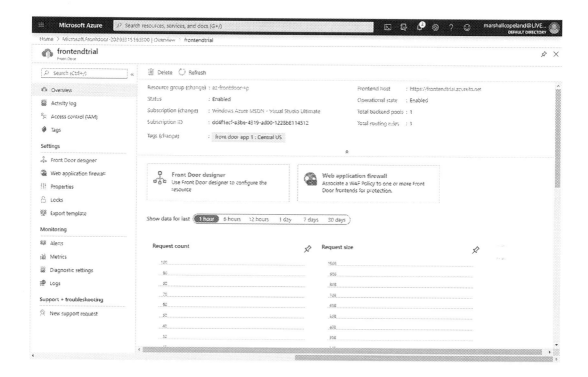

This concludes the Front Door exercise.

From the cyber security perspective, one of the benefits is that TLS termination is provided at the Azure network edge; it is included automatically by leveraging the Azure Front Door service. You can easily customize support for branding a domain name you own with support to built-in certificates or uploading your own TLS certificates. The Azure Web Application Firewall (WAF) rules can be customized to protect your web apps from cyber security exploitation like spoofing the client IP address. Some applications are developed to use the client IP address to enforce access controls, rate limits, or administration access. If the HTTP request header is used to change or "spoof" the IP address, Azure Front Door protects the workload and enables a different method of rate limit (other than using the HTTP header) to combat any malicious bot traffic against your company brand.

Remote Access Management

Accessing a VM running in Azure from your on-premises network can be challenging because of the security risks of a public IP open on the Internet. The use of a jump server would be one approach, and the VM should be hardened to limit open ports with services which limit the access if compromised. The basic approach requires enabling access to VM that is using a public IP address. If the connection supports RDP with port 3989 or SSH with port 22, the public IP address is a vulnerability access point for bad actors. You could enable and disable both the public IP address and the remote port using PowerShell, but never forget to disable access because of the lightning speed of brute-force attempts to gain access.

Azure supports an administration feature that is called the Just-in-Time (JIT) VM access that enables remote access to a VM using a "dynamic" public IP with a conditional time limit. The Just-in-Time access can be enabled for one or more VMs deployed with Azure Resource Manager (ARM) through the Azure API which includes PowerShell, CLI, and Azure Portal Network blade and using Azure Security Center. You want to support compliance validation for internal and external auditing, so JIT supports auditing activity on the VM.

JIT is enabled after you upgrade to the standard SKU in Microsoft Azure Security Center. Security Center supports many needed security features including Just-in-Time remote access. See Chapter 5 where Security Center configuration and cost assessment are provided as a dedicated chapter. The security risk exposure is reduced but not eliminated entirely with the automatic enabling and disabling of the Internet access to public IP. Now that you know what JIT is, you need to know how to leverage this feature to receive the benefit.

You should become familiar with all three components of Just-in-Time VM access to benefit this security feature. The areas to consider are

- Enabling

- Request access

- Auditing

There are two prerequisites before you continue to use JIT VM access with one being mandatory and the other an optional security best practice. If Just-in-Time access is to be used, it must first be enabled by upgrading Azure Security Center to the standard SKU. And second, you should consider setting up least-privileged access to JIT-enabled VMs and no other operations.

The VMs you would like to identify as your admin jump box would have a Network Security Group configured, either at the VM or subnet level.

ENABLING AZURE JUST-IN-TIME FROM SECURITY CENTER

1. From the Azure Security Center view, select the Just-in-Time VM access and select the not configured tab.

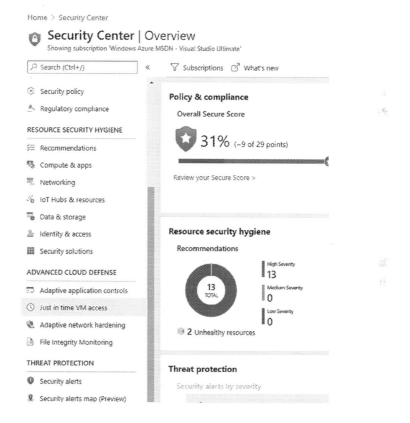

2. Select the VM to enable and then click enable. This enables JIT on one of the VMs; note this example shows one selection.

Virtual machines

Configured   Not Configured   Unsupported

VMs for which the just in time VM access control is already in

87 VMs

3. Select the VM by clicking the displayed ports to edit details (enter the port number 22-SSH for Linux, 3389-RDP for Windows OS), limited IP subnet allowed and time limit for remote connection. Then click OK.

4. Select SAVE to enable the JIT parameters you configured to Azure.

Note that your VM must have a Network Security Group enabled, and not in a restricted security policy at the subscription or resource group level.

Accessing the VM with JIT is now supported after completion of the JIT exercise. During the exercise, you will have successfully configured one or more VMs to allow Azure JIT. You can use Azure Security Center or navigate through the Azure VM pane to request access. When you saved the customized JIT configuration, it became an attribute of the VM. In the next exercise, you will learn to connect to the VM in a different method than connecting with Azure Security Center. Connecting from the VM pane in the Azure portal could be a security procedure that supports the remote access security policy.

ADMIN REQUEST ACCESS TO JIT-ENABLED VM

1. In the Azure portal, open the virtual machine pane, and under the settings option, select Connect.

2. From the right side of the pane, select the correct protocol option, RDP: Remote Desktop Protocol in this exercise (SSH: Secure Shell for a Linux system).

3. In this exercise, you should reconfigure the source IP for "My IP". (Note: Most remote workers are working from a branch or home office, and this choice reduces your Azure subscription attack surface.)

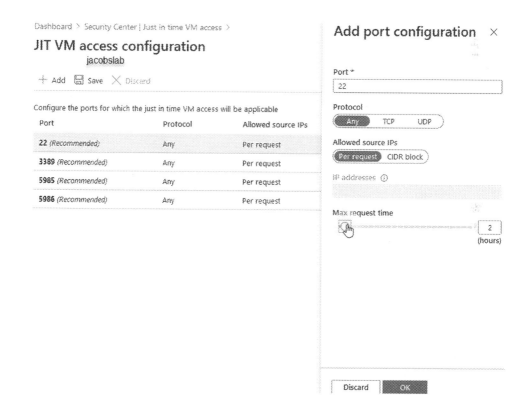

4. Select Request Access, and the Azure API enables the dynamic public IP address for the requested time limit.

The integration with Azure Security Center creates rules that specifically deny all inbound traffic when access through JIT is not requested. These rules are created on the NSG or the Azure Firewall rules to restrict and defend the ports from cyber security attacks.

When you request access to a virtual machine protected by Just-in-Time VM access, Security Center processes validate that Role-Based Access Control (RBAC) permissions are authorized. Security Center dynamically configures the NSG and Azure Firewall to allow inbound traffic for the specific time.

A key security point to take away from the use of Just-in-Time VM access is to build two security processes. Once you have decided that JIT is the correct solution to reduce security risks, consider creating two different roles to follow the least-privileged access by separating team members that can configure access and team members that can access VMs only:

- Configure JIT policy for VM

- Request JIT access to a VM

The JIT policy role requires actions assigned at the subscription or resource group level.

```
Microsoft.Security/locations/jitNetworkAccessPolicies/write
Microsoft.Compute/virtualMachines/write
```

The JIT access role requires actions assigned at the subscription or resource group level.

```
Microsoft.Security/locations/jitNetworkAccessPolicies/initiate/action
Microsoft.Security/locations/jitNetworkAccessPolicies/*/read
Microsoft.Compute/virtualMachines/read
Microsoft.Network/networkInterfaces/*/read
```

POINT-TO-SITE REMOTE MANAGEMENT OPTION

Another option could be to provision a point-to-site (P2S) connection using self-signed certifications that support connection security without exposing a public IP address. The P2S in Azure supports both Windows OS and Mac OS using native clients. The routing inside VNets needs to be planned, and distributing the certificates is a security risk, especially if a laptop goes missing that has the point-to-site certificates installed. It would be best to have a more secure remote connection option that just works, like Just-in-Time remote access (https://ShortenedURLMarshallCopeland/cyberlanguage).

Azure Bastion Host

A great option is to create an Azure bastion host and connect through the Azure portal without the need for a public IP address. One of the limitations to consider is that there is no file transfer, but that will change soon. Also, if you have a client Internet firewall, it may block some needed WebSocket traffic; if the Azure network has user-defined routes (UDR), they are not supported on the bastion host, and IP version 6 is not supported.

CREATE BASTION HOST

1. Open the Azure portal and search for bastion host; select create.

2. Enter the resource name, name of the instance, region, and virtual subnet to use the bastion host.

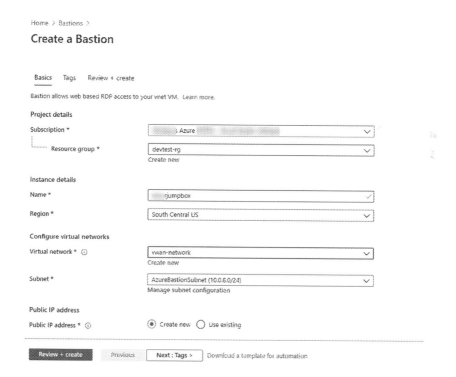

3.   Select Next: Tags and enter the project name and other tags; select
     Review + Create.

4.   The VM creation takes a few minutes; it is a hardened VM that locks the system
     down and allows connection from the bastion host to other VMs. The other VMs
     in your network do NOT require a public IP address. The bastion host connects
     using RDP and the private IP address.

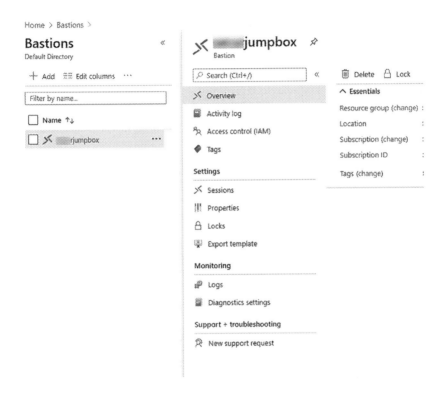

The use of bastion host allows a more secure connection to any VM without the need to create
a public IP address for any VM other than the secure jump box, aka bastion host.

Summary

In this chapter, you learned about the Azure Virtual Networks; this is an area that is foundational for all Azure infrastructure design. You begin with an overview and then into the deployment and security of VNets and IP subnets. You now know how to secure the IP subnets and VNets using Network Security Groups (NSG) and how to leverage the Azure Virtual Hub. You then learned about the support for network peering using the Azure Hub and Spoke network architecture.

You then gained a deeper knowledge of the Azure support for Network Security Groups compared to the Application Security Groups. Remember the Application Security Groups allow you to connect using Azure monikers, and they remove the editing of IP subnets to an NSG. You ended the security conversations with support for global deployment using Azure Front Door services and remote access with Just-in-Time VM access and how to configure bastion hosts.

CHAPTER 3

Reduce Cyber Security Vulnerabilities: IaaS and Data

In this chapter, you learn about the security requirements to maintain consistency to reduce vulnerabilities in the infrastructure. The infrastructure for Microsoft Azure includes VM, network, storage, and deployment options. Conversations with many customers have provided the focus to deploy Azure services using Infrastructure as Code (IaC). In this chapter, the areas you learn include

- Secure Infrastructure as Code (IaC)

- IaC deployment

- Hardening virtual machines (VM)

- Patching

- Endpoint security

- Azure database security

- Storage container security

There is a great deal to securing the data for the business, and this chapter provides an overview of all the Azure security features you should learn to be protected with the cyber security focus.

© Marshall Copeland and Matthew Jacobs 2021
M. Copeland and M. Jacobs, *Cyber Security on Azure*, https://doi.org/10.1007/978-1-4842-6531-4_3

Azure Security with IaC

This is a subject that you have read in our other publications about Microsoft Azure deployments. The deployment of Infrastructure as Code (IaC) is often an easy conversation with the development or DevOps team because their daily work includes using Visual Studio or another development platform to write code.

Continuous Integration and Continuous Delivery (CI/CD) require the Azure infrastructure team to adopt similar types of tools used in engineering development. Not only for Azure cloud but the same tools are used to deploy IaC in any major cloud. The audience for the topics covered in this chapter is the Azure security architects and cloud administrators that have a deep subject-matter expertise that should embrace this topic and use consistent templates to deploy cloud services instead of using the Azure portal. IaC is a process that provides the framework for a codified workflow to create, recreate, test (including internal penetration tests), and redeploy a software infrastructure. The Azure infrastructure includes software-defined networks (SDN), and the cloud infrastructure changes quickly so deployment using software tools is needed to create a secure environment.

The workflow process for IaC engineers requires the adoption of the same agile development methods and creates a corporate standard integration with application code workflows like Azure DevOps and the underlying Git versioning commands including GitLab and other CI/CD pipeline tools.

You normally deploy to an on-premises data center with hardware and software versions, current patching, and application configured for day 1. This first deployment is labeled as a "known good" deployment, providing a starting point, because over day 2 and beyond the problem of change from the original deployment and can sometimes be labeled as drift. When physical servers are deployed, and operating systems installed, the environment changes. Cloud operations should be included in the day 1 deployment and day 2 operations mindset.

The engineering term 'immutable' is used within IaC conversations to support the foundation of repeatability and reduces the number of systems that are out of compliance. Security is also required to be the first and last focus for all Azure services that follow the systems through their life cycle.

Azure Resource Manager (ARM) supports deploying ARM templates from PowerShell, the Azure CLI, and automation scripts. The security configuration for ARM templates includes reusable code, and the services they create are supportable.

The next step is to deploy software-defined networks, VNets in Azure, and provision idempotent configurations in your Azure subscription. ARM templates are defined in a JavaScript Object Notation (JSON) format to define the infrastructure and configure the application project. The ARM template uses a declarative syntax to deploy network infrastructure, storage, and virtual machines to Azure. The declarative JSON templates call the Azure REST API

Security architects use IaC for version control to support known security controls and create lower-risk stability. Development teams can then use the known infrastructure code for every product they build for the business. The infrastructure is validated and tested to prevent deployment inconsistencies. As an example, to enable an IaC self-service model in an IT service management (ITSM), deploy the requested Azure code from the form of Microsoft Azure Blueprints.

- ServiceNow Azure Cloud Management Blueprint

The security team, cloud operations team, and developer team should work together to create a battle-hardened repository of code for the Azure infrastructure. The tools needed for development should be adopted, and CI/CD pipelines should be used to support a library for future development test environments.

ARM Development

PowerShell scripting can be used to deploy the Azure software infrastructure templates. ARM is the Azure management layer that enables resources in Azure to be created, updated, and deleted. Infrastructure as Code resources in a template support

- Software-defined networks

- Load balancers

- Virtual machines

- Containers

- Kubernetes

Azure security supports fine-grained access using Azure Role-Based Access Control (RBAC), which is a direct feature of the Azure resource management layer integration with Azure Active Directory (AAD). ARM templates work to create the virtual foundation, and additional tools are used to configure the applications for consistency and compliance.

Some of the open source community tools like Ansible, Chef, and Puppet are great applications for management. These tools are used on-premises and in the cloud by the operations team after the network, server, and security infrastructure have been deployed. ARM templates use JSON files that define the configurations in Microsoft Azure in a declarative manner. Using templates in a software-defined format of JSON files ensures the deployment is consistent and predictable.

There are many design areas supported by the JSON file format, specifically for ARM. However, for this chapter, you need to be aware of only a few:

- Resource provider and version

- Resource location

- Parameters and variables

The application programming interface (API) layer of the Azure provider is where the method servers, services, applications, and users interact with the resource. As the API features are updated, the changes are reflected in version numbers of the resource provider. Each Azure region has resources supported for deployment that are used when deploying IaC.

As an example of considerations to create a repeatable library of templates, you need to design an ARM template to include the number of resources for performance or specific Azure pricing tiers for high availability (HA). Azure Resource Manager requires a text-based document that prescriptively enables the API layers to create, update, and delete Azure resources. ARM templates and version controls enable DevOps for Continuous Integration and Continuous Deployment (CI/CD) across subscriptions and across Azure regions.

JSON documents include many defined objects that are used in the software creation of Azure networks, virtual machines, and database services. Some of the types of object values are numbers, strings, Boolean values, and other objects. From an ARM template, I can call another ARM template. This is called a nested ARM template and allows the use of many IaC library modules.

You should be aware of the hundreds of Azure QuickStart Templates available in GitHub and updated by both Microsoft and the community. These are the same templates from GitHub ARM templates, but in an easy-to-search format.

You may also choose to use HashiCorp Terraform and support the business using the IaC libraries through that type of standard framework. The same Visual Studio Code integrated development environment (IDE) is supported for both ARM and Terraform. Versions of VS Code are available to run on Mac OS, Linux, and Windows OS.

ARM is free and the HashiCorp Terraform community version is free. The open source software (OSS) edition is an easy download as a single executable and can be installed on your local machine.

You can start to use the Infrastructure as Code deployment using the integrated command-line terminal from inside the Azure portal and watch the commands execute in the command shell.

You may also choose to use Microsoft Visual Studio Code for the installation to help you get started with developing ARM templates to build the secure library and use deployment for a more secure Azure deployment.

INSTALLING AZURE VISUAL STUDIO CODE EXTENSION

1. Open Visual Studio Code from your client system installation.

2. Choose the Extensions option.

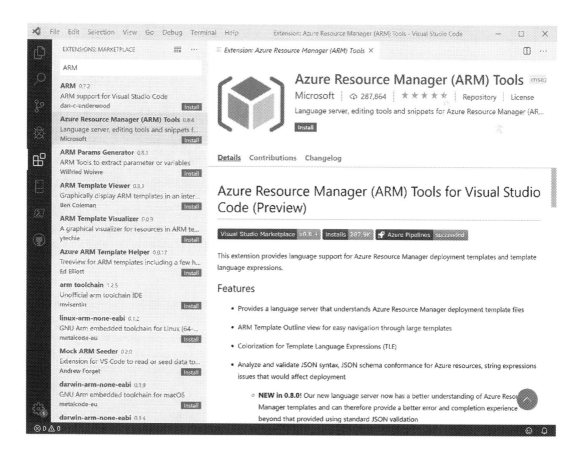

3. Search for the Azure ARM extension and note the one identified as created by
    Microsoft and not another developer or corporation. Select the Install option.

4. Verify that the Terraform extension is installed by using the search bar and
    typing the text: @installed

5. The extension should appear in the list of installed extensions.

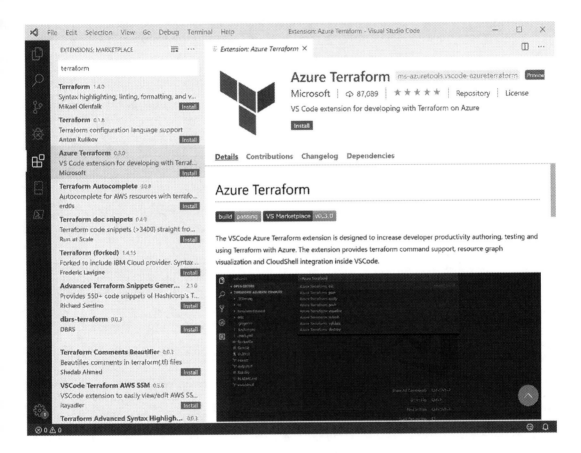

6. As a note, as Microsoft upgrades extensions and providers, the version
    numbers continue to increase.

Once the Terraform template is created, it is deployed from the Visual Studio Code
PowerShell or Azure CLI terminals.

THREAT INTELLIGENCE INFORMATION

There are several key annual security publications that should be required reading. This list is not all that should be reviewed, but it is a good start for publications published yearly and biyearly. Infrastructure teams new to security should start with this list, reading the most current publication and then reading the reports from the previous three years. The value of reading the current publications is to understand current cyber attacks. As you read the older publications, you will notice the commonalities of the bad actors and families of malware. What is sometimes seen is the resurgence of previously successful attacks but with modifications and new signatures.

The following list is a starting point for cloud architects who are new to cyber security:

- InfraGard is an FBI and private sector partnership: www.infragard.org/.

- MITRE ATT&CK Navigator knows how cyber security threats attack your business: https://mitre-attack.github.io/attack-navigator/ enterprise/.

- Microsoft Security current advisory and security updates: www.microsoft. com/security/blog/incident-response/.

- Verizon Data Breach Investigations Report (DBIR) 2020: https:// enterprise.verizon.com/resources/reports/dbir/.

- IBM-sponsored Ponemon 2020 Cost of Data Breach Study: www.ibm.com/ security/data-breach.

- Cisco has 2020 CISO Benchmark Report: www.cisco.com/c/en/us/ products/security/ciso-benchmark-report-2020.html.

- FireEye M-Trends 2020 Annual Security Report: https://content. fireeye.com/m-trends.

- Red Canary has a free 2020 Threat Report that ingested 200 billion endpoints (per day), 6 million leads, and 15,000 configured threats into a single report: https://redcanary.com/.

- National Council of ISACs, sector-based information sharing: www.nationalisacs.org/.

- SANS.ORG (SANS) is a not-for-profit organization; it supports free membership to access detailed white papers and threat intelligence: www.sans.org/reading-room/whitepapers/threats/paper/39395.

You, as a security professional, must stay aware to show support for the boards of directors as they significantly increase their focus on cloud information security, hybrid network cyber security, and IT risk management. Your security team requires up-to-date resources that provide a global view of international cyber armies, with in-depth information about their attack vectors, weaponized payloads, and industry-specific targeting.

Harden Azure VMs

Many administrators spend the majority of their efforts focused on keeping attackers from penetrating our edge and external facing devices. Subsequently, we lack development of an internal standard for creating security controls within our virtual machines. We can leverage the process of VM hardening to limit, without impeding normal operations, some of the policies and features that can be enabled on our virtual machines. A virtual machine that is responsible for only one role can be considered more secure than a VM that is responsible for multiple roles. For example, if you have a virtual machine that is responsible for running as an ADFS Web Application Proxy, you would notice if suddenly it starts trying to send emails. Unlike traditional on-premises data center deployments where VMs can be licensed in bulk and the cost of resources is bound by the amount of hardware that you have available, the temptation to get the most out of your Azure resources is real and something every organization faces. Don't fall into this mindset. Layering multiple services and functions into one VM can get out of hand especially when dealing with complex deployments that have interdependencies.

One of the many ways we can harden our VMs in Azure is by leveraging best practices derived from publications by well-tested and trusted organizations such as the National Institute of Standards and Technology (NIST) and the Center for Internet Security (CIS). NIST publication 800-123, Section 4, lays out guidelines for securing a server's operating system. Subsection four provides supporting documentation on removing unnecessary services, protocols, and applications that are not used for the primary role of the server. The following are noted in NIST 800-123:

- File and printer sharing services (e.g., Windows Network Basic Input/ Output System [NetBIOS] file and printer sharing, Network File System [NFS], FTP)

- Wireless networking services

- Remote control and remote access programs, particularly those that do not strongly encrypt their communications

- Directory services (e.g., Lightweight Directory Access Protocol [LDAP], Network Information System [NIS])

- Web servers and services

- Email services (e.g., SMTP)

- Language compilers and libraries

- System development tools

- System and network management tools and utilities, including Simple Network Management Protocol (SNMP)

CIS creates and releases a series of standards that they refer to as "benchmarks." "CIS Benchmarks are best practices for the secure configuration of a target system. Available for 100+ CIS Benchmarks covering more than 14 technology groups, CIS Benchmarks are developed through a unique consensus-based process comprised of cybersecurity professionals and subject matter experts around the world. CIS Benchmarks are the only consensus-based, best-practice security configuration guidelines both developed and accepted by government, business, industry, and academia." (`www.cisecurity. org/cis-benchmarks/cis-benchmarks-faq/`) Starting from the CIS Benchmarks, we can create baselines that are tailored to our organization's unique needs. Applying these benchmarks can be done in two ways: prebuild and postbuild. In a prebuild scenario, we can leverage hardened images that are deployable via the Azure Marketplace or when creating a VM within your tenant. To create a VM based on a CIS Benchmark, select "Browse all public and private images" when selecting the image. Type CIS in the search bar and select the appropriate image. Refer to Figures 3-1 and 3-2.

Be sure to read through the CIS Benchmark you are deploying. It will save time and headache by knowing that configurations are enabled or disabled in the image, which differ from a standard out-of-the-box deployment.

When applying CIS Benchmarks to an existing VM or postbuild, we will need to rely on Group Policy to configure and enforce these settings. Using Group Policy will allow us to make a baseline policy once, duplicate it to tailor for our organization's needs, and deploy it consistently when new VMs are joined to our domain. Our Group Policies can be deployed through Azure Active Directory Domain Services, which mirror the same management style as an on-premises Active Directory Group Policy.

Create a virtual machine

Basics	Disks	Networking	Management	Advanced	Tags	Review + create

Create a virtual machine that runs Linux or Windows. Select an image from Azure marketplace or use your own customized image. Complete the Basics tab then Review + create to provision a virtual machine with default parameters or review each tab for full customization. Learn more ⧉

Project details

Select the subscription to manage deployed resources and costs. Use resource groups like folders to organize and manage all your resources.

Subscription * ⓘ | Azure subscription 1 ⌄ |

   └ .... Resource group * ⓘ | rsg-IT ⌄ |
                              Create new

Instance details

Virtual machine name * ⓘ | WebAppSRV01 ⌄ |

Region * ⓘ | (US) East US ⌄ |

Availability options ⓘ | No infrastructure redundancy required ⌄ |

Image * ⓘ | Windows Server 2016 Datacenter - Gen1 ⌄ |
                              Browse all public and private images

Figure 3-1. *Image selection during VM creation*

You can transition to another option.

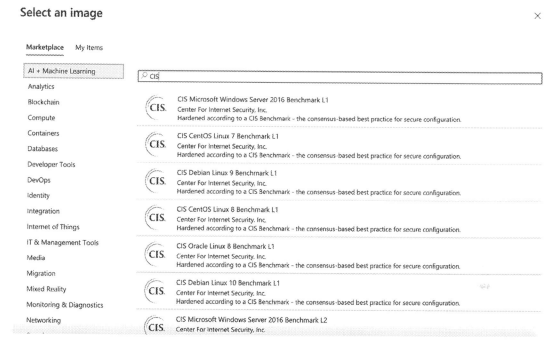

Figure 3-2. *Search for a CIS Benchmark image*

REAL-WORLD EXAMPLE

Working with company A, an audit firm was brought in to identify potential shortcomings in their cyber security posture. One of the key items that was brought to light was the lack of a server hardening standard. Several colleagues worked together to develop a standard template that could be applied across all servers in the organization both physical and virtual. However, it became evident that due to some servers being in a highly specialized environment with several layers of third-party automation between them, the standard had to be written in such a way that it would not interfere with normal operations. In the end, once the standard was agreed upon and written into policy, a documentation was provided for each server that was built, and exceptions were written for servers that didn't meet the policy verbatim. An exception is a notation that indicates why a deviation exists from an agreed-upon policy, usually backed by a business justification for its occurrence. When an internal audit was conducted a year later, it was well understood why certain exceptions existed. The point of the example is that exceptions aren't a bad thing within a security posture. Business justifications can ultimately provide evidence for atypical configurations, if the risk is understood and accepted.

Although it should go without saying, part of reducing your cyber security risk in Azure should include a well-documented and routinely executed patching process for all virtual machines. Collectively over the past several years, over 50% of companies that have acknowledged a data breach can trace the entry point to a device that was exploited due to a missing security patch. A third of these organizations had previously detected and were aware that the vulnerability existed within their organization's infrastructure. Due to the evolution of existing technology and the emerging threats of tomorrow, organizations will always face the inevitable gap that exists between when a vulnerability is discovered and when a security patch is developed and released. As we shift toward always-on and always accessible data centers in the cloud, we add an even more daunting workload to our administrators.

Traditionally, we deploy patches through the use of third-party vulnerability scanning and patching solutions. While that is still a valid option to use within our tenant, this creates yet another pane of glass to monitor and administer outside of Azure. We can leverage some of the built-in features of Azure to patch our VMs through automation. There are four main ways to deploy patches using Azure, with each option being unique to how much or how little your Azure tenant and subscriptions have matured. All of the outlined in the following assume you have an Automation account or will set one up inside of Azure, and there is always the option to patch using the native update management software inside of the VM operating system.

Patching the VM Directly

The mechanisms by how you patch are just as important as why you patch and what process you use to do it. For organizations that do not have a well-defined patching process, you can start with guidance from another National Institute of Standards and Technology (NIST) publication. NIST SP 800-40 Revision 3, a Guide to Enterprise Patch Management, provides some insight around why you should patch, some of the obstacles an organization needs to consider, and an overview of the different technologies that make a successful patch management process. As outlined in Section 2 of NIST SP 800-40r3, "Patch management is required by various security compliance frameworks, mandates, and other policies. For example, NIST SP 800-53 requires the SI-2, Flaw Remediation security control, which includes installing security-relevant software and firmware patches, testing patches before installing them, and incorporating patches into the organization's configuration management processes.

Another example is the Payment Card Industry (PCI) Data Security Standard (DSS), which requires that the latest patches be installed and sets a maximum timeframe for installing the most critical patches." Creating and maintaining an effective patch management process going forward will be one of the key items in thwarting attacks and ensuring a maximum amount of compliance in your environment.

You have the flexibility to use Update Management in Azure Automation to manage the OS update for both Windows and Linux VMs. This extends to updates for on-premises and other clouds. There are simple requirements like linking to a Log Analytics workspace and the Automation account. The updates are accomplished with Desired State Configuration (DSC) and Microsoft Update Catalog and Windows Server Update Services (WSUS). Learn more about this feature at `https://docs.microsoft.com/en-us/azure/automation/update-management/update-mgmt-overview`.

Patching systems often requires reboots, so one of the best practices for high availability for IaaS is using multiple servers deployed in Azure in different update domains and fault domains.

VM Security and Endpoint Protection

Virtual machines deployed in Azure are used to deploy many Infrastructure as a Service (IaaS) workloads, compared to on-premises infrastructure deployments. The operating systems include many different versions of Windows and Linux OS and include multiple languages.

With the flexibility of a VM, the cost-per-minute usage reduces the physical hardware resources to support the host systems. You can refocus some of the resources to enhance the layers of security of servers including node protection, encryptions, and network traffic security.

Endpoint protection is supported using a VM agent with Azure extensions to communicate through Azure API commands to protect from malware and viruses. Many of the vendors created easy deployment from ARM templates and through the Azure portal deployment including

- Microsoft

- Symantec

- Trend Micro

Virtual disk encryption is supported with the Azure Disk Encryption deployment of BitLocker for Windows and dm-crypt for Linux OS and data disks. Azure Disk Encryption is managed through an integration with your Azure Key Vault subscription.

Azure operations teams can take advantage of Azure Backup to protect the applications running on the VMs.

Azure Site Recovery (ASR) is a cloud-native solution to support virtual machine replication and failover of workloads. Other recovery solutions include Business Continuity and Disaster Recovery (BCDR); ASR supports cloud to cloud and on-premises to cloud disaster recovery strategy.

Compliance for VMs is supported through Azure Policy, Azure Blueprint deployment, and Azure Security Center. Refer to Figure 3-3 for an overall view of the composite view of security.

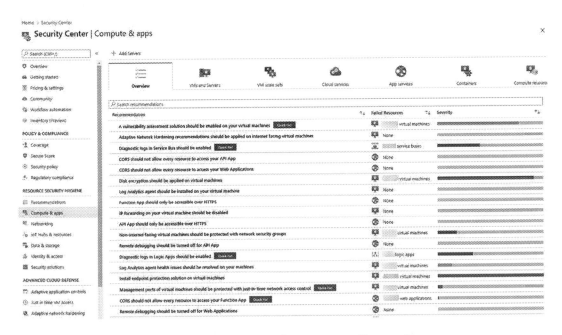

Figure 3-3. *Security Center compute and apps overall security*

There are options to click the Quick Fix to remediate to quickly improve the overall security score and improve your security posture.

Azure Blueprints are in the control of the Azure team to implement and adhere to business standards with a combination of the following:

- Least-privileged access

- Policy deployment

- ARM templates

You can read more about the use of Azure Blueprints and support for compliance standards at `https://docs.microsoft.com/en-us/azure/governance/blueprints/overview`.

A few examples of Azure Blueprints, which include security control examples ready for you to test and customize for your Azure deployment, include

- HIPAA and HITRUST

- IRS 1075

- ISO 27001

- PCI-DSS

Azure IaaS supports the business life cycle deployment, and the same standard is supported using Azure Blueprint deployments.

Database Security

Azure cloud is about choice, and when your business requires a database, the security to store critical information is one of the top priorities. Benefits for Azure SQL Database and Azure SQL Managed Instance are two options with security features. There are many database options to choose in the Azure Marketplace, so let the guidance focus on two from the Azure SQL Server family.

A SQL Server database is referred to as a single database. It can also be used in different Azure deployment methods. Azure SQL Managed Instance is a separate product, not just a deployment option of the SQL Server database. Refer to Figure 3-4 to view the different deployment options of a database to help decide the security required for the business.

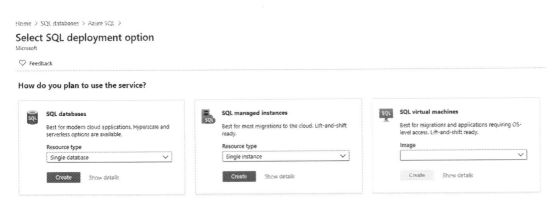

Figure 3-4. *Azure SQL Database deployment options*

Azure SQL Database can be automatically deployed as a single database with a separate set of resources and separate managed server. The managed server is not configurable other than selecting a purchase model, which you would do based on the workload estimate. The single database can be enabled and created on a serverless compute tier which is a purchasing model.

The security for the database is another layer of the overall security model. It is the layer of security that helps maintain the private information for the business. The security for the data applies to both Azure SQL data and Azure SQL Managed Instance.

IP firewall rules grant or deny access to the databases based on the IP address of the source (similar to Network Security Groups). The source IP address can be from the Internet (if allowed) or from Azure cloud. The firewall supports two levels of rules, the database level and the server level.

If you have one database or many databases, the server-level firewall rules are configured to maintain access control – up to 128 server-level IP firewall rules for each server and not each database hosted on the server. The individual firewall rules, for this management access, are stored in the master database.

If you have many databases, using the database-level IP firewall rules can be configured and applied to manage different access for each database. The IP firewall rules are stored in the individual database.

Advanced Data Security (ADS) is a package of security for the Azure SQL database, Azure SQL Managed Instance, and Azure Synapse Analytics (which is not part of this chapter). The automatic discovery and classification of data are supported in the Azure services. This security feature is discussed in Chapter 7.

Advanced Threat Protection, part of the ADS offering, can be applied to Azure SQL Database to detect Incidents of Compromise (IOC) and anomalous activities that could exploit data. This level of protection is used to identify

- SQL injection

- Unusual location access

- Access from unfamiliar ID

- Harmful application

- Brute-force SQL credentials

You should consider a Proof of Concept (POC) to test the value of enabling the Advanced Data Security for your business. Include in your measurement the savings cost of the current database security that is not cloud native or not even Internet access enabled.

DB Best Practices

You should use the database-level IP firewall rules whenever possible. Using this security setting allows the database to be secure, and you can now migrate the database and maintain the security rules. Security configuration is completed for each database if they have the same access requirements or different access requirements.

You should consider using server-level IP firewall rules when many databases required the same access rights. The configuration at this level minimized the configuration needed.

Database dynamic data masking is a security feature for Azure SQL Database, Managed Instance, and Synapse Analytics. Dynamic masking limits exposure of potential sensitive data to nonprivileged users. This masking is applied at the application layer (minimal impact on performance) and is policy based. Masking policies include

- SQL users excluded from masking

- Masking rules to apply

- Masking functions

The masking functions support control of data based on types such as credit card, email, and custom fields.

DB Authentication

The access of a user or an administrator to the database server and the database itself can leverage Azure Active Directory (AAD) or SQL authentication. Azure supports a user account name and password and can enable access based on the Azure roles the user is authorized to access.

SQL authentication uses a username and password stored in the master database of the SQL Server. The user is linked to the database to allow access. There is a difference between a login and a user.

An individual account stored in the master database is classified as a login. The credential is stored with the login information, and the user account can then linked to one or more databases.

An individual user account can be in any database, not just the master database, but does not have a requirement to be linked to a login. Because the user account is not linked, the credential information is self-contained and stored in the user account in the individual database. Refer to Figure 3-5 to view the two settings.

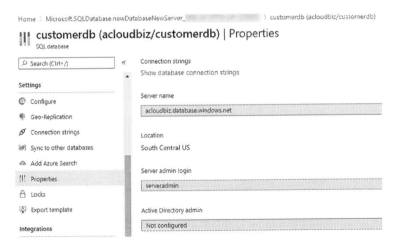

Figure 3-5. *SQL Server login and Active Directory admin view*

You can leverage AAD authentication for cloud-only (AAD only) and hybrid identities (sync with on-premises Active Directory). Developers can be allowed access using Azure AD authentication if they connect from SQL Server Management Studio with Multifactor Authentication enabled.

Database Auditing

Auditing tracks access to and inside the database with events. These events are written to the audit log that is stored in the Azure storage account and Log Analytics workspace. The business need for SQL auditing support includes the need to retain events that include access to and editing of the database and data access. This information can be used for reporting for security and compliance and analysis reports for suspicious events. Auditing can be managed by

- Server level
- Database level

Server-level auditing supports the security administration, but at the logical SQL Server, management introduces some different challenges. The server can be in different regions than the resource group for the auditing of the database.

Auditing the server can apply to current databases installed or newly created databases on the servers with the policy applied. The server policies applied for auditing always apply to the database. Enabled auditing on the database does not override settings on the server auditing; refer to Figure 3-6.

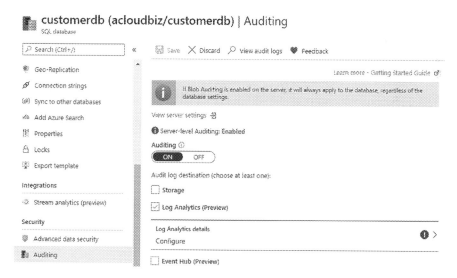

Figure 3-6. *SQL Database auditing for server level or database level*

The auditing data can be saved to many different collection points: Log Analytics workspace, event hubs, and storage containers. Audit logs in Azure Blob storage are written to the Append Blobs, so creating an immutable log store is necessary for compliance support.

Figure 3-7 shows the server-level auditing enabled. With server-level auditing enabled (on), the audit applies to all the databases on that server.

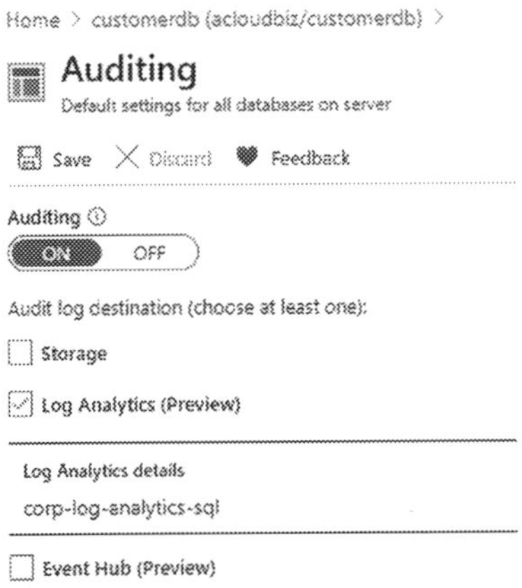

Figure 3-7. *Default auditing settings for all databases on the server*

Note   The best practice is to enable auditing for one level (server or database) but not both.

Storage Accounts

One of the most significant services to use is the Azure storage account. This service provides the flexibility needed to store data that has different properties and uses – in addition to storage for objects like

- Blobs (binary large objects)
- Files
- Queues
- Tables

Storage accounts are also used to store virtual disks for virtual machines. Access to storage is available from inside your Azure subscription and can be configured to allow Internet access. Access can be over HTTP or forced to HTTPS only, and there are many uses for massively scalable storage. Creating a storage account (refer to Figure 3-8) has some considerations to choose the best option for the data to be stored.

Instance details

The default deployment model is Resource Manager, which supports the latest Azure features. You may choose to deploy using the classic deployment model instead. Choose classic deployment model

Storage account name * ⓘ	devstorageacct007 ⌄
Location *	(US) South Central US ⌄
Performance ⓘ	⦿ Standard ◯ Premium
Account kind ⓘ	StorageV2 (general purpose v2) ⌃
	StorageV2 (general purpose v2)
Replication ⓘ	Storage (general purpose v1)
Blob access tier (default) ⓘ	BlobStorage

Figure 3-8. *Azure storage account view of v1 and v2 options*

There are additional considerations, like features supported by selecting the general-purpose v2 accounts for basic storage needs or general-purpose v1 which may need to be updated in the future. This discussion is needed for logging differences between the major objects.

Azure storage automatically encrypts data in the storage account using AES 256-bit encryption. The encryption is applied at the data storage level of the Azure storage service. All data written into the Azure storage account is encrypted and decrypted, and the process is transparent to the end user. No changes are needed to applications; this is just security by design.

Diagnostic logging is affected by the version selected during the creation. Often, the types of stored items are decision-making rules, and the different alerting and diagnostics should be considered from the Azure Security operations team. Service operations for logging support include the following:

- Blob storage supports v1 and v2.

- File storage supports v1.

- Table storage supports v1.

- Queue storage supports v1 and v2.

Note   Please review the details of Azure storage accounts at `https://docs.microsoft.com/en-us/azure/storage/common/storage-account-overview?toc=/azure/storage/blobs/toc.json`.

Data protection is available to leverage the Azure Resource Manager (ARM) features for security enhancements. Refer to Figure 3-9 for a visual representation of security features that also support disaster recovery issues.

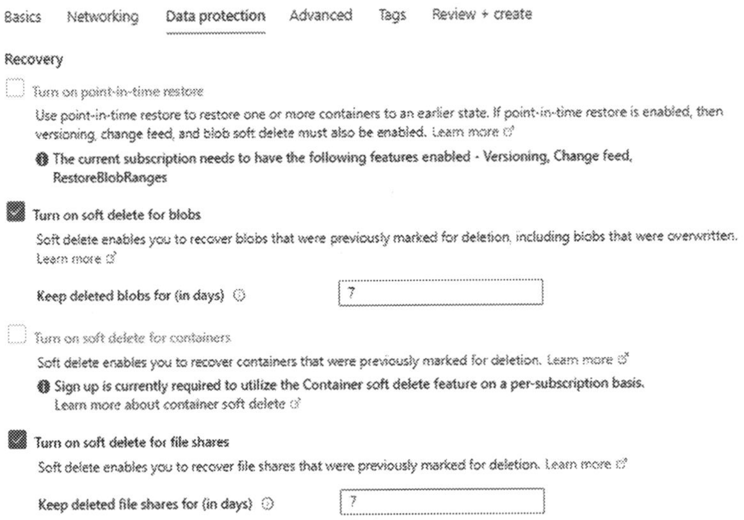

Figure 3-9. *Storage account data protection view*

You can enable features like soft delete for

- Blobs

- Containers

- File shares

Notice also you can turn on point-in-time restoration features for one or more containers. However, you do have prerequisites before this feature can be enabled. In the wizard, the length of time can be kept at default, 7 days. However, the options are from 1 day to 365 days retention. One final feature is to enable tracking for the versioning of Blob storage; refer to Figure 3-10. You may have requirements for compliance or insider threats that force this option.

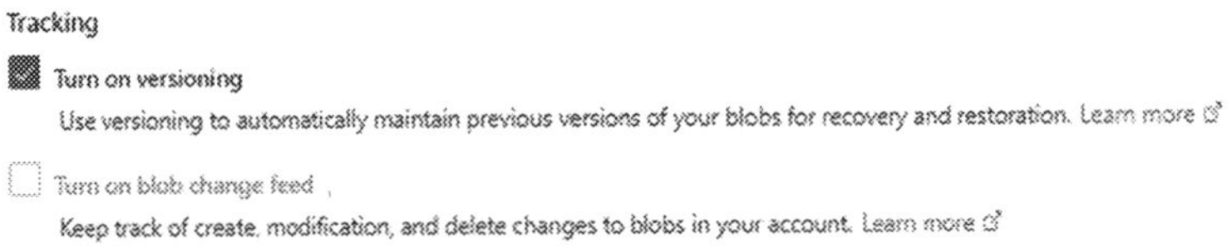

Figure 3-10. *Tracking and versioning to enable recovery points*

Creating the storage account includes features to protect the data in transit and also allow you to set the minimum security level for the TLS transport. Refer to Figure 3-11.

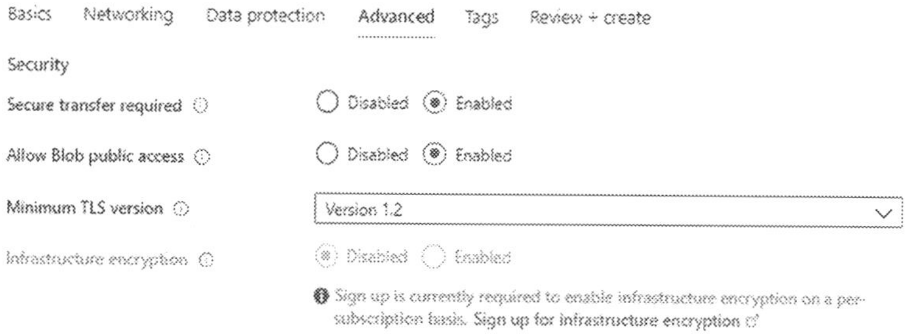

Figure 3-11. *Security feature view for the TLS version*

The secure transfer option uses HTTPS only and rejects any REST API calls that attempt to use HTTP. Forcing the Transport Layer Security (TLS) version can also be achieved using Azure Policy deployment.

Notice the option to first register to use the infrastructure encryption, and it may take several months for access to be approved in limited Azure regions. This security feature supports encryption at the infrastructure level, in addition to the data at the service level.

Authorizing access to Azure storage is easily accomplished using Azure Active Directory and can be logged for review and alerting in Azure Monitor, Security Center, and Azure Sentinel. Each of these configurations is included in Part 2 of this publication.

You should also be aware that access to Azure storage can be achieved by allowing access from the Internet using shared access keys or through a shared access signature, which you will learn next.

Shared Access Signatures

Storage services can optionally be available for public access using shared access signatures (SAS). The most granular access support is with the integration of Azure Active Directory. However, often, partners require access to data shared between the two companies, and access using permissions and a shared key is useful.

Note   The Azure policy can be used to force public IP address for Azure storage to be audited; The options include: TLS, HTTPS, and disabled.

The way the shared access signature works is by using a signed Uniform Resource Identifier (URI) to connect to the service. The token includes the resource allowed access, and the signature is signed with the key that was used to create the SAS. Shared access signatures (SAS) are supported on Azure storage blobs, files, queues, and tables. The use of SAS as an access method is often implemented for general-purpose access on the storage account and also the following contexts:

- User delegation SAS

- Service SAS

- Account SAS

The shared access signature is supported with two permission types:

- Ad hoc SAS

- Service SAS with stored access policy

The ad hoc created supports both start and end times, and the permissions are included in the SAS Uniform Resource Identifier (URI). The account stored access policy can be used to manage access to one or more services that are shared. There are two parts, and together they make up the shared access signature, URI, and SAS token; refer to Figure 3-12 for settings.

Figure 3-12. *Shared access signature services, permissions, expire times*

Key Management

In this example, once the Generate SAS connection string option is selected, the SAS key is generated, as shown in Figure 3-13.

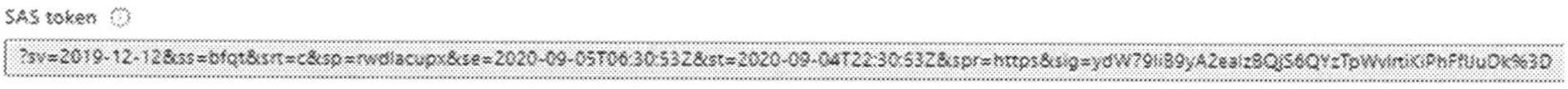

SAS token ⓘ

?sv=2019-12-12&ss=bfqt&srt=c&sp=rwdlacupx&se=2020-09-05T06:30:53Z&st=2020-09-04T22:30:53Z&spr=https&sig=ydW79IiB9yA2eaIzBQjS6QYzTpWvlrtiKiPhPfUuDk%3D

Figure 3-13. Shared access signature generated SAS token

You can gain a closer insight by reviewing the simple but real SAS displayed in Listing 3-1.

Listing 3-1. Begin and end access time with the signature key

```
?sv=2019-12-12&ss=bfqt&srt=c&sp=rwdlacupx&se=2020-09-05T06:30:53Z&st=2020-
09-04T22:30:53Z&spr=

https&sig=ydW79IiB9yA2eaIzBQjS6QYzTpWvlrtiKiPhFflJuDk%3D
```

Note   If a SAS is lost, saved with code in the GitHub repository, it can be used by anyone who obtains it, which can compromise your storage account.

The SAS token is generated on the client side and shared with client applications that need access to the Azure storage. When you configure Azure, the application provides the SAS URI directly to Azure Storage.

The Azure file service connection without encryption fails, and this includes SMB 2.1 and SMB 3.0 that are not using encryption. This is true for both Windows and Linux SMB client connections.

Best security practices include

- Create a revocation plan

- Use short-lived SAS times

- Force clients to renew SAS

- Always enable HTTPS

As you review the topics one more time, you begin to realize that as Azure services are deployed, there are many opportunities to deploy them inconsistently and insecurely. Always use the Infrastructure as Code deployment to maintain versioning and battle-tested configurations and improve your security posture.

Summary

There are important topics in this chapter. You learned about the value of the Infrastructure as Code day 1 deployment, using a consistent known deployment model, and configuration versions that can be supported. Then you learned about the way to harden a virtual machine and keep the VM patched. In addition, the support for security with endpoint management for Azure was shared.

Then you learned about securing the Azure Database and database services using firewalls and auditing features. Finally, you learned about the Azure Storage container security using both Azure Active Directory and shared access keys.

PART II

Azure Cloud Security Operations

In Part 2, the focus is clearly on identifying the vulnerabilities from a red team perspective (aka black hat) and how the blue team (white hat) could defend from the attack. The topics for cloud security are in alignment but, the "red team" goal is to help train the blue teams defense on specific cloud targets. During the chapters in Part 2, the reader is guided through many attack matrices from https://attack.mitre.org/ and C2 Matrix examples of attackers and their attack techniques.

Guidance on using the Azure cloud-native services like Azure Security Center, Azure Sentinel, and the value of Azure policies is included. Additional sidebars are used to identify how your cloud network, and hybrid network design, is a target to attackers. Where in the past, network hardware was on-premises. In the case of Azure, software defined network appliances with discussions on security best practices to defend against known and unknown vulnerablities.

CHAPTER 4

Configure Azure Monitoring for Blue Team Hunting

This chapter provides guidance about what data is available through Azure services, how to configure usage of this data, and how to enable performance and security alerting. The use of Azure cloud-native services for data analysis begins in this chapter and extends through other chapters into Azure Security Center and Azure Sentinel. Your focus is security analytics, so you need to understand the difference between logs and metrics from the Azure resources and what the resource costs are to consume the information and create actionable security data.

This chapter begins to answer your question by connecting the individual Azure services to best configure the data for reporting and later cyber security proactive monitoring. Also, this chapter begins Part 2 of the journey, and includes the next three chapters, to directly support the blue team cyber security hunters. As a cyber security defender, you fall into the "blue team" group of professionals that are held accountable for analysis supporting Azure network, Azure applications, and data integrity. You may or may not be a member of the Security Operations Center (SOC), but part of your work is to identify security flaws and validate security controls. Threat hunting falls squarely in the blue team skill set. You actively search Azure for intruders and proactively review Azure metrics and logs for Incidents of Compromise (IOC), using digital forensics to improve detection.

As a blue team security hunter, you need to extend your skills to the Azure cloud; you need to understand what data sources are available, what each specific Azure data feed provides, and how to leverage that information to find outliers, anomalies, and Incidents of Compromise. Using the information from all chapters in Part 2 provides

M. Copeland and M. Jacobs, *Cyber Security on Azure*, https://doi.org/10.1007/978-1-4842-6531-4_4

a foundation to support Microsoft Azure Sentinel. Azure Sentinel is a cloud-native Security Information and Event Management (SIEM) solution. Sentinel consolidates all data points from Azure metrics, logs, and diagnostics collected from the Azure platform and the applications for your business into a security orchestration service. You can use Azure Monitoring from the individual Azure resource like a VM; however, Sentinel correlates security events across all the different log sources and can ingest different Microsoft cloud security services, Advanced Threat Protection (ATP), and on-premises products. Azure Sentinel is covered in more detail in Chapter 5.

In this chapter, your cyber threat skills expand into the Azure platform, and you will learn to leverage resources including

- Azure data platform

- Logs and sources

- Metrics and sources

- Azure Monitor and Log Analytics enablement

- Guest OS metrics and logs

- Azure Analytics

Some Azure customers find the documents for Azure Monitor and Log Analytics confusing; the documents to use and deploy the services are similar but not the same. Not to oversimplify the powerful Azure Monitor service but the relationship can be visualized this way. Log Analytics is a component service within the Azure Monitor solution. Similarly, as another example, Microsoft System Center is the overall solution; System Center Operations Manager is a component of System Center.

Azure Monitor is the current service to receive, store, and display Azure data. The consolidation supports a more consistent approach to collect metrics in a single view for both Azure IaaS and PaaS deployments. Azure Monitor Log data is stored in a Log Analytics workspace. The Log Analytics service supports editing and executing queries to analyze the log data. The actual work of the queries is the "Analytics" just like the work of the Azure Application Insights service, which are both components of Azure Monitor. There may be a little confusion because the term Log Analytics has changed to Azure Monitor Logs. This was done to support a consistency with metrics identification consumed by the Azure Monitor service.

Before the adoption of cloud services, data was collected from hardware, operating systems (OS), and software applications. Information included servers, desktops, laptops, and mobile devices. Subject-matter experts (SME) knew the exact data center rack of servers that provided detail log information for the identity platform, application health, and encrypted file storage. When you move applications into the Azure public cloud, you need to learn new methods to validate applications are performing as expected and be alerted if an admin change made your data vulnerable to attacks. The integrity and availability of applications and the Azure data platform are identified using Azure logs and metrics.

Azure Data Platform

Identity and business applications run 24/7, and so does the need to analyze issues faster and create alerts that are actionable for the Security Operations Center (SOC) teams. Logging of hardware-specific data and the hypervisor information and alerts are managed by Microsoft, and everything else is up to the Azure subscription owner.

To better understand how the data is categorized in the data platform, which is included as part of your Azure services, you need to learn where data is collected and how it is aggregated. The more challenging requirement of the security team is the understanding of where, inside Azure, does data streams come from. More importantly, you need to know the costs associated with analyzing and storing the data. The virtual machine in the cloud still has a financial cost when running; the VM has virtual CPU, memory, network, and data storage requirements, just like a VM running in your on-premises data center. Other on-premises monitoring includes applications for application analysis, visualization of user connections, dashboard views, log monitoring, and security alerting.

There are two major categories of data described from the Azure Monitor data platform:

- Logs

- Metrics

These two types are used as labels or descriptors for the types of information that are collected and aggregated from a variety of sources inside Azure. Both logs and metrics are collected for utilization through Azure Monitor. Refer to Table 4-1 to review a few characteristic differences between logs and metrics.

Table 4-1. *Characteristics to identify metric data and log data*

Logs	Metrics	Characteristic
Numeric and text	Numeric	Data type
Service workload driven	Regular intervals	Collection times
Log Analytics/Monitor	Metrics Explorer	Where to review in Azure portal

As your cloud network team members add more VNets and IP subnets, traffic flow needs to be measured and alerted as the cloud network expands. When projects are created to include virtual machines and applications, the insight for server and application health should be analyzed, and alerts need to be enabled. To put workflow into perspective, networking uses VNets, and Azure compute includes VMs. The VMs run on a host but depend on an operating system (OS) so they are the guest OS metrics and logs. Applications installed on the guest OS may be SQL applications or custom applications. The VM, OS, and applications are all different and provide different forms of metrics and logs that dictate what type of data is created and how it can be used to alert. Now you need to consider the maturity of application services in the cloud. Please review the information in Figure 4-1 for a visual representation of the Azure Monitor services; this diagram is used to demonstrate information aggregation as part of the Azure data platform.

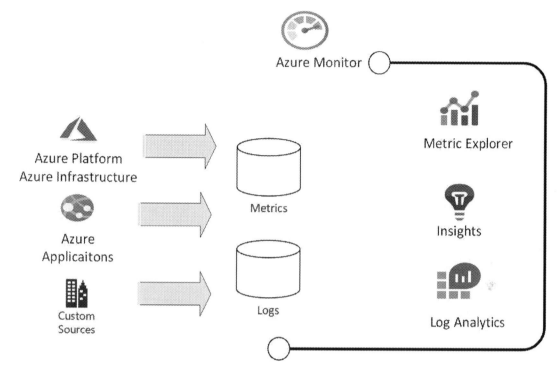

Figure 4-1. *Azure data platform visual representation*

If you expand this topic for Azure compute, the information provided includes Azure Kubernetes Services (AKS), Azure Spring Cloud, and Azure Functions. More service metrics and logs are added for analysis. These are compute services that are requested using the Azure portal journey to collect input and make the services available. As the Azure architect or operations team, you did not build the VMs, networks, and applications for any of these services. However, the Security Operations Center (SOC) is still required to monitor and secure the services. When any of the services are not performing optimally or unauthorized data access is being attempted, alerts are required to inform those responsible. Now you are provided with some of the best methods to leverage Azure Monitor.

Note   Azure Function is marketed as a serverless service which means the service runs on a VM core that you do not manage but that VM writes log and metric data in Azure you must use.

You have learned that the Azure platform sends logs and metrics to Azure Analytics workspaces (one or more) and archives storage and Azure Event Hubs. Now you continue to gain insight into the platform logs, metrics, and their sources of data.

Azure Logs

Azure Monitor is the updated cloud-native service and has the advantage of being the single cloud solution that your Azure operations team can utilize for analysis and alerting on the correlated data derived from the many cloud data sources. Data that are classified in Azure as logs are numerical or text (or both) with information like a timestamp and label. You may read online documentation that refers to diagnostic logs, but the name has changed to resource logs. However, there may still be a little confusion because the configuration label is "Diagnostic Settings" in Azure, which is used to enable the collection of resource logs.

Most operational data are stored to a resource log and can be used by Azure Monitor to perform data analysis. As a single example of the complexity of log data, let us review platform logs. Logs in Azure Monitor are stored in a Log Analytics workspace, and data is written in a time that matches the system load. A busy workload with many clients connected or reports being created generates more volume of data, a large log data amount for storage in the workspace. Please review the information in Table 4-2 to gain a better understanding of the Azure Monitor Log sources.

Table 4-2. *Major sources for Azure Monitor Logs*

Source	Data	Description (Log Analytics)
Tenant and subscription	Azure Active Directory audit logs, diagnostics, management groups, and subscriptions	Integrated AAD logs with Azure Monitor for each directory
	Activity logs	Install Activity Log Analytics, to be written automatically in a native store

(continued)

Table 4-2. (*continued*)

Source	Data	Description (Log Analytics)
Azure resources (cloud only)	Resource diagnostics including resource logs	Configure diagnostic settings for data diagnostics to be written
	Monitoring solutions	Writes data collected to a workspace
	Metrics (logs)	Platform metrics for Azure Monitor, can connect to Azure Sentinel
	Azure Table storage	Azure storage resources (Blob)
Virtual machines	Agent data	Linux and Windows OS (with Azure agent installed), events, performance data, and logs
	Monitoring solutions	Various solutions data writes to log collection
	System Center Operations Manager (SCOMS)	Connect Ops Manager Management Group to Azure Monitor
Applications	Requests and exceptions	Requests, page views, exceptions
	Usage and performance	Requests, browserTimings, performanceCounters
	Trace data	Distributed tracing tables
	Availability test	Summary data of availabilityResults table

A cloud operations team member can create a diagnostic setting to allow platform logs and metrics to different locations; please review the note.

Note   The security team should be aware that each Azure resource can support a separate diagnostic setting, one per Azure service, and each Azure service has different destination log options.

Azure Metrics

Data that is classified in Azure as metrics will always be a numerical value. All metric data is collected at a point in time and includes needed information including a timestamp, name, and other identifications. Metrics are most effective for correlating and trending data over a span of time and used to create a baseline. Metrics are critical for quick alerting on issues detected as a deviation of the baseline or an anomaly when compared to that baseline. You should become familiar with the level tiering classification of data and metrics; please refer to Table 4-3 for the Azure data tier classification.

Table 4-3. *Sources of Azure Monitor metrics*

Source	Data	Description (Log Analytics)
Platform metrics	Azure resources for health and performance: every 60 seconds	Distinct metric set per resource (autoconfiguration for VM host)
Guest OS metrics	VM OS: Windows/Linux	VM metrics must be enabled by VM agent extension: Windows Diagnostics Extension (WAD)/InfluxData Telegraf Agent (Linux)
Application metrics	Enable Application Insights for data	Detects application performance, issues, and trending usage including server response time and browser exceptions
Custom metrics	Enabled in custom applications (Application Insights custom data)	Custom metric API usage (autoconfiguration)

Metric retention resources are stored for 93 days for the majority of sources but not all metric sources. That is true for guest OS metrics created when you enable them for Azure Resource Manager (ARM) Windows OS and Linux OS VMs, so their monitor metrics are in this 93-day timeline. Diagnostic data is collected in Azure Storage divided in tables and blobs through a "data sync" process. If data is needed for a longer timeline because of regulatory compliance, additional data sync processes are needed to move the necessary metrics.

Log Analytics agents collect some of the guest OS metrics, like performance counters, and send them to a Log Analytics workspace for only 31 days. You can extend the time to 2 years, but beyond that timeline, you need to create a long-term storage option using automation scripts that move metrics into the Azure Blob storage. Application Insights' log-based metrics for event logs are stored for 90 days.

Next, you learn to use Azure Monitor as a single view to correlate all the individual service availability and performance data. As you enable an Azure service, the Monitor is automatically enabled to provide views of data analysis using both metrics and logs specific to the service you just enabled. The Azure data foundation is the workflow for logs, metrics, and their data sources that are collected. A service can write to a Log Analytics workspace (logs) or a metrics database. Depending on the Azure service, the Monitor writes to both logs and a metrics database.

Azure Monitor and Log Analytics Enablement

You have learned, in this chapter so far, that Azure Monitor collects data from platforms and services. Data included is stored in a metrics database, and the data is numerically sampled and includes a time series attribute. If we use a virtual machine as an example, the data stored can be divided into four major categories: virtual CPU, memory allocation, disk utilization, and network traffic. Log data is event information as events that have an activity to a subscription, platform data enablement, and resource-level information for services residing inside the Azure resource group.

As you create Azure resources, you enable either metrics or logs depending on the type of Azure service used. There are two methods to review the type of data from inside the resource:

- Monitor (Log Analytics)

- Monitor Metrics

It is important to monitor the environment of the hosted applications with Log Analytics and use Application Insights to also monitor the applications. The data collected and saved by using Azure Monitor (includes logs and metrics) are stored based on the types of data as discussed earlier.

When the Azure subscription is created, there is no configuration required and no cost for Azure Active Directory logs. It provides tenant-level activity history of a user's sign-in. The management group activity is automatically written to the activity log. Logs are updated when you create resources or modify the Azure resource. The overview page shows the automatically collected platform metrics.

All individual log resources created by the separate Azure Services used in the Azure portal can be consolidated into a single Log Analytics workspace. This log repository collects data from guest operating systems, Azure Monitor insights, and all the logs that Azure automatically enables logging. Creating the workspace does have a cost for the individual data collected for data ingestion and retention for analysis.

Note   The only prerequisite is to search the Azure regions for availability to support the Log Analytics workspace.

CREATE AZURE LOG ANALYTICS WORKSPACE

1. From the Azure portal, click all services and search for Log Analytics workspaces. Click the service to load the landing page. Click the + Add button to create a new Analytics workspace.

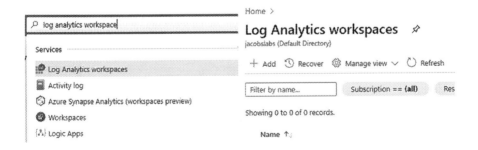

2. Enter the name for your Log Analytics workspace, in the example, CorpAnalyticsWorkspace1.

3. Select the Azure subscription and create a new resource group to maintain the life cycle of all the logs and metrics to be collected.

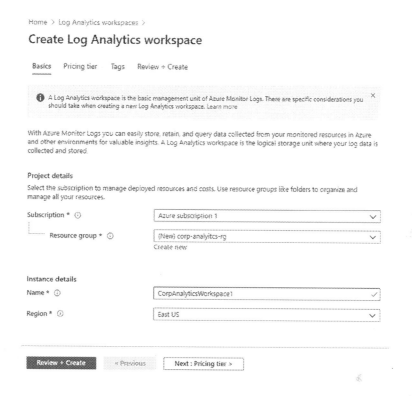

4. Enter the location to store the workspace and click Review and Create. The pricing tier is preset to pay-as-you-go, so this example does not reflect changes or entering a tag for business purposes.

The Log Analytics workspace is created in a few moments.

Now that you have configured your Analytics workspace, the configuration settings for all diagnostics can be configured. This next exercise enables the diagnostic settings to enable both log and metric details.

Azure platform metrics are automatically sent to the Azure Monitor metrics. However, the diagnostic settings for certain Azure services with logs need to be enabled at each resource log diagnostic menu. The next exercise walks you through configuring Azure Monitor Logs for analysis with other monitoring data using log queries for platform and resource discovery.

ENABLE PLATFORM LOG STORAGE IN LOG ANALYTICS WORKSPACE

1. Open the Azure portal; from the search menu, type monitor and press enter. Click the Monitor icon.

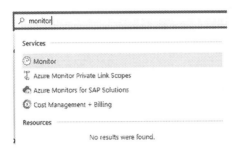

2. The Monitor landing page opens. Scroll down the menu items on the left side, select Activity log, and select the Diagnostics settings gear icon.

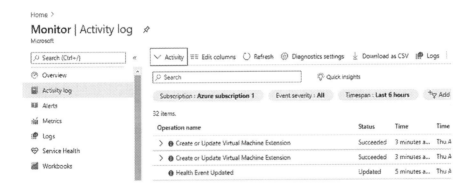

3. The Diagnostics settings landing page is displayed. Click the + Add diagnostic setting to begin selecting the logs and metrics.

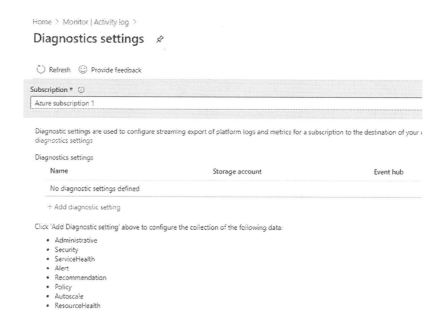

4. Select the logs to collect by choosing from the list under the category details. In this example, all logs are selected. You should enable the option to send to Log Analytics; this is the workspace you created in the earlier exercise.

5. Click the Save icon at the top left to update the diagnostics configuration
    settings in this step.

There are additional options to archive to a storage account and stream to an event
hub. You can select the Archive to storage account option to retain the data from 1
to 365 days.

---

6. To connect the data source of Azure Activity Logs to the workspace, scroll down
    from the Log Analytics workspace menu to the Workspace Data Sources menu,
    and select the Azure Activity log.

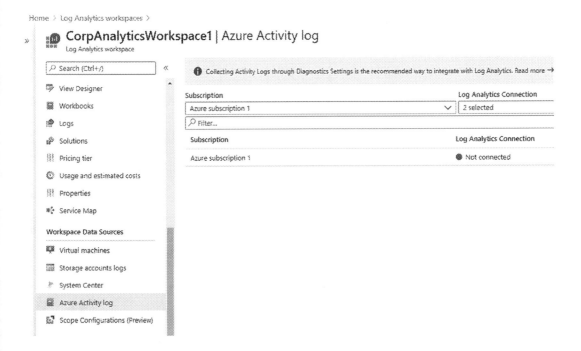

7. Click the Not connected text to display the status and click Connect from the upper-left menu. In just a few seconds, the Status should change to Connected.

Home > Log Analytics workspaces > CorpAnalyticsWorkspace1 | Azure Activity log >

Azure subscription 1
Azure Activity log

  🖉 Connect   🖉 Disconnect   ◌ Refresh

Status
Not connected

Subscription Name
Azure subscription 1

Subscription ID
cb54a82d-65d0-46e0-b9f6-00042c650b69

Message
Activity log is disconnected

If you archive to a storage account, review the length of days that was discussed earlier in this chapter. The option to stream to an event hub could be used for analysis outside of Azure.

Note   You can send the activity logs from a subscription to up to five Azure workspaces to support your monitoring requirements. However, to collect logs across different Azure tenants requires the deployment of Azure Lighthouse.

Log Analytics Workspace Security Strategy

The Log Analytics workspace used in production requires considerations for effective and efficient long-term deployment. The workspace is an Azure resource that collects data in an Azure storage container. You are not limited to a single workspace; there are many administrative guidelines to support your deployment decision. The type of data from the Azure resources can be selected based on the deployment model, centralized, decentralized, and hybrid. Figure 4-2 provides a visual representation of a decentralized workspace deployment model.

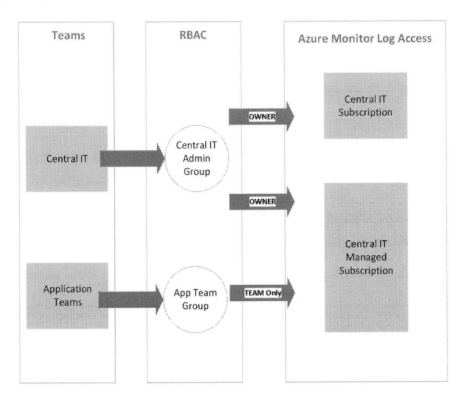

Figure 4-2. *Decentralized deployment of an Analytics workspace model*

Planning the Log Analytics agent deployment allows flexibility for the Windows agent to report to one or more workspaces. This allows different security access for different analytics teams. The agent supports writing to a maximum of four Analytics workspaces because the agent can be multihomed on the Windows OS, but the Linux agent can only report to one Analytics workspace.

Provision of a workspace should include the following areas:

- Azure region

- Security boundary

- Price-based retention

- Data capping

Azure Region: To deploy a centralized model, the configuration would require an Analytics Workspace deployed in the same region your Azure subscription services are deployed. Regional deployment of cloud resources should be influenced by business decisions such as compliance and data sovereignty. You should choose an Analytics workspace in the same region to avoid outbound data transfer charges supporting log data in separate regions as the Azure business services. A centralized team model supports secure access for the management and correlation of logs. The centralized organization of data is ideal for companies with a great quantity of metrics and log data.

Decentralized model allows different teams to manage access based on a resource group or specific log data workload. The Analytics workspace security generally follows the team access to the resource group. There might be delays when a cross-correlation of logs is needed to provide a wider view for more meaningful analysis. If security is the business driver, this decentralized model allows granular access control of the data.

A more complex multiregional (Azure regions) and multiresource group deployment is considered a hybrid model deployment of the Analytics workspace. You may have this model if your company has acquired companies, and their Azure subscriptions are moved to a single Azure Tenant model.

Security Boundary: Azure Active Directory supports the granular role-based security control known as Role-Based Access Control (RBAC). As a security blue team member, you want to follow the least-privileged access control for team members to require the data. The security boundaries refer to how users and groups access the Azure Analytics workspace and are supported by two different access control modes:

- Workspace context

- Resource context

Workspace context: This security context supports users that have permission to all the logs in the workspace including queries to all tables in the workspace. The access mode is scoped to the workspace for all logs selected from the Azure Monitor menu. Users access context from the Azure Monitor menu or the Log Analytics workspace.

Resource context: This is a very granular security context in supporting access to the workspace for a "selected" set of logs chosen, not from the Azure Monitor menu but the individual Azure resource log menu. Users access this context view from the Azure resource menu and with correct RBAC settings can access the limited resource data from Azure Monitor or the Log Analytics workspace.

Note   The Azure resource context allows query only from logs they are explicitly granted access and cannot query logs from resources they have no access.

Permissions are applied based on how the user accesses the workspace. To apply the permissions to using the workspace, follow the guidance from `https://docs.microsoft.com/en-us/azure/azure-monitor/platform/manage-access#manage-access-using-workspace-permissions`. If your model is to have granular RBAC control, then you need to allow permissions based on the Azure resource; please follow the guidance from `https://docs.microsoft.com/en-us/azure/azure-monitor/platform/manage-access#manage-access-using-azure-permissions`.

One final reminder that workspace permissions do allow granular access through Azure RBAC, so users with granted access at the workspace context have access to all the data in the workspace. Resource permissions follow the Azure "resource-context" mode to provide access to view logs only in resources you have access.

Price-Based Retention: The cost of data retention understanding begins at day 31. The total cost includes cost of data collected from each Azure Service log connected (some are low cost or no cost) and includes a small data ingested charge by the service plus the retention days beyond 31. You should be aware that one VM can minimize the monthly data ingestion to 1 GB if you limit the logs and metrics collected. That same VM can ingest 3 GB of data and metrics if all information is collected. There are options to save the cost of log and metric data storage by reserving a fixed capacity limit.

You can gain a greater perspective of the total cost of Log Analytics by going to your workspace and selecting the usage estimates as shown in Figure 4-3.

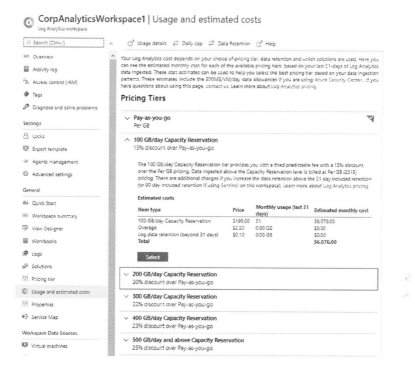

Figure 4-3. *Log Analytics pricing tiers and capacity reservations*

You need to have at least 31 days to collect information before the usage charts are populated with data. Once your data is ingested, you can select the query to evaluate the amount of data on a daily consumption rate to consider capping data.

Data Capping: This is an extreme cost measure used to place a hard cap on the daily collection. The use of this option does introduce some latency as the cap is approached. To set a daily cap, select the Log Analytics workspace, and select the Usage and estimated costs menu under the general section. Now select the Daily cap option at the top of the Usage and estimated costs pane as shown in Figure 4-4.

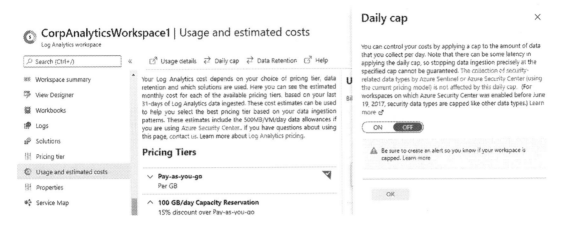

Figure 4-4. *Daily cap to enable a hard limit on the log collection*

You should take notice that enabling the daily cap setting does not affect the collection of security-related data logs and metrics. This includes Azure Sentinel and Azure Security Center. This is important because you don't want the data cap to affect cyber security notifications.

You can set an alert from Azure Monitor to be notified as the pricing tier capacity is nearing. The notification can go out through creating a ticket in your IT Service Management (ITSM) solution or a simple text message or email to a distribution group.

Guest OS Metrics and Logs

As you have learned, Azure Monitor is the single view for Azure platform data, logs, and metrics. For blue team hunting, you can use data stored in the workspace storage container (i.e., Analytics workspace) to provide real-time alerting, chartings, and routing from all the collective information.

Another source of data can support the correlation of Azure Monitor with the addition of Windows Azure Diagnostics (WAD) that collects metrics and logs from the guest operating system which is the OS from the virtual machine. You may be a little confused by the term guest OS, but this is not the Azure Hypervisor but the VM running on the host. Standard platform metrics for the host are already collected so you need to know how to enable the diagnostics extensions for your VM.

OS Guest Data: The Azure security operations team can enable metrics and logs from the guest operating system. This data can be written from the VM directly into the Azure Monitor metrics database store. The data collection is not enabled by default and can be validated from the Azure portal. Open the Azure portal and select any virtual machine and scroll down to the Monitoring section on the left menu. Select the Metrics view, and you notice without the agent installed, there is only data for the Hyper-V Host, identified as the Virtual Machine Host; please refer to Figure 4-5. Notice the Metric drop-down defaults to CPU Credits Consumed, aka how much US dollars has this VM cost to date.

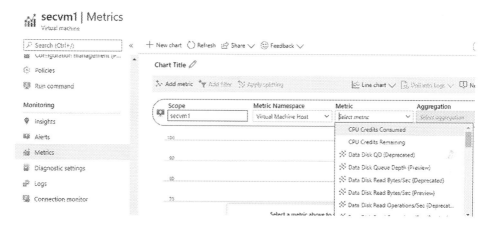

Figure 4-5. *Metrics for the Virtual Machine Host without OS guest diagnostics*

When you create a virtual machine, you can enable OS guest diagnostics during the VM portal journey, as shown in Figure 4-6; you can see the option to enable metrics and logs on the VM.

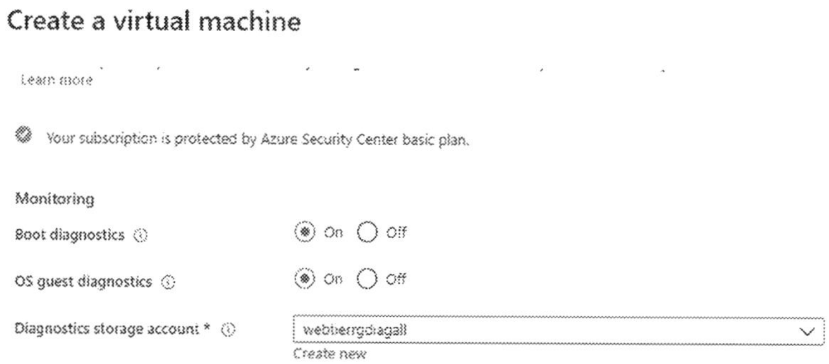

Figure 4-6. *OS guest diagnostics enabled during the VM creation*

Once the agent is installed, the metrics can be shared. Using the portal to view VM settings to share, open the landing page and scroll down to the left-side menu and select Diagnostic settings. You should have a similar view shown in Figure 4-7 to gain an understanding of the metrics, logs, and syslogs that are collected. Select the individual configuration options, make any changes, and then click the Save option. The diagnostic settings need to send to the Azure Log Analytics workspace using the example later in this chapter.

Figure 4-7. VM metrics and diagnostics collected

Note   The only prerequisite to follow the exercise to enable guest OS metrics is to have Windows VMs deployed and contributor access on the VM and contributor access on the resource group of the Log Analytics workspace.

ENABLE GUEST OS METRICS AND SEND TO AZURE MONITOR

1. Open the Azure portal and select the Windows VM to enable. Scroll down the menu on the left-hand side and select Diagnostic settings under the Monitoring section. The Overview blade will display; if you have not enabled a Diagnostics storage account for this VM, you can enable it now before you continue.

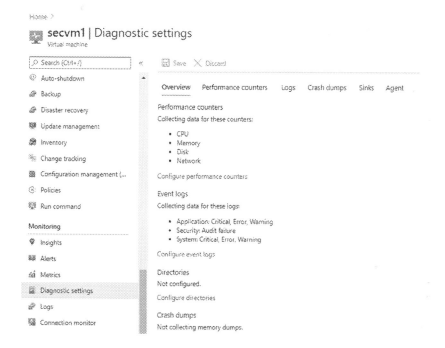

2. Select the Performance counters at the top of the menu on the right-hand side of the Overview blade. Once the Performance counters blade is displayed, select the Custom counter view.

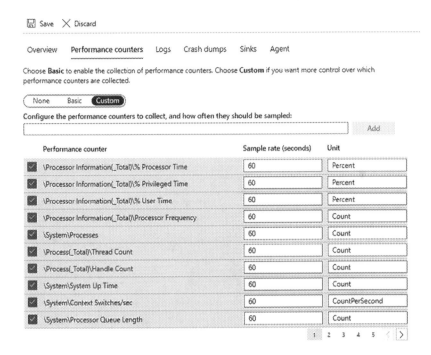

3. From this Custom view, you can use all selected performance counters (3 GB storage/VM per 24 hours), or you can unselect performance metrics to limit the amount of storage per VM. Once you have completed any changes, click the Save option on the top left.

4. Select the menu item Sinks. From this menu, you can enable diagnostics to be sent to Azure Application Insights. You can also choose to send these VM metrics to the Azure Monitor for a comparison of Azure resource metrics and these VM metrics.

5. Use your mouse to select the option to create a managed identity in Azure
AD for this VM to share data with the Azure Monitor. Set the Status to ON and
click Save.

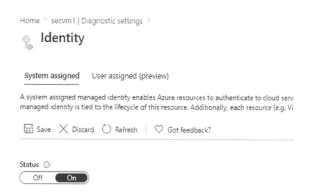

6. You will see a pop-up window that requires your consent to register the
selected VM with Azure Active Directory. By selecting to save this setting, you
are allowing the VM to be granted access to Azure AD. Select Yes to enable the
access. After the object ID is displayed, settings are complete; you should select
the Diagnostic settings menu.

7. From the Sinks menu back under the VM Diagnostics settings, you should
    choose the option Enabled to send diagnostic data to Azure Monitor. Click Save
    settings on the top-left menu. Updating the changes may take a few moments
    to complete.

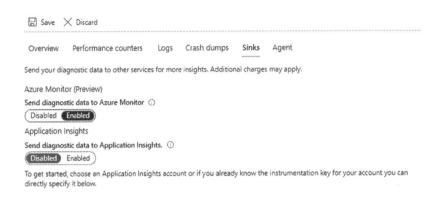

All selected performance counters' collection time begins once you click save, from this
moment in time moving forward.

Connecting Data Sources to Log Analytics Workspace

Monitoring the health, metrics, and performance of the Azure platform and the Azure
resources in use allows the single view of all the correlated data. This collection of data
from a variety of Azure resources allows us to leverage the power of Microsoft Kusto
Query Language (KQL) in a single window.

You can, of course, enable the collection of metrics and data from the individual
resource to be collected in Log Analytics. This next exercise enables multiple resource
data (logs and metrics) to be shared with the Log Analytics workspace without the need
to enable at each resource.

ENABLE INDIVIDUAL DATA SOURCES FOR LOG ANALYTICS WORKSPACE

1. From the Azure portal, search for Log Analytics workspace. Click the workspace icon and scroll down to the Workspace Data Sources menu on the left-hand side.

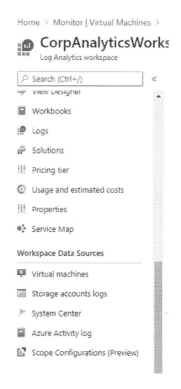

2. This example demonstrates connecting virtual machines, including the diagnostic data and storage account logs. Select the Virtual machines to display the VMs.

3. Click the text Not connected to present the view of the Status; select the option to Connect in the top-left menu. The update shows connecting after about 60 seconds.

4. Repeat step 3 for each VM you would like to connect with the workspace. You may want to limit the number of VMs to five as a Proof of Concept. (Once you have completed the validation, you should consider creating an Azure Policy to deploy agents on the VM and connect; refer to Chapter 7 for guidance on Azure policy.)

5. Return to the Monitor pane and select the Virtual machines view from under the Insights menu. Choose the option to Enable the Virtual machine. In this example exercise, there are three VMs not monitored by Azure Monitor services.

6. On the Azure Monitor Insights Onboarding pop-up window, choose Enable to allow the data collection validation to begin. This step takes over 60 seconds to complete.

7. If you close the pop-up window, the VM you just enabled may display, Enabling – Waiting for data. Click the Why? to get details about collecting data to Azure "Insights."

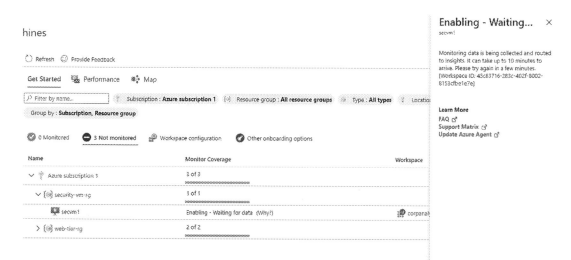

8. Close the Enabling – Waiting pop-up window and repeat step 5 for each VM you would like to monitor.

9. Next, this exercise connects a single Azure Storage account to the Azure Analytics workspace. From the left menu, select Storage account logs. Select the + Add.

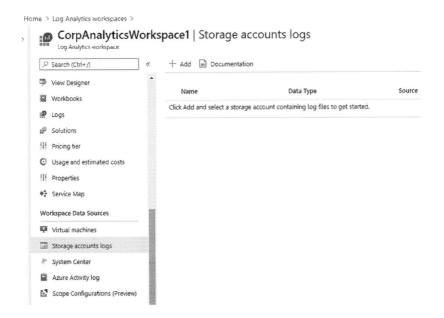

10. Use the drop-down menu to select the Storage account; in this example, we select jacobslabstorage1.

11. Select the data type drop-down menu, and select the data type based on the storage contents. Each data type enables a different source stored in the account:

- IIS logs [source = wad-iis-logfiles]

- Events [source = WADWindowsEventLogsTable]

- Syslog (Linux) [source = LinuxsyslogVer1v0]

- ETW logs [source = WADETWEventTable]

- Service Fabric Events [source = WADServiceFabric*EventTable]

12. This exercise selects the Events data type; click Save in the bottom left of the pane. You can select multiple storage data types.

13. You can now validate the storage accounts have been added to Azure Monitor. After the connection is configured, click the Storage accounts view and review the data displayed.

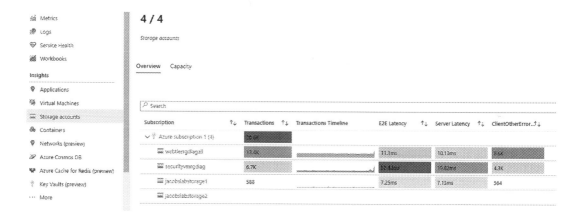

This exercise is the preferred method to follow for a Proof of Concept or in a lab environment. This method supports a steady state of data collection and validation of costs.

You now know that the Azure Monitor workspace is undergoing a consolidation of what first appears as redundant views of logs and metrics. The consolidation includes Log Analytics, Azure Application Insights, and Azure diagnostics to be used by Azure Monitor. If you focus the consolidation topic on support for Azure VMs, you are required to have on each VM at least two agents installed, two for each Windows or Linux OS. They are the Log Analytics agent and the Dependency agent. One of the agents you will see running on your VM is the Microsoft Monitoring Agent (MMA) that is installed when you enable Azure Security Center to manage VMs and collect data.

Note   There are multiple Azure Monitor agents; for further details, visit `https://docs.microsoft.com/en-us/azure/azure-monitor/platform/agents-overview`.

OPTIONAL EXERCISE: ADD INSIGHTS TO ANALYTICS WORKSPACE

Note   This is an optional exercise and demonstrates another method to configure Azure Monitor for VMs. If you choose to follow this exercise, the VM Insights management pack will be added to your Analytics workspace.

---

1. From the Azure portal, search for Log Analytics workspace. Click the workspace icon and scroll down to the Workspace Data Sources menu on the left-hand side.

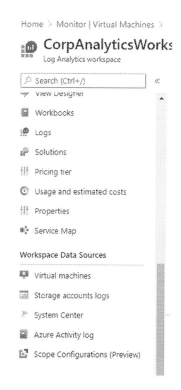

2. This example demonstrates connecting ALL virtual machines, including the
    diagnostic data and storage account logs. Select the Virtual machines to display
    the VMs.

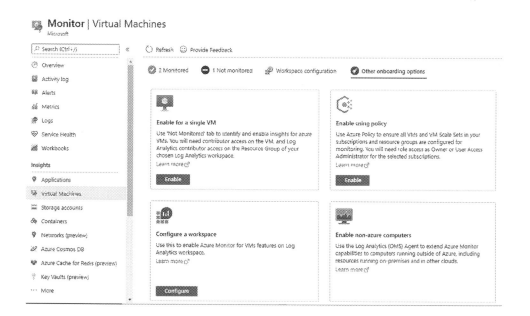

3. Click the text Other onboarding options (top right) to open the 4 x 4 matrix options window. Select the matrix "Configure a workspace" (lower left); click Configure to continue.

4. When the Azure Monitor Workspace Configuration window appears, validate the correct Azure subscription is selected and use the drop-down arrow to select the correct Log Analytics workspace. Click Configure.

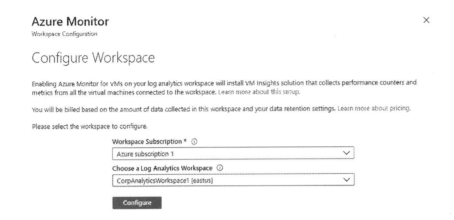

5. After a few minutes, the metric data is updated and can be validated using the Monitor Metrics view. This example changed the scope to a virtual NIC, network interface standard metrics, and bytes sent.

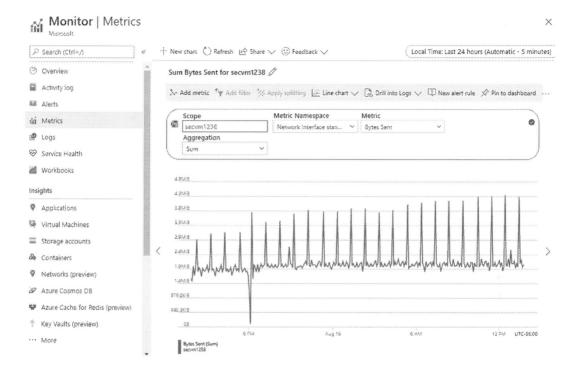

This exercise is optional because its updates are applied to any agent already connected to the workspace, whether or not it's enabled for Azure Monitor for VMs.

The Azure platform is continuously updated behind the visual display of the portal, and occasionally you are required to update services to continue providing the service. The Analytics workspace update that you may encounter is required; there is no opt-out. In this example, the option is to upgrade only, as shown in Figure 4-8, the notification.

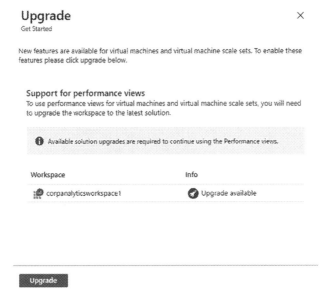

Figure 4-8. *Monitor view of virtual machines' required upgrade window*

ALERTING IN AZURE MONITOR

1. Open the Azure portal, select Monitor page, and select Alerts. Select the option + New alert rule.

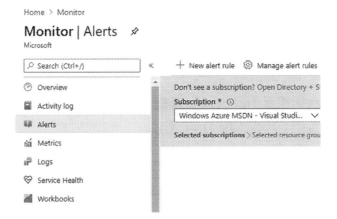

2. Select Resource link to select the target.

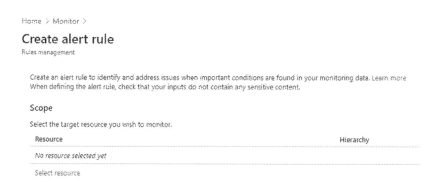

3. Validate the correct Azure subscription is selected and choose the Filter by resource type.

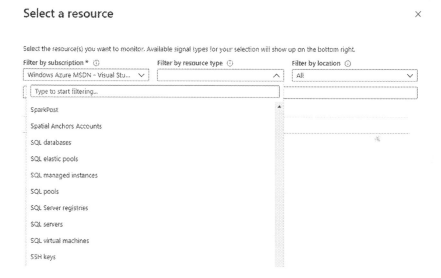

4. In this example, SQL servers is selected. Select Done.

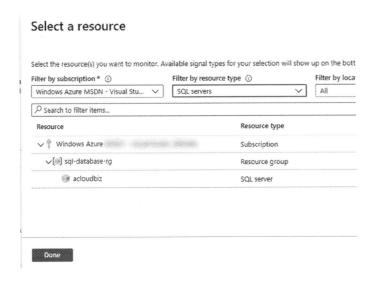

5. Select the condition option; notice for this example all SQL server alert options are displayed. Select All Administrative operations.

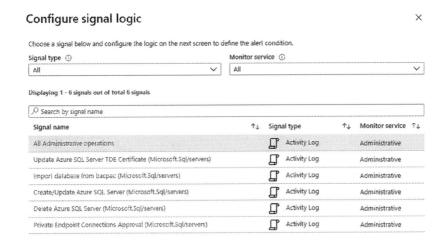

6. Leave the default settings for Event Level, Status, Event initiated by; select Done.

7. Select Action group to send notification by email or SMS messages.

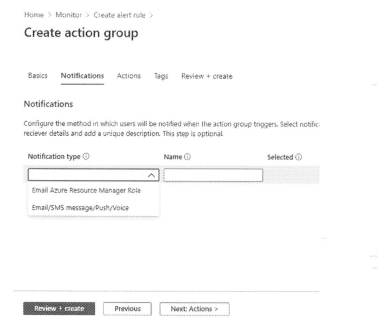

8. Select Create action group and select email/SMS messages.

9. After selecting the email and SMS, enter a valid email address and phone number.

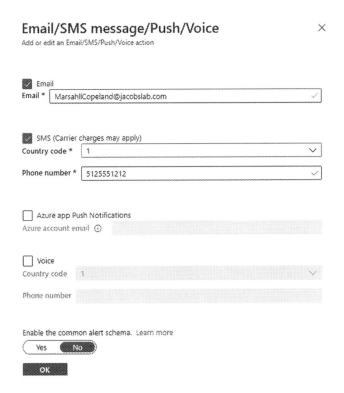

10. Select the Next: Action, leave the defaults as you complete the wizard screens, and select Create action.

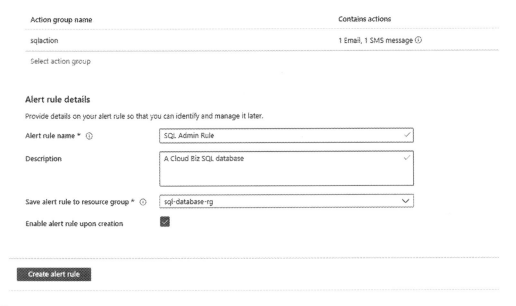

11. Enter the alert rule name and provide a description for the type of alert. Select Create alert rule.

In your production environment, create rules as necessary for both performance data and security alerts.

Setting up Azure Monitor alerting for all business services provides insight into the daily health of applications and Azure infrastructure to create internal business service-level agreements (SLA). You can track the availability of systems and ensure performance throughput maintains a steady flow. Setting security alerts, as in the last example, helps protect the data and privacy for the business.

It should take time, so plan accordingly to set up sources, instrumentation, and collections of logs and metric data to provide an overall analysis of the Azure platform and custom application health.

Summary

You have learned about the details of metrics and logs, with metrics defined as numerical data following a timeline. Azure logs include a mixture that consists of numerical data and text within a timeline. You learned that Azure Monitor is the single portal view to query information that is stored in an Azure storage container called the Log Analytics workspace. Now you know that Azure Insights and Log Analytics are components of the Azure Monitor service.

Next, you started to enable the Azure platform logs to be retained in the Azure Log Analytics workspace along with individual resource data. Azure resources using IaaS and PaaS can share both metrics and logs to be used with Azure Monitor for analysis using the powerful KQL predefined queries.

In the next chapter, you will configure Azure Security Center and Azure Sentinel to start consuming the data from the shared Log Analytics workspace. Each of the following chapters leverages the foundation you learned in this chapter about the Log Analytics Workspace. The Azure data collected provides threat hunting information for the cyber security blue team.

CHAPTER 5

Azure Security Center and Azure Sentinel

This chapter provides a foundation and configuration for both Azure Security Center and Azure Sentinel. Microsoft has expanded many of the Security Center features so you can benefit from these updates. Azure Sentinel is a Microsoft Security Incident and Event Management (SIEM) service. Together, Security Center and Sentinel provide a powerful Security as a Service in the Azure cloud.

Earlier in Chapter 1, you learned about managing the Azure tenant and Azure Active Directory and enabling additional layers of security like Multi-Factor Authentication (MFA). Privileged Identity Management was configured to protect assets in the Azure infrastructure. In Chapter 2, you learned about virtual networks and subnets, layers of security with Azure Firewalls, and Network Security Groups. Chapter 3 provided the VM security challenges with the IaaS deployment model and how to best secure SQL Servers and storage accounts to encrypt your data in Azure. Chapter 4 guided you through the configuration of the Azure Monitor platform. You learned how services that used log and metric data like Azure Insights and Log Analytics support the Azure Monitor powerful query service. In this chapter, we bring all the previous chapters' learning together to provide the Azure security data logs and metrics.

You will configure Azure Security Center first; it may take up to 24 hours for baseline data to provide security changes for securing the Azure infrastructure. The Security Center interface clearly identifies security risks and steps to remediate all cloud security professionals are confronted with. The recurring security themes are prevention, detection, and response.

This chapter leverages the 30-day free Azure Security Center standard tier trial specifically for testing Azure Security Center using jacobslab.com as a typical Azure cloud deployment example. The jacobslab network example has typical servers

© Marshall Copeland and Matthew Jacobs 2021
M. Copeland and M. Jacobs, *Cyber Security on Azure*, https://doi.org/10.1007/978-1-4842-6531-4_5

deployed into the TCP/IP subnet, and the typical infrastructure deployment includes virtual machines (VMs) in the perimeter IP subnet and infrastructure IP subnet and SQL Servers in the database IP subnet.

Next, you will configure Azure Sentinel to work directly with all the data sources you configured from Chapter 4 to include logs and metric data in the Log Analytics workspace. You configure Azure data connectors to then consume this data from

- Azure Security Center

- Azure Active Directory

- Azure Active Directory Identity Protection

- Common Event Format

- Microsoft Security Events

These are the Sentinel data connectors you will use in the configuration of data feeds; however, there are more than 54 total data connectors you will be aware of for your own data connectors for Azure deployment.

Let us begin by answering the question of why we configure Azure Sentinel with Security Center, it is so the Azure cloud cyber security vulnerabilities, created because of day 2 deployment, are exposed through alert detection, and the Sentinel playbook response can be automated. Azure Sentinel leverages the Kusto Query Language (KQL), threat intelligence data, and artificial intelligence to secure your Microsoft Azure business deployment.

Note   This chapter enables and configures Azure Security Center and Azure Sentinel. Unique use cases and deeper cyber security discovery are highlighted in each of the remaining chapters.

Cloud Security Challenges

Small-, medium-, and enterprise-scale companies as well as government agencies are moving to the public cloud to take advantage of the elasticity and commodity of scale from trusted providers. Companies need to enable the best cloud security methods to extend their on-premises security layering to protect customer data, systems, and assets in the cloud.

Cloud infrastructures, in most companies new to cloud management and cyber security, are greatly distributed, and management is sometimes difficult. Chief information officers (CIOs) and chief information security officers (CISOs) are still responsible for the security of these environments even though the cloud infrastructure is more dynamic. A CISO requires best practices for security from the on-premises environment integrated into the cloud. Customers with larger teams and longevity have on average 30 different security or cyber security–related solutions. Many of these tools create alerts that require attention, and the expertise required for each security solution creates another challenge for experts to use each solution and gain value from the data.

Sunset applications are ones that may no longer have engineering support, and these older applications are greater targets for cyber attacks. In fact, some of the older applications were created under non-agile methods and could take more time and resources to be reviewed by a current software assurance program.

Companies of every size, small and large, using Azure Security Center leverages continuous security data analyses from Azure-deployed virtual machines, virtual networks, Platform as a Service (PaaS) services (think Azure SQL Database), and partner solutions such as Barracuda, Fortinet, or Check Point. Companies gain visibility into the current security state, which extends across all subscriptions, so for customers that leverage parent-child Azure subscriptions, like a sandbox, those subscriptions may be used by system admins to improve their cloud knowledge.

Senior executives must rethink their approach to cloud security beyond traditional on-premises security expertise. Enterprise organizations may have greater numbers of staff members labeled as experienced cloud security experts; however, an investment in cloud expertise introduces new challenges. Moving data to Azure cloud resources challenges administrators in the management of access and auditing of cloud security for those assets. Small- and medium-sized companies have the same compliance requirements as larger organizations with the additional competitive struggle to attract and maintain crucial cloud security experts. In addition, the support for secure DevOps is challenging for companies that want application development to include cloud agility.

It is important to understand the attack targets that bad actors are attempting to compromise inside an organization. The same type of attack surfaces can be seen in the Azure cloud, as shown here:

- Impersonation of a user (social media)

- Credential theft and elevation of privileges (admin or developer)

- Installing code to enable backdoors

- Gaining access to data and data resources (cloud resources)

- Azure subscription owners (top-level administration)

- Pivot attacks from on-premises to the public cloud

- Cloud resource compromises by hijacking or other exploitations

- Privilege elevation to move between subscriptions

- Public storage secret credential keys (GitHub)

- Misconfiguration of credential keys

- Imperva "man-in-the-cloud" token synchronized

- Side-channel code enablement

- Ransomware on cloud resources

The added training requirements that are needed to ramp up for cloud administrators and the additional need to improve knowledge to extend cyber security expertise to the cloud can be overwhelming. Every organization that chooses Microsoft Azure as part of their hybrid infrastructure can leverage Azure Security Center.

Note   The first edition of *Cyber Security on Azure*, ISBN 978-1-4842-2739-8, has many detailed use cases for Azure Security Center. The interface has changed, but the services are still valid. Find it at `www.apress.com/us/ book/9781484227398`.

Enable Security

The services supported by Azure Security Center are constantly changing at the pace of cloud innovation, so even though you are reviewing virtual networks, virtual machines, and database services in the exercises, additional preview features on the road map include additional Azure cloud services, third-party services, and integration with cloud-native services like Azure Firewall Manager.

This first exercise is to enable Azure Security Center, install agents, and allow the collection of data to begin. It can take up to 24 hours to start collecting baseline information and making recommendations.

ENABLE SECURITY CENTER STANDARD TIER

You gain the benefit of additional security features when upgrading to the standard tier, and the first 30 days are part of a free trial. This provides the best opportunity to evaluate the Security Center functionality for your subscription.

1. From the Azure portal, search for Security Center and click the icon to take you to the landing page.

2. The interface has changed over the years; however, the strength and integration in the API configuration are where the improved features set are appreciated.

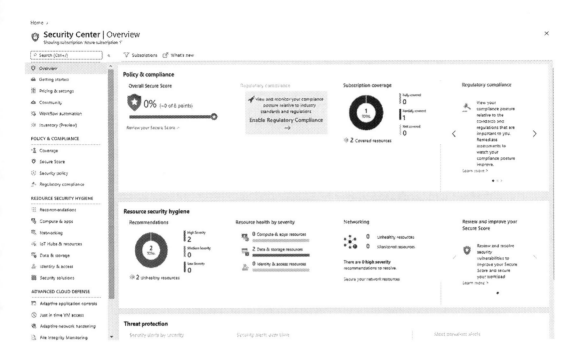

3. From the left menu, click the Getting started pane.

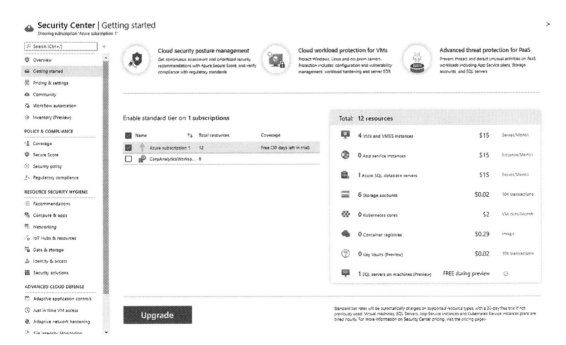

4. There is a preliminary review of the cost based on the current Azure deployment services. Select the entire subscription; note you can be selective if you have many subscriptions. Click the Upgrade option to begin your 30-day free evaluation.

5. You will gain information by choosing the option to install the agents. The Azure tenant is part of a trial subscription. Click Install agents. (Note you do have options to install manually or to test without installing agents.)

6. Return to the Getting started pane and select the CorpAnalyticsWorkspace (or your equivalent) and click Upgrade to share the Security Center data collected with the Azure Monitor service.

These two upgrade options change configuration through the connection to the Analytics workspace and all current and future VMs. Virtual machines provisioned in the jacobslab subscription automatically receive the Microsoft Monitoring Agent (MMA). This is called autoprovisioning, and it should be your default method to configure Security Center.

Azure Identity: Security Center leverages Role-Based Access Control (RBAC) provided by Azure Active Directory (AAD). There are two roles you should use with Azure Security Center:

- Security Reader

- Security Admin

The Security Reader role should be assigned to all users who only need read access to the dashboard. The Security Admin role should be protected as are other sensitive administrative credentials.

The Storage agent collects information and sends it to the Analytics workspace. Another great point about using the standard tier is you have up to 500 MB per day. If data exceeds 500 MB per day, additional charges will apply, similar to the data storage charge costs provided in Chapter 4. Security Center adoption considerations should include the length of time for data retained beyond 30 days. With the Analytics workspace, you have options to send to a BLOB storage for a portion of the data storage requirements.

Configuration Value

You should consider the standard tier price for some of your Azure resources, if not for all of the resources. In the updated analysis discussion about the overall cost of Azure Security Center from a business perspective, you could use Security Center to protect web tier and critical data. The focus is on more than just the pricing tier model and allowed chief information officers (CIOs) and chief information security officers (CISO) to gain insight into the total cost of support for Security Center as part of the security layering defense strategy. Before moving on to further configuration, you need to consider the difference between the two tiers:

- Basic (free)

- Standard (not free)

The next set of exercises shows how to configure the data collection storage account and enable the standard tier to start using the security service. The standard price is intentionally identified as a cost and helps you realize the value once you consider the consolidation of current security tools your company renews year after year that are not cloud friendly.

First, the way your company purchased the Azure subscription may affect the price, and you may use many Azure services at a discount if you have an enterprise agreement (EA) with Microsoft. Second, the prices change often as major cloud providers change prices for their cloud features to remain competitive. Third, you may see the retail price and, after a quick calculation, decide the overall cost is great value once you understand the full breadth of features provided by Azure Security Center. Undercutting the value of any security product without comprehending the fullness of features does a disservice to your company and how security features benefit the overall security posture. If you are a cloud security administrator, you should include the security architect in the decision-making process. Azure Security Center is not a solution that is used to simply check the box for security; it provides a breadth of value that should be evaluated based on merit. Figure 5-1 provides a view of the two pricing feature sets.

Figure 5-1. *Standard tier value for security benefits*

Standard Tier Advantages

As an Azure architect, you are undoubtingly evaluating the security features found in the standard pricing tier but may not have the background to understand the depth of the individual features and how Azure Security Center leverages the breadth of global information to protect server assets.

You should carefully consider the additional features beyond the free tier. Make sure to look at the standard tier features when evaluating other security products, which may not have the advantage of integrating with a cloud solution that is global in deployment and leverages millions of data sensor points.

Just-in-Time Access

You can lock down inbound and outbound RDP traffic to your Azure virtual machines with Azure Security Center and the Just-in-Time (JIT) virtual machine (VM) access feature, only available in the standard tier. This reduces exposure to attacks while providing easy access when you need to connect to a VM.

> Enable JIT: With your own custom options for one or more VMs using Security Center, PowerShell, or the REST API. Alternatively, you can enable JIT with default, hard-coded parameters from Azure virtual machines. When enabled, JIT locks down inbound traffic to your Azure VMs by creating a rule in your Network Security Group.

> Request access: The goal of JIT is to ensure that even though your inbound traffic is locked down, Security Center still provides easy access to connect to VMs when needed. You can request access to a JIT-enabled VM from Security Center, Azure virtual machines, PowerShell, or the REST API.

> Audit activity: To ensure your VMs are secured appropriately, review the accesses to your JIT-enabled VMs as part of your regular security checks.

Advanced Threat Detection

This feature is extremely informative to security teams because it provides details about sophisticated attack detection using the Microsoft cloud-based security analytics. The threat protection provided may be a tipping point for security professionals in favor of Azure Security Center because timely intelligent security data is a cornerstone that enables a successful solution. As an individual, you can become good at identifying intelligence from log files, accounts, and other security data. If you work in a team, the individuals combine the data points to make the discovery and decisions faster and more accurate. If you don't have a team of security specialists or the budget to hire them, then advanced threat detection provides insight that doesn't require the CISO or CIO to ask the board of directors for more money.

The advanced threat detection technologies and methodologies detect threats using machine learning analysis on big data. The security graph of data analytics aggregates what you as an individual may interpret as an anomaly, namely, recognized behaviors by the millions of data points of anonymized information. The daily collection from Windows Defender and behavioral sensors (individual contact points) alone is astonishing. With integration with Windows Defender, the daily data includes the following:

- Millions of Microsoft Windows devices

- Indexed web URLs

- Online reputation lookups

- Millions of suspicious files

Other methods of detection are included as individual components to support the overall detection effectiveness of Azure Security Center. For instance, atomic detection leverages the current information on the history of malicious patterns to provide known Indicators of Compromise (IoC). Atomic detection uses log entry data for software malware that, in the past historical data analysis, does not mutate. Atomic detection using log file attributes can most closely be correlated to active network packet analysis in an intrusion detection system (IDS). Because the patterns are known attributes, there is a very low level of false positive rates, and common malware can be found with this type of detection.

Anomaly Detection

The security graph of data analytics aggregates information in order to recognize certain behavior and detect threats. Building a system baseline is necessary to alert on deviations from the standard. It is possible that no alert is sent because the deviation did not have supporting evidence and no other attributes were detected to cause the alert threshold to be crossed.

Anomaly-based algorithms, such as repeated failed logon attempts based on statistically significant levels of failures, are identified. The type of information that can trigger an alert would include if the failed logon attempt was attempted with existing or nonexistent users.

Crash Analysis

Security Center analyzes data looking for future malware that is being designed and tested to compromise systems, including in results from system crash dumps. This analysis can find evidence of failed exploitation attempts and immature malware code.

Microsoft has integrated the crash dump data into Azure Security Center to detect indicators of failed attempts, and this crash data is surfaced to algorithms to identify potential failed attempts of threats on your systems.

Threat Intelligence

Microsoft has many global cloud services that provide threat intelligence telemetry such as Office 365, Microsoft CRM online, MSN.com, Azure, the Microsoft Digital Crimes Unit (DCU), and the Microsoft Security Response Center (MSRC).

Other partners have contracts with Microsoft to provide researchers with threat intelligence information including other cloud providers and third-party solutions. One of the many intelligence data points includes the communication from a compromised system to a known IP address of a malicious actor. Threat attributes include emerging threats or existing ones with specific indicators, implications, and other mechanisms. After the raw data is collected, it is augmented by a global team of threat protection "hunters" to analyze the data effectively and integrate it into Azure Security Center. The security team hunters run algorithms against customer data sets to validate results and reduce false positive alerting.

Behavioral Analysis

This form of analysis for threat detection is different than simply matching signatures and patterns; it focuses on "actions" taken by a suspicious programmatic behavior. The collection of data changes compared to patterns that are known and are not just signatures. Malware can quickly generate many variants, which means the hash tables change just as quickly. As bits and bytes change on the malware, a new signature is required to identify the same malware based on the current attributes. This is a major reason behavioral analysis is a strength of Azure Security Center.

With Security Center, the technology can correctly articulate the behavior actions of a variant of malware, which provides necessary identification without pattern matching. With future malware movements and unidentified behavior correlated, false positives can be detected because of the initial suspicious properties.

Configure Alerting

You should configure email alerting by adding the necessary email contacts. You can add security contact emails for On-Call@jacobslab.com, and another dual notification is required. There is not an escalation option to help support any internal SLA you may have with the security team or business.

Security Center will send an email notification on the first occurrence of the alert, but it only sends email for high-severity alerts.

CONFIGURE EMAIL NOTIFICATIONS

---

1. From the Azure portal, open the System Center pane. Click the Pricing and Settings menu.

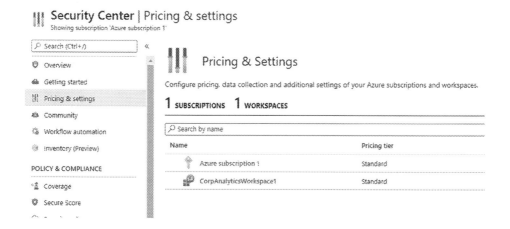

2. While viewing the Azure subscription, click the text to configure the email settings.

3. Select the Email notifications menu on the left-hand side of the pane.

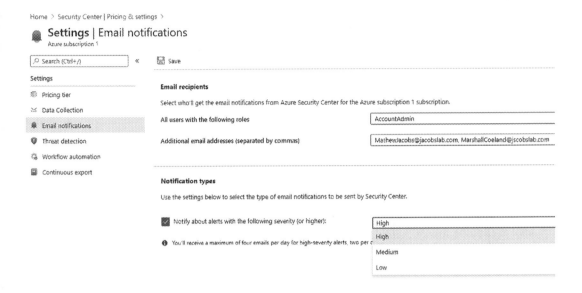

4. Use the down arrow to select the users and enter the email address of users (use a comma in between multiple email addresses) or user groups to be notified.

5. Enable the check box to be notified about alerts and select the severity for the notification type. Click Save on the top-left side.

Notice there is not a text message option for notification from Security Center. However, you do have a text message option from Azure Sentinel.

Using Security Center

Now that majority of configurations are enabled (you may need to wait up to 24 hours) for the initial Azure Security Center configuration, you should take the time to review the information that has been identified using this solution. The testing configurations would provide a different view than your Azure network infrastructure. In the jacobslab. com infrastructure, the information provided is centered around four virtual machines and several IP subnets; this represents a typical Azure first-use deployment.

Azure Security Center requires time to analyze your Azure VMs, VNets, web apps, and SQL-deployed applications. Baselines are created and used for recommendations to improve your security posture. First, you will look at the results of implementing the standard tier, and then you can begin a methodical process to follow the recommended prioritization of the Security Center items.

Security Center provides a dashboard view to clearly help with priorities: red = bad, green = good. Refer to Figure 5-2 to see an overview summary.

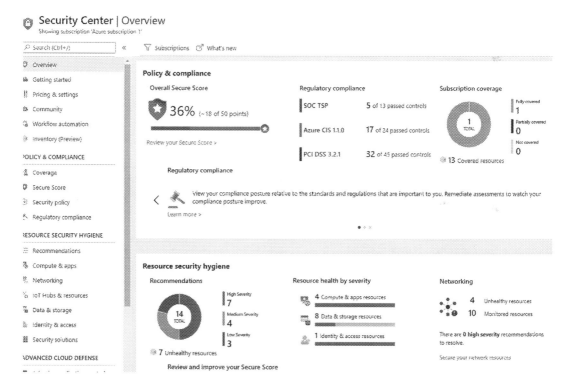

Figure 5-2. *Security Center overview page with resource security hygiene priorities*

From the Overview landing page, notice a few points of data; the overall security score is low at 36%, and high-severity resources need immediate attention. Security Center identifies all the missed configurations for each VM that has an agent installed and provides recommendations to protect the individual systems. You should take a short view of some of the major areas that Security Center has recommended remediation.

Compute and Apps

The information provided by this view is the type of data the security team needs to better remove security risks and maintain compliance standards. Also, this data is needed for Azure operations teams to support the business by improving the security posture for each VM deployed in the Azure subscription. This detailed view provides any major areas to help focus on security work; a few are listed here:

- Log Analytics agent installation

- IP forwarding

- Endpoint protection

- Vulnerabilities

- Disk encryption

These are just a few of the recommendations; each of these areas would be identified with a security health rating or severity because of the security data being analyzed. The color scheme is typical with alerting solutions in Azure:

- Red = high (critical)

- Yellow = medium (important)

- Green = none (OK)

These areas are color coded for security health, and a different scheme is used to show the priority of the component security recommendations. You will learn the details (refer to Figure 5-3) about the recommendations in other chapters.

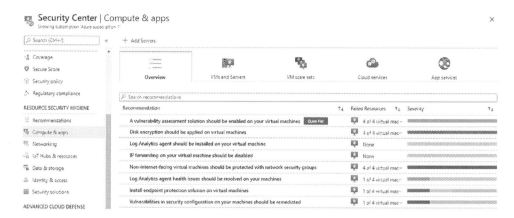

Figure 5-3. *Compute and apps view with recommendation and severity color*

Network

If you start from the Security Center menu, click the Networking resource security health bar the Networking dashboard will appear. This is a logical isolation view of the Azure cloud dedicated to the current subscription. Security Center identifies the Azure Virtual Networks available in your subscription; again, this may take time to report.

Security Center recommendations include changes needed to improve the overall security posture. Refer to Figure 5-4.

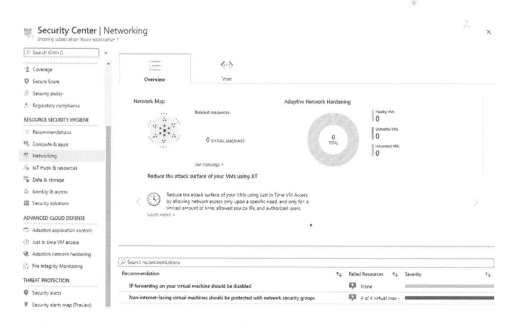

Figure 5-4. *Networking pane view of the overall network hardening value*

There are a few more interesting points for recommendations for IP forwarding at the bottom of this view.

Data and Storage

The Azure SQL and data view provides guidance on security recommendations that improve the business security and exposure created by Azure SQL Database default deployments.

In large corporations, this type of visual data is normally viewed only by the subject-matter experts in the networking team and select systems administration teams. The security health of SQL Servers, data, networks, and computers exposed to the Internet is identified as critical and requires changes to reduce the risk of the current configuration as shown in Figure 5-5.

Figure 5-5. *Data and storage view displaying vulnerability assessment findings*

The automation behind Security Center provides intelligent recommendations after an analysis of the events. These events could span the partner solutions as well as the virtual machines you build and place into different Azure IP subnets. A list of prioritized security alerts is presented in the console; an email is also sent with severity recommendations needed to prevent an attack. You can see a few examples of additional security events in Table 5-1.

Table 5-1. *Security Center anomaly and behavior examples*

Security Center Description	Security Consideration
Malicious SQL activity	SQL injection attempt
Failed RDP brute-force attack	RDP attack prevented by Security Center
Successful RDP brute-force attack	Attack not prevented
Suspicious process executed	Unidentified execution of an anomaly
System binary discovered in a dump file	Hacker code caused crash dump

MITRE ATT&CK FRAMEWORK

As a cyber security professional, you need to stay ahead of the attackers with the most current information to help defend your business. You need a blue team threat hunters' playbook, and you should begin with this framework since it is priced at "free." Start with the MITRE ATT&CK tools that are online at `https://attack.mitre.org/`. MITRE is the name of a not-for-profit company that was started in 1958, and please realize the name MITRE is not an acronym.

The MITRE company shares up-to-date globally adversary tactics and techniques based on real-world customer attacks and data gathered. The MITRE company and many global partners support the mission statement "make the world safer" and more through security. The ATT&CK (attack spelled with &) knowledge base is an open source framework and available to any organization at no charge.

The ATT&CK data is transferred into products using the current Structured Threat Information Expression (STIX) version 2, a language to exchange cyber threat intelligence (CTI). ATT&CK, STIX, and Trusted Automated eXchange of Intelligence Information (TAXII) are integrated in the Microsoft Azure Sentinel service.

The ATT&CK framework includes threat intelligence (TI), detection, and analytics on how an adversary uses red team cyber security attacks. Using this knowledge helps you identify techniques of adversary groups and correlate the types of attacks used. You can review the attack data collected and detailed against specific businesses like financial, hospitals, manufacturing, or hospitality. There are also details collected about cyber security attacker history, group name, attack motivation, family of attack software, and how you can improve defensive layers based on past cyber security attack methods. There are three levels to the framework:

Level 1: Start here if you are new to the framework.

Level 2: Mid-level teams maturing their security skills.

Level 3: Resources for advanced cyber security teams.

The ATT&CK framework follows the cyber security "kill chain" including reconnaissance, execution (i.e., payload), persistence, and exfiltration.

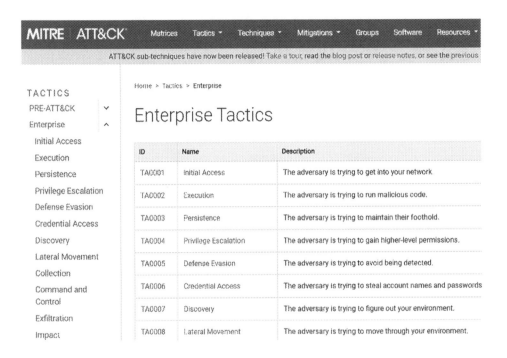

The cyber intelligence is used to learn about your adversaries; this is a homework to help you make better defensive security decisions. Choose a group to walk through the framework; you can review the listing at https://attack.mitre.org/groups/. This listing maps out groups and typical previous targeted companies. There is also a step-by-step guide on how to use the matrix at https://attack.mitre.org/docs/Comparing_Layers_in_ Navigator.pdf.

As an example, from the URL, select APT29; they have other names like Cozy Bear, The Dukes, and CozyDuke. (You may think they are not very original in the naming, but the threats are identified as being associated with the Russian government that compromised the Democratic National Committee in 2015; see the details in the following figure.)

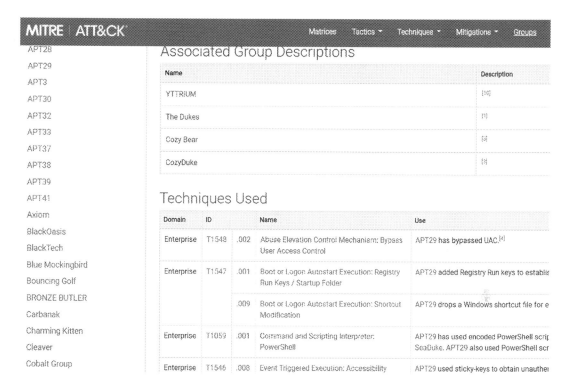

Use the threat intelligence framework to learn how adversaries attack your business, what cyber tools they use, and how you can mitigate the attacks listed in the framework.

If this is the first time to learn more than just the name, download the eBook on how to get started using the MITRE ATT&CK framework from www.mitre.org/sites/default/files/publications/mitre-getting-started-with-attack-october-2019.pdf.

As you become more familiar with the value of the MITRE ATT&CK framework, notice the "mitigation" security recommendations to improve security in your cloud infrastructure.

Azure Sentinel

Critical security data has the greatest value when it is provided in a very timely manner. When that specific data includes additional insight and preference guidance on the cause and resolution, the security service becomes a critical security service. With the introduction of Azure Sentinel, Microsoft provides security insights using all available root cause analysis and security vulnerability remediation in the first cloud-based Security Information and Event Management (SIEM) service.

Real-time analysis is a key part of any SIEM defense in depth feature that can identify potential threats and vulnerabilities in an enterprise. In addition, the solution should provide methods to remediate threats and improve the security posture for the business. Features included with Azure Sentinel are

- Integrate with other controls

- Artificial intelligence

- Threat intelligence feeds

- Compliance reporting

- Forensic analysis

- Investigative methods

Azure Sentinel provides real-time monitoring with the integration of other intrusion detection systems (IDS) and intrusion prevention solutions (IPS). You may have given pause to the feature of real time, so our definition is defined as "continuously updated streaming," with zero or exceptionally low latency. You should not get sidetracked with some of the logs and metric data concepts from Chapter 4. In some of the screenshots, the OS performance counters are collected every 60 seconds, but they are continuously streamed to the Log Analytics workspace, so they are in real time. The information is determined as the current state of the information.

The security team members that rely on the SIEM information to successfully protect the business from attacks and hackers are normally identified as the Security Operations Center (SOC). Not all security products are 100% SIEM solutions like Azure Sentinel. Some products and services are branded as a Security Information Management (SIM) service or Security Event Management (SEM) service. They are all designed to provide security alerts generated by users, applications, and networking events.

Microsoft Azure Sentinel is a cloud solution, so the time to implement reduces the traditional long-tailed configuration and integration. Exercises in this chapter show you how to enable and configure Azure Sentinel in minutes from the Azure portal. You use more resources in the adoption, learning curve, and alert tuning process. Also, you should have a good Azure cloud security foundation. Azure Sentinel provides actionable alerts with guidance; however, security experts are needed to analyze the data. Adoption can be slowed if the misconfiguration of the streaming data through connectors or other data streams is not effective. To help you realize the goals of a SIEM solution, you should first review the information in Table 5-2 to gain insight into the attacker events that may be triggered.

Table 5-2. *Attack classification and generic event sources*

SIEM Rule	Source of Event
Virus or spyware	Firewalls, antivirus (endpoint), identity system failed logon
Repetitive logon attack	Active Directory, LDAP services, Azure Active Directory, syslog, switches, routers
Repetitive firewall attacks	Firewall appliance (hardware and software), routers, switches
Virus detection	Antivirus, network anomaly detection, system anomaly detection, host intrusion prevention systems (HIPS)
Repetitive network attack	Network intrusion detection systems (IDS), network intrusion prevention systems (IPS)
Denial-of-service attack, distributed denial-of-services attack	Network intrusion detection systems (IDS), network intrusion prevention systems (IPS)

Azure Sentinel integrates with Microsoft solutions, as you would expect; however, many industry standard threat detection solutions are available for integration on day one of enablement. You will walk through the exercise to enable Azure Sentinel and have it ready to connect to all known data streams in minutes. Remember this service is a managed SIEM from the Azure cloud, and as a SaaS (Software as a Service) solution, there is no software EXE to install on servers. You are ready to review the Sentinel landing page; begin data streaming from as many data connectors as you need at the time you enable Sentinel in your own Azure subscription.

There is a security industry standard expectation in any SIEM solutions to include orchestration and automation (SOAR). The "R" is for response; orchestrated and automated response in Azure Sentinel includes security analytics and threat intelligence for more than just the cloud. If you have a hybrid network connection with an ExpressRoute or a site-to-site VPN for on-premises enterprise, Sentinel provides the right solution for alert detection, threat visibility, proactive hunting, and threat response.

ENABLING AZURE SENTINEL

---

1. In the Azure portal, search for Azure Sentinel.

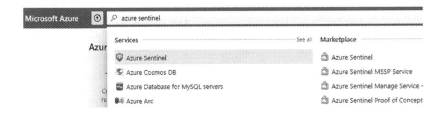

2. Select the + Add an Azure Sentinel Workspace; this example uses the
   Log Analytics that was created in Chapter 4. (If you want to create a new
   workspace, choose the option to create a new workspace and follow the
   exercise in Chapter 4 and then return to this exercise.) From the options,
   choose + Add to select the workspace.

Note   You can create a new Analytics workspace to gain insight to the cost of
metric and log storage for Sentinel consumption.

3. In this exercise, we choose to add the CorpAnalyticsWorkspace1 created from the Chapter 4 exercise.

4. Select the Workspace and add Azure Sentinel from the bottom-left menu. The Azure Sentinel landing page is displayed in about 60 seconds.

As a reminder, Azure Sentinel is a cloud-native SIEM, and using the Log Analytics workspace, the next exercise begins the simple tasks of data connectors to start populating query data.

Azure Sentinel Cost: The use of Azure Sentinel does not have a direct monthly fee to draw down Azure credits. The cost begins when you ingest data feeds to leverage the Microsoft cyber security AI automation. If you created a new (empty) Analytics workspace and want to keep the cost to a minimum, then select a few data connectors to reduce the data storage tier cost.

You should be aware that Microsoft allows the use of some data connectors that have low cost, and I've read a documentation that leads you to believe it is no cost, but that is not entirely true. Fist, all logs that are ingested by Sentinel and go through the workflow are adding to the cost of traffic ingestion. Second, some of the cost is included in many of the premium SKU (like Azure Active Directory P2/E5) that you have already purchased. The data from the connectors listed have minimum storage cost:

- Azure Activity (Azure platform logs)

- Azure Active Directory Identity Protection (AAD Premium P2)

- Azure Information Protection

- Azure Advanced Threat Protection (only alerts)

- Azure Security Center (only alerts)

- Microsoft Cloud App Security (only alerts)

- Microsoft Defender Advanced Threat Protection (monitoring agent alerts)

- Office 365 (logs)

You need to consider the cost of data connectors and the storage cost into the Log Analytics workspace. A free or low-cost option is good; however, for any SIEM solution to be successful, many other Sentinel data connectors are needed. The cost for streaming data and processing and storing charges are incurred for other connectors, for example:

- Ingesting data into Log Analytics

- Sending data through Azure Sentinel

- Optional use of Logic Apps for automation

- Optionally running your own machine learning models

- Optionally running any VMs as data collectors

The jacobslab.com Azure subscription uses pay-as-you-go (PAYG). If this is your model, you pay a fixed price per gigabyte (GB) consumed, and it is charged on a per-day basis. Microsoft has provided the option to use discounts based on the larger volumes of data. Choosing a different pricing tier to save money is a manual process.

Connect to Data Streams

Open your Azure portal, search for Azure Sentinel, and select it to reveal the Sentinel Overview page. Before you begin to see events, alerts, and incidents, you need to go through the steps to connect the logs and metrics provided by Azure from the data connector pane.

Once you have connected some of the data produced by Microsoft Azure in the next exercise, you will take a tour through the Azure Sentinel information summary to become familiar with the interface.

Note   If you did not enable the Azure VMs to allow connecting data source to the Log Analytics workspace, return to Chapter 4 and follow the exercises.

ENABLE AZURE SENTINEL DATA CONNECTORS

The prerequisites required "contributor" permissions to the Log Analytics workspace and "reader" permissions to any subscription logs to stream into Azure Sentinel.

1. From the Azure portal, search for Azure Sentinel, select the icon, and open the overview page. On the left menu, scroll down and select Data connectors.

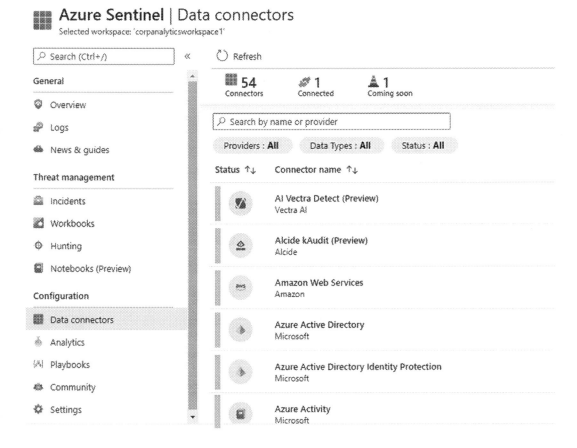

2. Your screen should have no data connectors active (this example displays one connected); select Azure Activity, and on the far-right pane, select Open connector page.

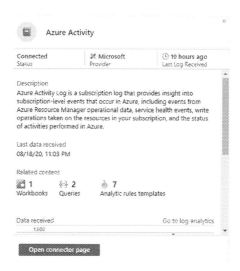

3. From the Data Connectors "Azure Activity" window, look at the far-right window and select the Connect option. The status will change from Disconnected to Connected. Data from the Azure Activity log is now streaming into Azure Sentinel.

4. You need to confirm the event data collected from the Windows Servers. This is accomplished from the Log Analytics workspace; however, you can navigate to the DATA location by selecting Settings on the bottom-left menu. Then select the Workspace settings at the top menu.

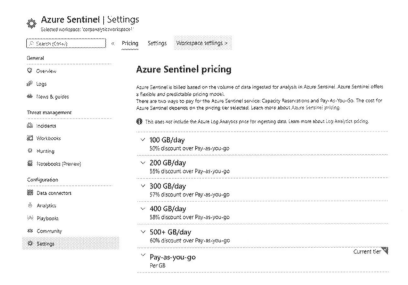

5. Select the Workspace settings at the top menu; this selection takes you to the Log Analytics workspace. Scroll down the menu to Settings and select the Advanced settings from the left menu.

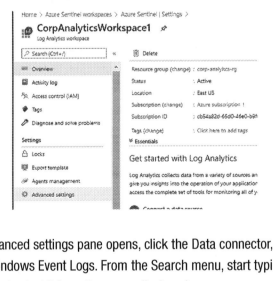

6. Once the Advanced settings pane opens, click the Data connector, and it defaults to Windows Event Logs. From the Search menu, start typing the word Application and select it from the menu displayed.

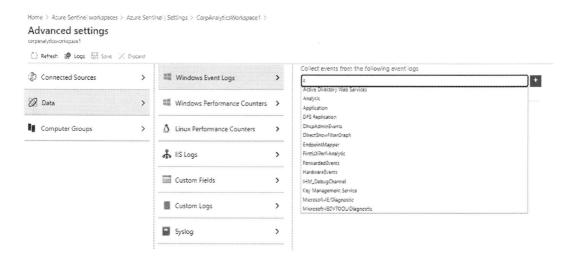

7. Select application and click the + button to add. You can leave all the defaults checked, Error, Warning, and Information. Repeat the search for Setup and System.

8. That completes the setup for this exercise. Before returning to the Azure Sentinel Overview page, take a moment to select each of the other options.

The Azure Activity log displays subscription-level events from the Azure Resource Manager data, the API operations: DELETE, PUT, POST.

If you click Computer Groups, select WSUS or SCCM; notice you have the option to import data from these systems into Sentinel. Customers that have deployed SCCM to manage their systems can import the SCCM database information to help populate

Sentinel with workstation and server data. Customers that have deployed WSUS in their production systems can also share the information collected (refer to Figure 5-6). The data collected is used by Sentinel to have an individual machine inventory beyond current patching levels.

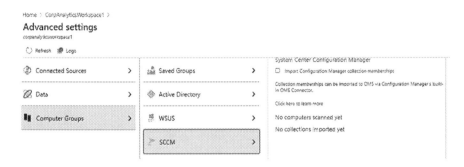

Figure 5-6. *System Center Configuration Manager import options*

The information available from the Azure platform through the data connection exercise allows all Azure Activity logs to flow into Azure Sentinel and perform the AI analysis on the information. The data provides event data to display when an edit was made by an identity (user or system), what was the edit, and when it changed. Follow the enable data connector exercise a few more times to enable more (low-cost) data analytics by enabling these connectors:

- Azure Active Directory

- Azure Active Directory Identity Protection (enabled from Chapter 1)

- Azure Information Protection

- Azure Advanced Threat Protection

During a Proof of Concept (POC), you should enable data connectors that have a cost associated with the data service. Enable these connectors in production once you have chosen to purchase the Azure Security Center standard tier for your Azure subscription or a few individual Azure resources.

- Azure Security Center (standard tier pricing required)

You may have additional data connectors to complete in your production environment. From the Azure Sentinel Data connectors pane, scroll up to Amazon Web Services, Cisco, CyberArk, and Forcepoint and down past Okta, Symantec, and Zscaler. Each connector has a guided installation process to allow you to leverage all the data from many current security solutions in place.

In our jacobslab site, we have six connectors streaming data into Sentinel (refer to Figure 5-7), and for the next few topics in this chapter, you gain a deeper insight into the strength of Azure Sentinel as a cloud SIEM solution. Topics covered in the remaining chapters use the configuration in both Azure Security Center and Azure Sentinel to continue blue team hunting with real-world examples.

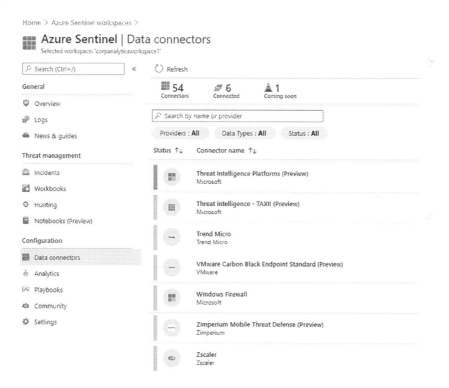

Figure 5-7. *Sentinel data connectors that are connected and streaming data*

If you'd like to validate data is being streamed, from the Sentinel Overview page, click settings on the lower-left menu. A data graph like the one shown in Figure 5-8 should be displayed. In the exercise, you connect to a small subset of data connectors, and the best practice is to collect data that is meaningful to your business. As different solutions gather large volumes of data, you should consider the cost of storing duplicate data. Send relevant data that can be viewed as actionable for the Security Operations Center (SOC) teams.

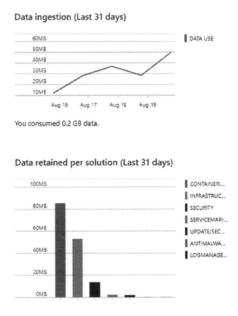

Figure 5-8. *Data ingestion and data retained (last 31 days)*

The next section teaches you some of the areas provided by a SIEM solution with additional examples guiding you through the remaining chapters.

Using Azure Sentinel

You may need to wait up to 24 hours for the connected data streams to start processing in the Sentinel AI engine. Open the Azure portal, search for Azure Sentinel, click the icon, and review the Sentinel overview. You may see something similar to Figure 5-9 from the jacobslab.com site.

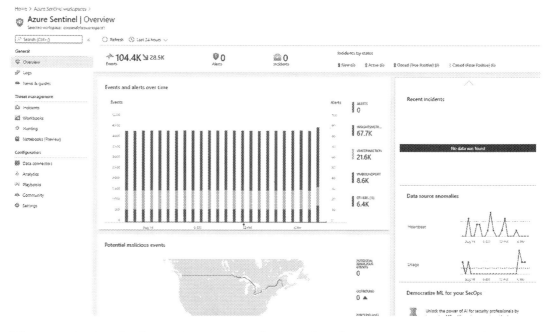

Figure 5-9. *Sentinel overview page 24 hours after data streams connected*

You will learn about each of the major views of Azure Sentinel through each topic as your journey continues.

Logs Pane

When you first go to the Logs blade, the example queries are displayed and are a good start to begin learning how to formulate Kusto Query Language (KQL) queries. You should see a view like Figure 5-10 for the Logs page. You should take time to try the individual sample queries to gain insight into the query syntax and if there is any initial data in the logs for Sentinel to display. Remember if you're not collecting the data, there are no results in the predefined queries.

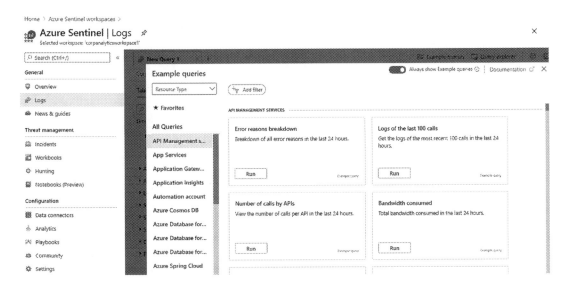

Figure 5-10. *Sentinel Logs page with example queries*

Click the X on the top right of the Example queries screen (not the X to close Sentinel) to remove the Example queries screen. This Example queries screen can get redundant to review this screen after learning more about the queries. Another way to review some of the KQL syntax is to use the Query explorer on the top-right side of the Logs page; please refer to Figure 5-11 to enable the Query explorer.

Figure 5-11. *Query explorer view, settings "gear" and help icons*

Click the Query explorer icon to display the many different queries to reveal data logs. Figure 5-12 shows the expansion of some of the solution queries tree view. The Query explorer button allows you to add your custom queries to this listing. You can mark any of the queries as favorites by using your mouse and enabling. If you click any of the trees and expand some of the page icon views, the query displays back the logs view so you can run the query. Each time you click a query, a new tab opens.

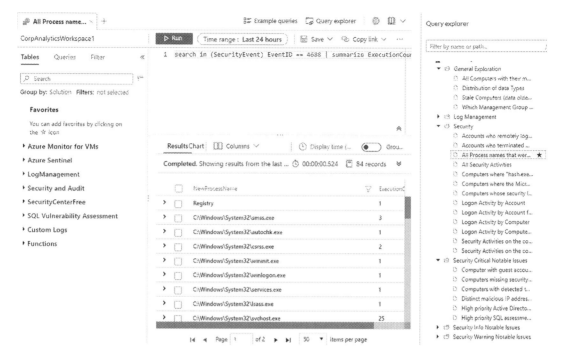

Figure 5-12. *Query explorer displaying solution queries examples*

If you click under Security, as shown in Figure 5-12, and run "All Process names that were running," there is a list of processes running on systems. As you go through additional Azure security topics, more queries are provided in this book.

Note   With a Microsoft email account, you can learn KQL skills at a free demo site at `https://portal.azure.com/#blade/Microsoft_Azure_Monitoring_Logs/DemoLogsBlade`.

Analytics Pane

Analytics integrates with artificial intelligence (AI) and machine learning (ML) to assist and provide you with relevant information and reduce the raw number of alerts that are required to be investigated as a cloud security team member.

Azure Sentinel has many rules that are not enabled by default, and before you enable them, you can test each based on the rule and data you are collecting in your Log Analytics workspace.

ACTIVATE ANALYTICS RULE TEMPLATES

1. From the Sentinel Overview page, click the Analytics menu on the left-hand menu and select the Rule templates at the top of the screen.

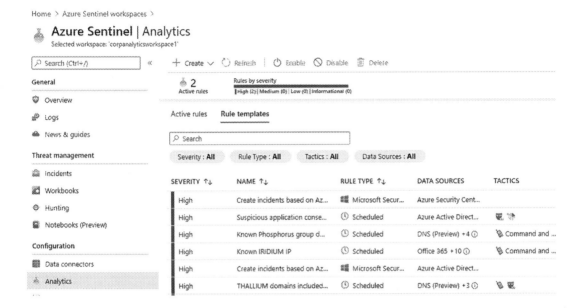

2. The default view provides all four severity level rules to display. Click Severity and unselect all but medium rules.

3. Use your mouse to click the Severity pop-up window behind the selection
    options and click OK.

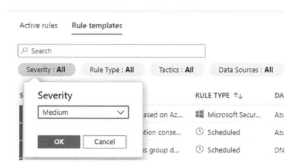

4. Now only the Medium Severity rules are displayed. As an example, click the
    RDP Nesting rules to expand the window on the right-hand side and start to
    create a rule journey by clicking Create rule.

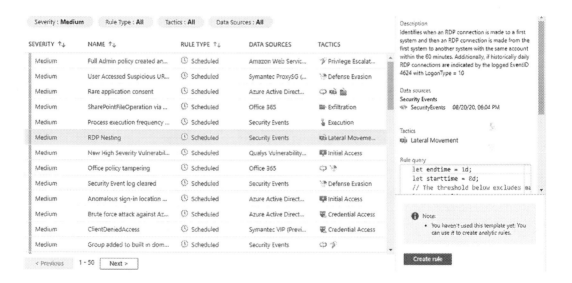

5. Review the Analytic rule wizard information. You can change the Severity here;
    click the down arrow next to severity, if your business identifies RDP sessions
    made, as a higher or lower severity. Click Next: Set rule logic.

Analytic rule wizard - Create new rule from template
RDP Nesting

General   Set rule logic   Incident settings {Preview}   Automated response   Review and create

Create an analytic rule that will run on your data to detect threats.

Analytic rule details

Name *

> RDP Nesting

Description

> Identifies when an RDP connection is made to a first system and then an RDP
> connection is made from the first system
> to another system with the same account within the 60 minutes. Additionally, if

Tactics

> Lateral Movement   ∨

Severity

> Medium   ∨

Status

(**Enabled**   Disabled)

[Next : Set rule logic >]

6. Review the Set rule logic options; notice the query schedule attributes and
   adjust the query if your Azure environment requires different scheduling. Click
   Next: Incident settings.

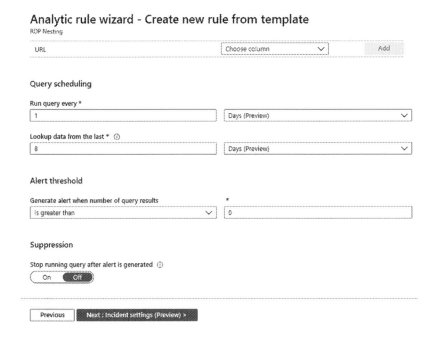

Analytic rule wizard - Create new rule from template
RDP Nesting

URL   Choose column   ∨   Add

Query scheduling

Run query every *

> 1   Days {Preview}   ∨

Lookup data from the last * ⓘ

> 8   Days {Preview}   ∨

Alert threshold

Generate alert when number of query results   *

> is greater than   ∨   0

Suppression

Stop running query after alert is generated ⓘ

(On   **Off**)

[Previous] [Next : Incident settings (Preview) >]

7. Notice the Incident settings will create an alert when this rule is triggered. If you are TESTING a rule to validate how much noise it will create, disable this option. Select the Next: Automated response to continue.

Analytic rule wizard - Create new rule from template
RDP Nesting

General   Set rule logic   Incident settings (Preview)   Automated response   Review and create

Incident settings (Preview)
Azure Sentinel alerts can be grouped together into an Incident that should be looked into.
You can set whether the alerts that are triggered by this analytics rule should generate incidents.

Create incidents from alerts triggered by this analytics rule
(**Enabled** Disabled)

Alert grouping
Set how the alerts that are triggered by this analytics rule, are grouped into incidents.
Grouping alerts into incidents provides the context you need to respond and reduces the noise from single alerts.

Group related alerts, triggered by this analytics rule, into incidents
(Enabled **Disabled**)

Limit the group to alerts created within the selected time frame
| 5 | Hours |

Group alerts triggered by this analytics rule into a single incident by
(●) Grouping alerts into a single incident if all the entities match (recommended)
( ) Grouping all alerts triggered by this rule into a single incident

[Previous]   [**Next : Automated response >**]

8. There are no other changes needed, except the defaults through the "Automated response," and the rule is created.

You begin to create playbooks and hunting exercises in additional chapters.

There is a great deal of work to review with Azure Sentinel, and you may agree it requires a technical how-to book on this subject and the pages would be full. One of the focus topics you learn is the graph that incidents the scope of the intrusion and provides the root cause to the incident. Review Figure 5-13 to see the investigation pattern and all the known systems affected.

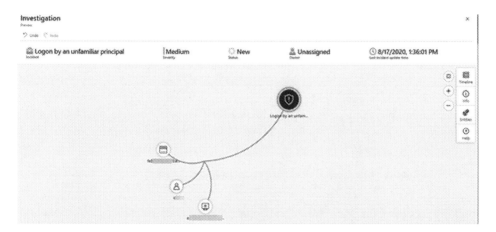

Figure 5-13. *View of the Investigation graph display logon by an unfamiliar principle*

This short introduction continues in the remaining chapters; however, you look at hunting before you continue. If you have a new deployment of Azure Sentinel, there may not be incidents to investigate. There are many powerful built-in hunting queries to begin the automation of the investigation.

Hunting

Cyber security blue team hunting is a critical component and can be exceptionally difficult in the Azure Cloud VNet hunting ground. Hunting for security threats in Azure Sentinel highlights the most powerful features within Azure Sentinel. Cloud security team members are responsible for investigating threats and ending them as soon as possible in the cyber security "kill chain." Acting on alerts is mainly a reactive response; however, Azure Sentinel provides early warning of Indicators of Compromise (IOC), as anomalies are discovered in your Azure subscriptions. Refer to Figure 5-14 to see the default hunting pane from jacobslab.com.

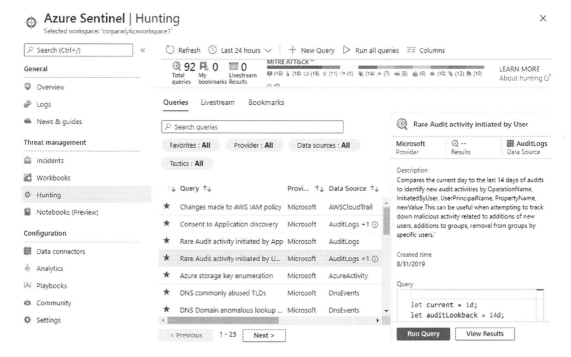

Figure 5-14. *Azure Sentinel Hunting pane using the MITRE ATT&CK matrix*

Azure Sentinel's hunting feature offers

- Built-in queries

- Kusto Query Language

- Bookmarks

- Notebooks

Microsoft continues to invest 1 billion US dollars a year in cyber security R&D. The Sentinel queries are developed by Microsoft security researchers and offered as an example library to start blue team hunting. The use of KQL with Log Analytics and Azure Sentinel hunting for attacks and compromised systems allows you to build queries to identify and track down anomalies quickly. Using the Log Analytics Workspace data with Sentinel, you create your own bookmarks for queries that can be quickly reused. You should review the hundreds of KQL queries and playbooks in GitHub (now owned by Microsoft); there is a full list of KQL examples on the Azure Sentinel hunting repository at `https://github.com/Azure/Azure-Sentinel`. Microsoft has reengineered and customized the Jupyter Notebook used with the support of the Azure Machine Learning (AML) platform for analyzing your security data in Azure Sentinel. Jupyter Notebooks are workflows with a specific use case to check.

Azure Sentinel is a SIEM server in the cloud that supports the centralized management of inventory software that collects and responds to security events occurring in the Azure Tenants, subscriptions, and IaaS and PaaS services. Azure Sentinel provides alerts, filters data, and more for your cyber security blue team hunting.

Summary

In this chapter, you configured Azure Security Center by enabling the clients to be installed on the existing VMs, and you migrated to the standard tier to obtain the most benefits using Security as a Service. You enabled email notification and began receiving security health summaries.

You enabled Azure Sentinel and connected to the Log Analytics workspace created in Chapter 4. The data connectors available in Sentinel continue to show the integration value of the Security Center security discovery. Next, we expand on the cyber security findings and remediation from Azure Sentinel as you continue to learn about Azure security optimization.

CHAPTER 6

Azure Kubernetes Services: Container Security

In this chapter, you learn the business use case for Azure Kubernetes Services (AKS), understand the fundamentals of containers, and learn how to maintain a secure Kubernetes cluster. You need to understand the underlying container ecosystems and how Kubernetes supports the management of hundreds and thousands of containers.

The main focus in this chapter is the velocity that a microservices management platform of Kubernetes provides for the business and the need for Azure operations teams to manage and secure Kubernetes services in Azure. The processes to support Infrastructure as Code (IaC) improve cloud maturity processes. IaC includes the processes that mature companies need, to enable Virtual Machines in the cloud. VMs are created using repeatable automation deployment processes, scaling to hundreds of VMs, which is **measured in minutes**. As a comparison, Microservices, like containers in the cloud, are created using repeatable automation processes, scaling to thousands of containers, which is **measured in seconds**. The velocity to build a business DevOps platform can be finalized in minutes or seconds.

To better understand how to secure a container cluster in the Azure cloud, you must first know how to deploy, scale, and update clusters. To create an Azure container cluster you must gain knowledge using Azure container instances and designing a compute strategy for Azure Kubernetes Services (AKS). Containers are the de facto microservice architecture companies are leveraging. Docker containers and Kubernetes management work together. You gain an understanding of microservices and gain a brief lesson on how containers started and gradually increase your knowledge and security best practices for AKS along the way. In this chapter, you learn

- Microservices
- Containers, Docker, and Kubernetes

© Marshall Copeland and Matthew Jacobs 2021
M. Copeland and M. Jacobs, *Cyber Security on Azure*, https://doi.org/10.1007/978-1-4842-6531-4_6

- Azure Kubernetes Services and security

- AKS security with Security Center and Sentinel

- Kubernetes security with Azure Policy

First, you are introduced to microservices to gain an understanding of this architecture and how it is the foundation of containers. As you learn microservices management, you begin to realize it is one of the fastest development skill sets needed in the market; you need to know why containers are beneficial and how to secure them for your business. You learn how microservices relate to containers, Docker, and Kubernetes and how the microservice architecture can be secured. You then are provided with methods to secure the containers in an AKS deployment, design, and verify the security using Azure cloud security services.

Microservices

Before adopting a microservice architecture, you need to understand the components that make up a microservice; rather than provide you a definition, understanding may be best if you learn what business, DevOps, and security problems a microservice solves. A microservice is a small code and runs on a small virtual compute instance. The use of many small code instances together is sometimes referred to as a design pattern. Using a logical description, you can begin to define a microservice as a small application, a single service, or several small services running in an isolated process. The service is very lightweight and used for business capabilities (i.e., applications or services), and because it is independent, it can be deployed and redeployed without interruption of the overall business application.

Deployment of the lightweight service also introduces isolation of the service. The services are decentralized, so governance and management are needed. Another concern is data management and data confidentiality; they are both a security consideration also. The microservice infrastructure should be autonomous and self-supporting with an overall design to self-heal from failure. One of the main benefits of a Microsoft architecture is the support of DevOps to increase deployment speed without compromising the system.

There are many publications on the history of software engineering that start with monolithic methods, waterfall methods, and up through agility deployment. Software deployment has always had the need to be a high-quality solution to provide value to customers and businesses. Software development life cycle needs to be as short as possible and continuously improved.

The adoption of a microservice architecture helps to minimize the cost but also reduce the complexity of the multimonth development time. A DevOps team can use the individual services as software projects to rapidly produce a product. All the mini services coupled together become the business solution. Beyond the components that define the microservice, how does adopting microservices benefit the business? A composable architecture leads to the use of containers as the delivery foundation for a microservice. Refer to Figure 6-1 to gain a visual representation of a historical monolithic architecture vs. a microservice architecture with service separations.

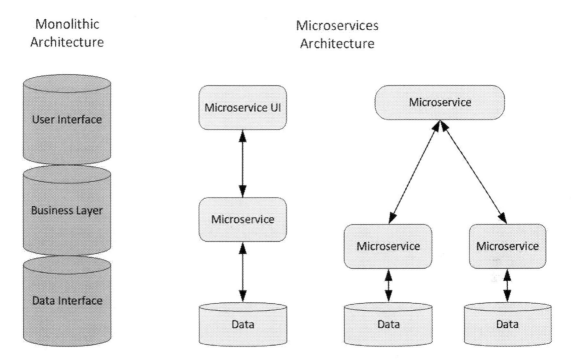

Figure 6-1. *Monolithic and microservice architectures with separation of services*

A new term you should begin to appreciate is "disposable," because when adopting microservices, each service is quickly instantiated, cloned (for elasticity), and destroyed. The modularity of a microservice supports the programming team and application deployment team by using many tiny modules. There are many small moving parts that are easy to develop but still require updating and expanding. One of the challenges includes the functionality to support Continuous Integration (CI) and Continuous Deployment (CD). Microservices support individual services to be destroyed and replaced with updated services using an automated Continuous Integration/Continuous Deployment pipeline.

One of the challenges for adoption of microservices architecture includes DevOps, Agile, and Lean methodologies. You need to create processes that support a single model that allows tool and platform adoption. However, adopting microservices supports a large ecosystem of tools for code development and release management. The toolchain for cloud deployment with microservices is the correct infrastructure to support both the code repository and disbursement of DevOps team members.

You also need to be aware of the term "immutable" in a computer system or services. Immutable systems are services that are not susceptible to change. In contrast to the term immutable is the requirement for microservices to be part of a mutable infrastructure. This type of infrastructure is continually updated, changed, and tweaked to support the service requirements. A "Day One" deployment is a known state of configuration. Changes that create modifications or "drift" of a known state are labeled as "Day Two." Cloud services are constantly undergoing change. When you want to update an "immutable" Microsoft Azure Kubernetes Service (AKS), the control plane allows AKS administrators' permission to create, update, and destroy the microservice. With version control for immutable objects, the underlying structure is easier to support and reproduce. Testing and replication just became easier because of the immutable infrastructure components.

Containers, Docker, and Kubernetes

You can relate the use of a virtual machine (VM) running on a shared computer host using a hypervisor and the use of containers in the same host using the same hypervisor. The difference is that a VM has traditionally been used for business infrastructure, replacing physical infrastructure servers with virtualizing servers. The VM includes all physical server features, whether you need them or not. For example, VMs support disk drives, Universal Serial Bus (USB), serial communication links, video, and options to add more hardware (or add more virtual hardware). Containers are built for application developers and are essentially and exceptionally lightweight processes when running. Containers do not have the overhead of additional features that a VM supports.

Containers are built as Platform as a Service (PaaS) with the product labeled as "image." Virtual machines are built as Infrastructure as a Service (IaaS) with the product also labeled as image. Containers, however, are created by layering of software when an image is built. Only software that supports the application will be installed and running on the container. Containers are often purpose built based on requirements of the developer application. Containers do not support all potential applications that could be required to run on a VM.

A container has less overhead and lighter weight than a virtual machine. A VM includes the entire operating system (OS), while a container is a small, self-contained, and complete software package that runs on an operating system. It is like a VM in that it was designed to run on a shared OS host and supports the benefit to run on almost any virtual host, Hyper-V, VMware, Azure, and AWS. A VM has the application package, libraries, and dependencies included already to run any application supported by the OS. The container has only the application dependencies required to run the application.

Refer to Figure 6-2 to gain a visual representation of the difference between a VM and a container.

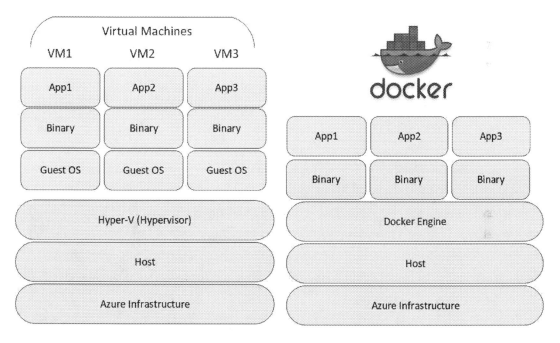

Figure 6-2. *Visual representation of a VM and container*

Docker is a PaaS product that requires a virtualized host to run the container. Docker supports a software method to build, run, and store container images. Containers, by default, are isolated from other containers so they include all the libraries and configuration files to run. This isolation is referred to as a namespace. Each container runs in a separated namespace which limits the access to that specific container. Containers were initially created to run on Linux servers and today are supported and deployed on Windows OS as well as most hypervisors' software. Docker created a complete solution and container utilization. Docker is a market leader and often is synonymous with the process to build, host, and store container images. There are four major components of Docker:

- Docker process
- Docker objects
- Docker images
- Docker registry

The software process that runs the container is often a Linux daemon; on Windows OS, it is a service. The process that runs the container is called "dockerd" and often referred to as the Docker Engine. This process manages the container, listens for requests, and allows user interaction. Docker objects are images, containers, and other services. For the purpose of this discussion, you can refer to them as container. A Docker image is a read-only template used to build the purpose-built container. Finally, the registry is a repository for all the images that have been finalized. The Docker registry supports the download of any image, which is called a pull. And if you create an image, with Docker "compose," you can push an image into the registry. The management of Docker containers is supported through Docker Swarm. Swarm management features include listing nodes in a cluster, creating new nodes, and removing nodes from a cluster. Docker Swarm had some initial shortfalls when managing containers at scale, so that allowed the container market an entry for Kubernetes.

Kubernetes created a foundation for managing containers, and the business model was designed to ease requirements of developers to host, share, update, and remove containers at scale. Remember the velocity of container deployment to thousands of containers is measured in seconds.

Kubernetes is an open source container orchestration system. And, like Docker, it has specific definitions of individual components that work together to deploy, manage, and scale applications. The design of Kubernetes, originally at Google, and now maintained by Cloud Native Computing Foundation, is loosely coupled and extensible for different workloads. This supports the use of Kubernetes on Azure, Google, AWS, VMware, and so many other platforms. Kubernetes has several individual resources, including for our Azure security learning:

- Management plan
- Nodes
- Pods

When you see the term Kubernetes, you need to visualize in your mind this is the entire cluster service and not an individual component. Refer to Figure 6-3 to gain insight into the Kubernetes solution.

Note   Learn more about Kubernetes at `https://kubernetes.io`.

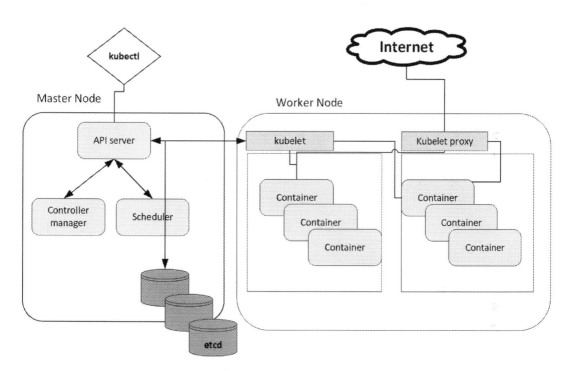

Figure 6-3. *Kubernetes components with control plane and worker nodes*

Kubernetes is deployed in a cluster which can be divided into two main areas of work distribution. The two areas of Kubernetes are the control plane and worker node; together they create the cluster. For our security conversation, you do not need to know the details of all the objects but what service they provide. You first need to know that the Kubernetes control plane is composed of services that are like any stand-alone computer OS. There is an interface to send and receive commands, API server, scheduler (to assign new pods to run in a node), and "etcd," a highly available key store to manage cluster data.

Another term the Azure cloud security and operations team need to remember is "ephemeral." The definition can be associated with temporary, as in a container is ephemeral when added to a pod to accomplish a specific action. For another comparison, Azure supports an Ephemeral OS disk to support stateless workloads using a Shared Image Gallery. Ephemeral containers could be used to provide an inspection service; once inspected, the container is removed.

Kubernetes runs one or more than one container in a collection which is called a pod. The worker node is a virtual machine, managed by the control plane. The control plane manages one or more containers that all share the storage and networking.

On the node runs the agent called a "kubelet," and it runs on every node in the cluster. The kubelet is responsible for running healthy nodes. From a security view, Azure would need to leverage the health through the use of kubelet data and some add-on daemon services. As an example, the Domain Naming Service (DNS) is an "add-on" service, which is required by the Kubernetes service to identify pods and containers in the pods. Another add-on is the container resource monitoring service to provide metrics about the cluster. Security controls for each of these "add-on" services can be resource challenging.

Finally, you should be aware of the pod security settings that are applied to limit privileges and access control on a per-pod basis. The enforcement is completed through policy-based definitions. The pod security policy is a cluster-level security control. The augmentation of security and possibly the replacement of the pod security policy are security points of interest for Azure Kubernetes Service. There is an exercise at the end of this chapter that demonstrates the engineering complexity of open source security policy inclusion with Azure Policy definitions.

Azure Kubernetes Services and Security

Azure cloud services host the Kubernetes control plane and nodes as a service so you do not need to build the individual container objects like the API server, schedule, kube-controller-manager, cloud-controller-manager, and etcd key-value store. As you have learned about Docker containers and Kubernetes cluster management, the authentication and authorization are used to secure these services. With the integration in the cloud, Azure Kubernetes Services (AKS) offload the responsibility to the Azure services. You can gain a greater insight by using the Azure portal to create an Azure Kubernetes Service deployment.

AZURE KUBERNETES SERVICE CREATION

This example uses the basic network configuration to gain a perspective of the AKS automation features quickly. Additional security considerations for the advanced network configuration are discussed in this chapter.

1. From the Azure portal, search for Kubernetes services. Select the + Add option to Add Kubernetes cluster.

Home >

Kubernetes services 📌
jacobslabs (Default Directory)

+ Add ∨   ⚙ Manage view ∨   ○ Refresh   ⤓ Export to CSV   ⌁ Open query | ⊘ Assign tags | ♡ Feedback

+ Add Kubernetes cluster

+ Register a Kubernetes cluster with Azure Arc

Showing 0 to 0 of 0 records.

Name ↑↓	Type ↑↓	Resource group ↑↓	Kuberne...

all)   Type == (all)   Resource group == (all) ✕   Location == (all) ✕   ⊽ Add filter

No Kubernetes services to display

2.   Since this may be the first time you create a cluster through the portal, select the subscription to create AKS. Enter a new resource group name to allow easy cleanup after the testing. Enter a unique Kubernetes cluster name. Leave the version default, but select the down arrow and take note there are older and new versions that could be created. Change the node count = 2 and select Next: Node pools.

Home > Kubernetes services >

Create Kubernetes cluster

Azure Kubernetes Service (AKS) manages your hosted Kubernetes environment, making it quick and easy to deploy and manage containerized applications without container orchestration expertise. It also eliminates the burden of ongoing operations and maintenance by provisioning, upgrading, and scaling resources on demand, without taking your applications offline. Learn more about Azure Kubernetes Service

Project details

Select a subscription to manage deployed resources and costs. Use resource groups like folders to organize and manage all your resources.

Subscription * ⓘ | Azure subscription 1   ⌄ |

Resource group * ⓘ | (New) jacobsaks-rg   ⌄ |
                                      Create new

Cluster details

Kubernetes cluster name * ⓘ | jacobslab-aks   ✓ |

Region * ⓘ | (US) East US   ⌄ |

Kubernetes version * ⓘ | 1.16.13 (default)   ⌄ |

Primary node pool

The number and size of nodes in the primary node pool in your cluster. For production workloads, at least 3 nodes are recommended for resiliency. For development or test workloads, only one node is required. You will not be able to change the node size after cluster creation, but you will be able to change the number of nodes in your cluster after creation. If you would like additional node pools, you will need to enable the "X" feature on the "Scale" tab which will allow you to add more node pools after creating the cluster. Learn more about node pools in Azure Kubernetes Service

Node size * ⓘ   **Standard DS2 v2**
                                     Change size

Node count * ⓘ   ○⸻⸻⸻⸻⸻⸻⸻⸻⸻⸻⸻ | 3 |

[Review + create]   < Previous   [Next : Node pools >]

3. There is no option to change from the default settings; however, you should be
    aware that if you enable the virtual nodes option, Azure can burst the number of
    serverless nodes. Select Next: Authentication.

Home > Kubernetes services >

Create Kubernetes cluster

Basics   **Node pools**   Authentication   Networking   Integrations   Tags   Review + create

Node pools

In addition to the required primary node pool configured on the Basics tab, you can also add optional node pools to handle a
variety of workloads Learn more about multiple node pools ☐

+ Add node pool   🗑 Delete

Name	OS type	Node count	Node size
☐ agentpool (primary)	Linux	3	Standard_DS2_v2

Virtual nodes

Virtual nodes allow burstable scaling backed by serverless Azure Container Instances. Learn more about virtual nodes ☐

Virtual nodes ⓘ   ⦿ Disabled ◯ Enabled

VM scale sets

Enabling VM scale sets will create a cluster that uses VM scale sets instead of individual virtual machines for the cluster nodes.
VM scale sets are required for scenarios including autoscaling, multiple node pools, and Windows support.
Learn more about VM scale sets in AKS ☐

VM scale sets ⓘ   ◯ Disabled ⦿ Enabled

                                  ❶ VM scale sets are required for multiple node pools

[Review + create]   [< Previous]   [Next : Authentication >]

4. Leave the default settings so Azure creates a new Service Principal Name to be managed by Azure Active Directory. Leave the default selection to leverage the Role-Based Access Control. Select Next: Networking.

Home > Kubernetes services >

Create Kubernetes cluster

| Basics | Node pools | **Authentication** | Networking | Integrations | Tags | Review + create |

Cluster infrastructure
The cluster infrastructure authentication specified is used by Azure Kubernetes Service to manage cloud resources attached to the cluster. This can be either a service principal ☐ or a system-assigned managed identity ☐.

Authentication method   ⦿ Service principal ◯ System-assigned managed identity

Service principal * ⓘ

[(new) default service principal   ]

Configure service principal

Kubernetes authentication and authorization
Authentication and authorization are used by the Kubernetes cluster to control user access to the cluster as well as what the user may do once authenticated. Learn more about Kubernetes authentication ☐

Role-based access control (RBAC) ⓘ   ⦿ Enabled ◯ Disabled

AKS-managed Azure Active Directory ⓘ ◯ Enabled ⦿ Disabled

Node pool OS disk encryption
By default, all disks in AKS are encrypted at rest with Microsoft-managed keys. For additional control over encryption, you can supply your own keys using a disk encryption set backed by an Azure Key Vault. The disk encryption set will be used to encrypt the OS disks for all node pools in the cluster. Learn more ☐

Encryption type

[(Default) Encryption at-rest with a platform-managed key   ⌄]

[Review + create]   [< Previous] [Next : Networking >]

5. Change the Network configuration setting to Basic, leave the other settings to their default, and select Next: Integrations.

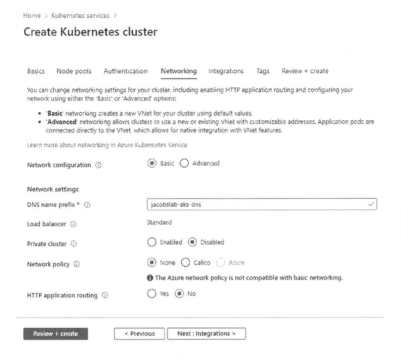

6. The default setting is to enable container monitoring; in this exercise, we selected the same Log Analytics workspace created in Chapter 4 exercises. Skip the Tags page and select Review + create.

7. If there are no validation errors, select Create.

Once the deployment is complete, select the option to go to the resource.

AKS provides many benefits by running Kubernetes as a service to reduce the manual work like security updates; Azure takes this action to upgrade etcd. Maintenance upgrade clusters are backup and support of autoscaling. The provision of services in the PaaS uses the underlying elasticity of the Azure cloud platform. The monitoring of cluster health is required for the entire architecture and is included with Azure services like Azure Monitor, Log Analytics, Security Center, and Azure Sentinel. Refer to Figure 6-4 to review the deployment of AKS from the completed exercise.

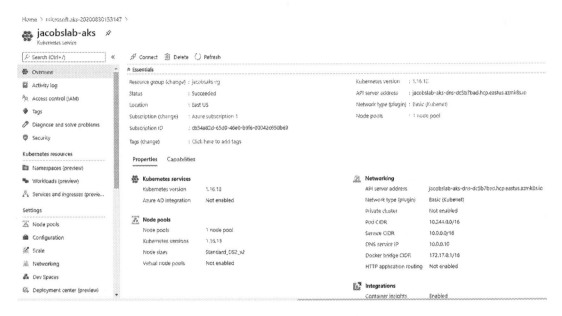

Figure 6-4. *AKS deployment in the jacobslab subscription*

AKS SECURITY WITH KUBERNETES ATTACK MATRIX

You learned in Chapter 5 about the MITRE ATT&CK framework as a knowledge base of known tactics and techniques used by adversaries to attempt cyber attacks against your business. The matrix also includes in the body of knowledge mitigation to prepare, put in place, and defend your business. The framework is designed to follow the kill chain; attackers start reconnaissance (recon) on the left-hand side (kill chain figure) and attempt to exploit an application or configuration vulnerability. They want to remain persistent in your network, come back later by installing a "back door," and steal your company data during exfiltration.

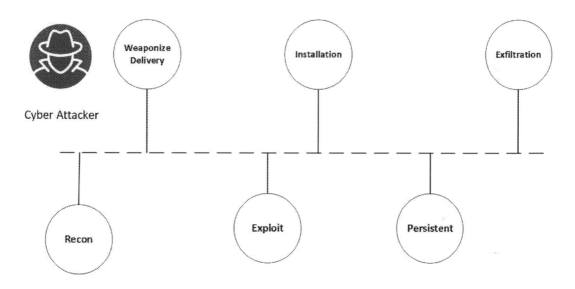

Kill chain figure

As a cyber security expert, you attempt to identify and eradicate the attacker closer to the left side of the kill chain, a phrase called "shifting security left." Stop the attacker early in their kill chain processes. You do have an attack matrix for the overall infrastructure and application security; what about a security matrix for microservices?

An Azure Kubernetes Service (AKS) is a service that requires Microsoft to support customer deployment of AKS to have adequate detection and mitigations. Kubernetes is a microservice with many parts that require security controls. Microsoft has created a Kubernetes ATT&CK-like matrix to help with addressing the security control focus.

Initial Access	Execution	Persistence	Privilege Escalation	Defense Evasion	Credential Access	Discovery	Lateral Movement	Impact
Using Cloud credentials	Exec into container	Backdoor container	Privileged container	Clear container logs	List K8S secrets	Access the K8S API server	Access cloud resources	Data Destruction
Compromised images in registry	bash/cmd inside container	Writable hostPath mount	Cluster-admin binding	Delete K8S events	Mount service principal	Access Kubelet API	Container service account	Resource Hijacking
Kubeconfig file	New container	Kubernetes CronJob	hostPath mount	Pod / container name similarity	Access container service account	Network mapping	Cluster internal networking	Denial of service
Application vulnerability	Application exploit (RCE)		Access cloud resources	Connect from Proxy server	Applications credentials in configuration files	Access Kubernetes dashboard	Applications credentials in configuration files	
Exposed Dashboard	SSH server running inside container					Instance Metadata API	Writable volume mounts on the host	
							Access Kubernetes dashboard	
							Access tiller endpoint	

Kubernetes attack matrix

You can read more about the Kubernetes threat matrix at `www.microsoft.com/security/blog/2020/04/02/attack-matrix-kubernetes/`.

In Chapter 4, you learned how to enable Azure Monitor services, and AKS is also a PaaS hosted service that has hooks in Azure health monitoring and maintenance. The AKS automated deployment service supports automation to standup Kubernetes clusters with the control plane and agent nodes. You need to know the technical processes and configurations of AKS security features including

- Authentication
- Container registry security
- Container security
- AKS isolation
- AKS automatic updates

Authentication

You begin with Azure identity services, like all Azure services, leveraging Azure Active Directory (AAD). Azure Kubernetes Services authentication and authorization is supported for Kubernetes using Azure Role-Based Access Control (RBAC) to grant users, groups, and service accounts permission to services. The service accounts are granted only the access needed following your least-privileged access policy. You can secure the cluster access to developers and operators.

Kubernetes allows access through role permissions; to deny permissions, an identity is not included in a role. The Kubernetes design has no processes to block or deny access; you simply have access from a role, or you do not have access because you are not granted a role.

The role permissions are part of the namespace security you learned earlier in this chapter, and users are granted permission to access each individual namespace. ClusterRoles grant permissions across the entire cluster that is separate from the given namespace.

Individual defined role permissions to Kubernetes resources are assigned with RoleBinding. Azure Active Directory binds the roles to the Azure AD users to execute work or take actions inside the cluster based on the individual namespace.

Kubernetes supports service accounts, and they are managed by the Kubernetes API. Access to services requires credentials that are managed as a Kubernetes secret. Service accounts complete work by authorizing pods to request the API server to provide an authentication token for the service account.

The Kubernetes architecture was not designed to support user accounts for humans in support of administrative duties or developers in the same way as Microsoft Active Directory Domain Service (AD DS). Instead of using a rudimentary key-value pair to store a username and password, external identity solutions integrate into the Kubernetes cluster. Azure Kubernetes Services integrate with Azure Active Directory to perform human users' identity stored activities. Refer to Figure 6-5.

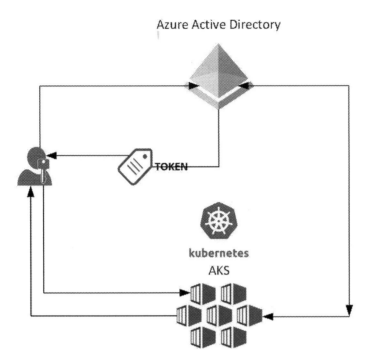

Figure 6-5. *Picture of AAD and API server integration*

AKS providers have four built-in roles to mirror the Kubernetes built-in roles. The master node is the control plane that includes the API server, schedule, controller, and etcd.

Note   etcd is a reliable key-value store for critical data (learn more at `https://etcd.io`).

You can download at the AKS secure baseline reference implementation on GitHub: `https://github.com/mspnp/aks-secure-baseline`.

Container Security

When the Azure Kubernetes Service completes the configuration, there are security features you should be aware of. You learned about the Docker container registry earlier; however, with AKS, you now have a private Azure Container Registry. The private container image repository is used to pull into your Azure Kubernetes clusters.

The container can be accessed from the AKS administrative commands from the web API requests, so all images use the private registry. Additionally, developers no longer need to have all the Docker compose software installed; they can use Azure Cloud Shell. Just to remind you, this text is focused on security, and so resources are limited, and created containers and image deployment can be found on the books on the GitHub account.

One of the best practices to build secure images is to only include applications that are up to date and include static and dynamic scanning on all DevOps platforms. Use runtime libraries that do not include exploited vulnerable tools including the Linux package managers. Malware can include Remote Access Trojan that installs a back door into your images.

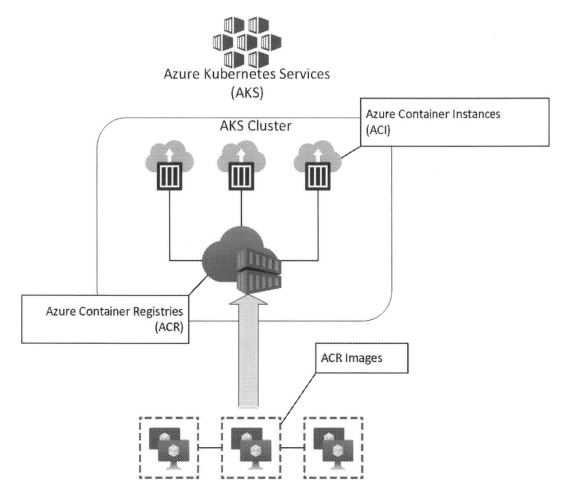

Figure 6-6. *Azure Kubernetes Services visual model view*

215

During the AKS installation exercise for testing or a Proof of Concept (POC), the basic network option was selected to demonstrate the easy automation that Kubernetes services running in Azure may provide. Production environments may require additional options that may be selected to allow for a greater bursting of nodes into thousands or hundreds of thousands. Refer to Figure 6-7 to gain a better view of the customized networking option in the AKS journey.

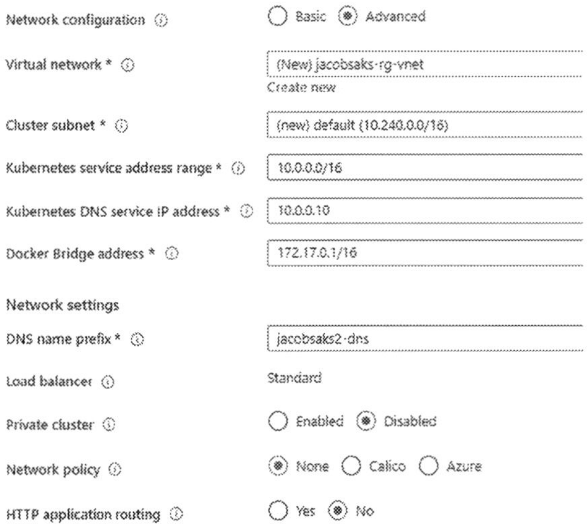

Figure 6-7. *Advanced networking settings in Azure Kubernetes Services*

You first need to look at the default Classless Internet Domain Routing (CIDR) sizes of the clusters, Kubernetes services, and Docker bridge addresses. All three are set to /16 range or address space. Azure requires a reservation of 5 IP addresses, but if you take the raw numbers, there are 65,534 nodes (pods), service addresses, and bridge addresses. There can be no IP subnet overlap at the address space or subnet level.

Security configurations include Network Security Groups (NSG) and user-defined routes (UDR), of which Azure automatically updates based on the dynamic clusters created. It is recommended to allow AKS to manage the network; however, you can preconfigure virtual networks to customize the inbound and outbound services. In addition, DNS and HTTPS traffic are additional services that can be customized.

Before this topic is closed out, there are additional details to consider when customizing the network IP traffic. Remember that Kubernetes is an open source community–supported service, and the use of network policy can include Azure or Calico. Project Calico allows different Calico network policy APIs for different and more granular policy controls. Learn more about Project Calico at `https://docs.` `projectcalico.org/getting-started/kubernetes/managed-public-cloud/aks`.

Finally, choices for many of the Azure Kubernetes customization must be chosen during the creation of clusters. Policy changes and advanced network settings rolled back to basic network settings are not supported. For these two security-related architecture decision reversals, you must destroy your AKS deployment and recreate.

Note   For a very detailed explanation of AKS network management options, refer to `https://docs.microsoft.com/en-us/azure/aks/limit-egress-traffic`.

AKS Security with Security Center and Sentinel

Azure Security Center (ASC) is a cloud-native security service that you can enable to protect container hosts like virtual machines running Docker, Azure Kubernetes Services (AKS), and the Azure Container Registry (ACR); refer to Figure 6-8. During the AKS creation exercise earlier in this chapter, the integration with Azure Security Center (ASC) was enabled because this Azure subscription is being secured with the ASC standard license.

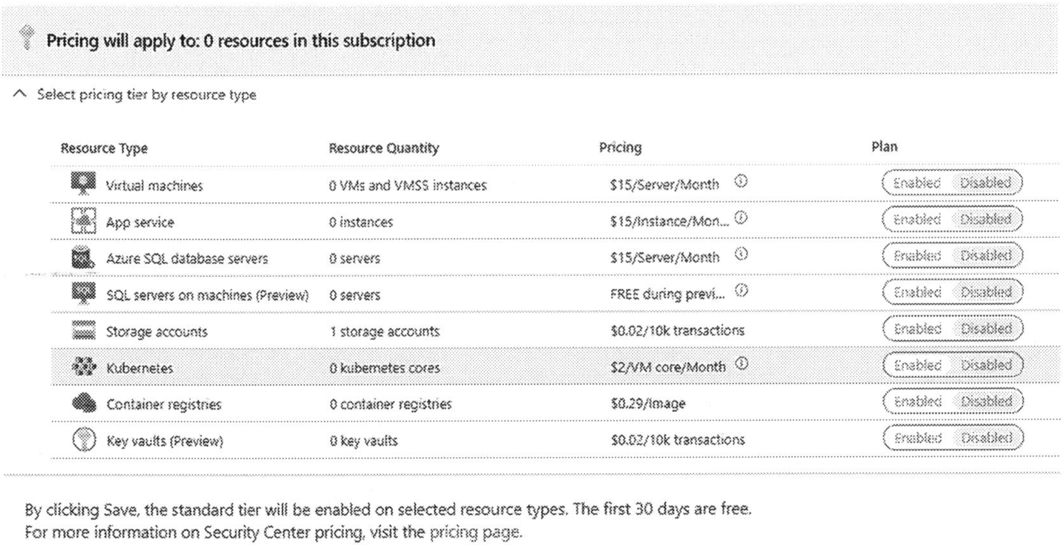

Resource Type	Resource Quantity	Pricing	Plan
Virtual machines	0 VMs and VMSS instances	$15/Server/Month	Enabled Disabled
App service	0 instances	$15/Instance/Mon...	Enabled Disabled
Azure SQL database servers	0 servers	$15/Server/Month	Enabled Disabled
SQL servers on machines (Preview)	0 servers	FREE during previ...	Enabled Disabled
Storage accounts	1 storage accounts	$0.02/10k transactions	Enabled Disabled
Kubernetes	0 kubernetes cores	$2/VM core/Month	Enabled Disabled
Container registries	0 container registries	$0.29/Image	Enabled Disabled
Key vaults (Preview)	0 key vaults	$0.02/10k transactions	Enabled Disabled

By clicking Save, the standard tier will be enabled on selected resource types. The first 30 days are free. For more information on Security Center pricing, visit the pricing page.

Figure 6-8. *Security Center pricing for Kubernetes core monthly*

This integration provides visibility into the AKS nodes, cloud traffic, and other security controls. There are several objects in the AKS deployment, so knowing what is projected is important. Azure Security Center uses the same Log Analytics agents on IaaS VMs to secure and enable threat protection on the AKS nodes. Additional Kubernetes subsystems including logs are available in Azure. Security Center access can be granted to allow Security Center to pull data already collected by the AKS management plane.

Protection includes security recommendations for the individual virtual machines. As vulnerabilities are shared by the threat intelligence (TI), updates and patching can be automated; refer to Figure 6-9. Another monitor feature is hardening of the clusters and Docker configurations. Real-time alerts to threats and malicious activities are provided at the host and cluster level.

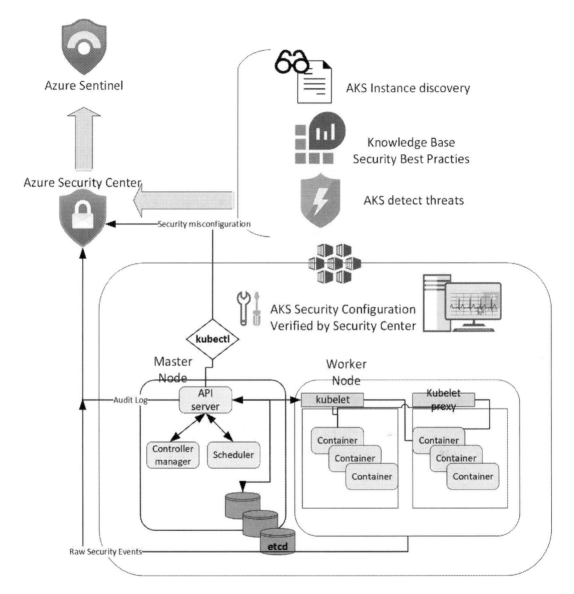

Figure 6-9. *Azure Security Center integration view with Azure Kubernetes Service (AKS) clusters*

Security Center scans Docker configuration provided in any misconfigurations identified. Guidance is provided to help resolve issues. Azure Kubernetes Services are integrated, and you gain visibility in the Azure Container Registry (ACR), so images and access are scanned. With the ASC Scanning options enabled on the Container Registry, the images are scanned for vulnerabilities.

Azure Security Center provides a built-in integration process with Azure Sentinel through the use of a Sentinel Security Center connector. This integration provides additional log visibility to automatically create alerts and provide blue team hunting incidents. The Azure Security Center data stream, metrics, logs, and other data streams like MITRE ATT&CK use all the data to detect Incidents of Compromise (IOC). Figure 6-10 shows some of the out-of-the-box container log files.

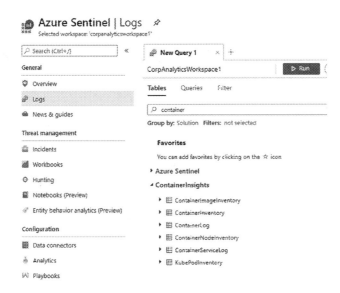

Figure 6-10. *Azure Sentinel container insight log file headers*

The high-level view in Figure 6-11 can be expanded out to search for details like pod container last status, repository, and node-specific information.

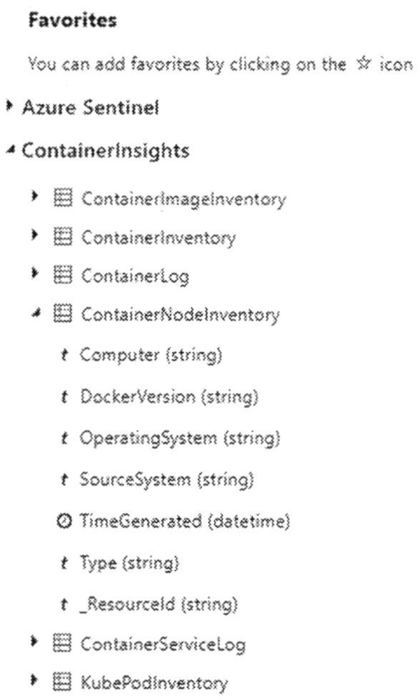

Favorites

You can add favorites by clicking on the ☆ icon

▶ **Azure Sentinel**

◢ **ContainerInsights**

   ▶ ⊞ ContainerImageInventory

   ▶ ⊞ ContainerInventory

   ▶ ⊞ ContainerLog

   ◢ ⊞ ContainerNodeInventory

      t Computer (string)

      t DockerVersion (string)

      t OperatingSystem (string)

      t SourceSystem (string)

      ⊘ TimeGenerated (datetime)

      t Type (string)

      t _ResourceId (string)

   ▶ ⊞ ContainerServiceLog

   ▶ ⊞ KubePodInventory

Figure 6-11. *Container node inventory log data for KQL queries*

Azure Security Center and Azure Sentinel work together to provide real-time scanning, alerting, and hunting playbooks.

Kubernetes Security with Azure Policy

Your business relies on security policies to maintain governance and legal requirements. The business also is dependent on a microservice architecture with containers managed through Azure Kubernetes Services. You should review the automation of enforcement and consistency with specific Kubernetes policy and predefined initiative using the Azure Policy service.

As you have learned in this chapter, the use of Kubernetes to manage the container deployments allows the Azure Security architect to support the decoupling of policy decisions from the DevOps teams and directly support the business. This support for Kubernetes through Azure Policy service today is accomplished with an Open Policy Agent (OPA) using the extension of a community controller webhook called Gatekeeper.

The Azure Policy service is supported using the current Azure support model, and any of the community extensions are part of the service. The use of Azure policy with Kubernetes clusters includes

- Azure Kubernetes Service

- Azure Arc enabled Kubernetes

- AKS Engine

Note   The example enables support for policy while the community add-on Gatekeeper is in preview. You should still use the Kubernetes policy in Azure and look for updates at `https://github.com/open-policy-agent/gatekeeper`.

ENABLE AZURE POLICY FOR KUBERNETES

The Azure Policy use for Kubernetes clusters requires the service features to be enabled.

1. Open the Azure portal and search for subscription; select the subscription. Select the Resource providers menu on the left-hand side; filter the providers by typing Kubernetes.

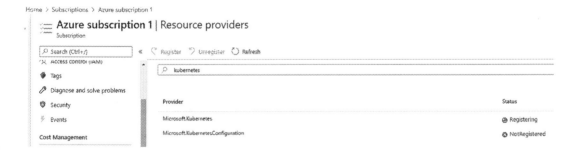

2. Select one at a time, Microsoft.Kubernetes, then select the Register action, wait a few moments, and select Refresh to validate registration completed. Select the Microsoft.KubernetesConfiguration, then select the Register action.

3. Once both providers have registered, search for policy. Select the Policy home page and then select Join Preview (note this policy provider may no longer be in preview).

4. Select the Subscription to include and click the Opt-in button.

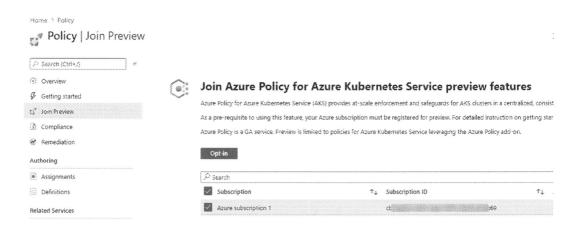

5. The add-on feature is registering; this may take several moments.

6. Remove the add-on option; this will disable the button on the AKS cluster under the Policies page.

Note   AKS clusters must be version 1.4 or higher before the policy scripts validate the AKS cluster.

---

7. From the Azure portal search option, search for Kubernetes services. Select your AKS cluster, select Policies on the left menu, and click the Enable add-on button.

8. Install the Azure Policy add-on for the AKS Engine. Download and install the Azure CLI tool version 2.0.62 or later (follow this URL: `https://docs.microsoft.com/en-us/cli/azure/install-azure-cli`).

9. On the Azure CLI tool, log in to your Azure subscription; type: az login. After you have logged in, from the same Azure CLI window, type: az provider register --namespace 'Microsoft.PolicyInsights'.

10. Create a role assignment for the cluster service principal. From the Azure CLI window, type: az role assignment create --assignee <cluster service principal app ID> --scope "/subscriptions/<subscriptionId>/resourceGroups/<aks engine cluster resource group>" --role "Policy Insights Data Writer (Preview)" Replace with your Azure subscription ID.

If the Enable add-on button is grayed out, the subscription has not yet been added to the preview.

Once the exercise is completed, you have enabled the `Microsoft.ContainerService` and the `Microsoft.PolicyInsights` resource providers. You also installed the Policy add-on for the AKS Engine. You can now deploy the policy definitions; refer to Figure 6-12 for the examples available.

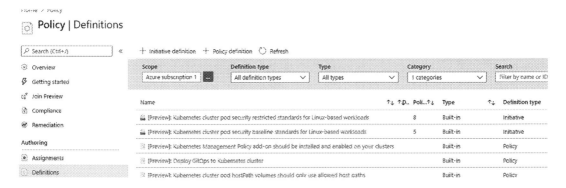

Figure 6-12. *Azure policy view of Kubernetes definitions and policies*

You should take the next few moments to review the individual initiatives that are predefined and policies to gain some detailed security policy view. As an example, scroll to the policy with the title "Kubernetes clusters should not allow container privilege escalation." Open the policy and scroll to the constraintTemplate section, as shown in Figure 6-13.

```
"constraintTemplate": "https://raw.githubusercontent.com/Azure/azure-policy/master/built-in-references/Kubernetes/container-no-privilege-es
```

Figure 6-13. *JSON code in the policy, to review the Gatekeeper add-on code*

These webhooks included in the policy cannot work because you enabled the needed resources in the exercise:

```
apiVersion: templates.gatekeeper.sh/v1beta1
kind: ConstraintTemplate
metadata:
  name: k8sazurecontainernoprivilegeescalation
spec:
  crd:
    spec:
      names:
        kind: K8sAzureContainerNoPrivilegeEscalation
  targets:
    - target: admission.k8s.gatekeeper.sh
      rego: |
        package k8sazurecontainernoprivilegeescalation

        violation[{"msg": msg, "details": {}}] {
            c := input_containers[_]
            input_allow_privilege_escalation(c)
            msg := sprintf("Privilege escalation container is not
            allowed: %v", [c.name])
        }

        input_allow_privilege_escalation(c) {
            not has_field(c, "securityContext")
        }
        input_allow_privilege_escalation(c) {
            not c.securityContext.allowPrivilegeEscalation == false
        }
        input_containers[c] {
            c := input.review.object.spec.containers[_]
        }
        input_containers[c] {
            c := input.review.object.spec.initContainers[_]
        }
```

```
# has_field returns whether an object has a field
has_field(object, field) = true {
    object[field]
}
```

This is just one example of the security features for Kubernetes that is provided when using Azure policy for Kubernetes.

Summary

In this chapter, you began learning about the microservice architecture and the impact of the shift from traditional monolithic application services. Before diving into Azure services, you learned about the intertwined dependencies of containers, Docker, and Kubernetes.

You walked through an example to build a Kubernetes cluster and deploy nodes and the management plane. You then learned that security features are integrated through Azure Security Center and Azure Sentinel. You are also aware of the future integration for Kubernetes clusters using Azure Policy to add additional governance to all Azure Kubernetes Service deployments.

CHAPTER 7

Security Governance Operations

Azure cloud governance is a process that includes business leadership and Azure Automation with technical configuration. The executive leaders of your company should be the key stakeholders for the policies needed in the Azure tenant and subscriptions. The Azure security operations team should be responsible for presenting the governance challenges and methods to audit or adhere to governance policies. As a best practice, you should schedule quarterly meetings with the internal leadership team and present the Azure governance challenges with a proposed remediation using Azure policy and other technical automations. Business leaders decide and own the policies deployed in Azure, so the IT and cloud operations teams are not deploying policies on their own. The business owns the policies deployed; the cloud operations teams ensure they are deployed and provide the security posture results from the built-in auditing.

In this chapter, you learn about

- Azure governance

- Management group architecture

- Azure policies

- Compliance reporting

- Azure Blueprints

- Role-Based Access Control

- Azure Cost Management

- Data governance

© Marshall Copeland and Matthew Jacobs 2021
M. Copeland and M. Jacobs, *Cyber Security on Azure*, https://doi.org/10.1007/978-1-4842-6531-4_7

A policy is a fundamental service to implement business governance in Microsoft Azure. Configuration and application are needed to correctly understand the difference between the built-in policy and custom policy.

As you continue through this chapter, the architecture of governance unfolds and supports the Azure security framework with additional layers of security in Azure as they work together. Governance is supported through top-level management groups and policy enforcement through assignments. The ability to create your own Blueprints including both policy and ARM templates is a way to enforce security and remain flexible for DevOps requests.

Azure Governance Architecture

You need to understand the change that Azure cloud provides and adopting the cloud policy framework using automation technologies is fundamental. The security team is leading the agility practices to embrace the agile development techniques for Infrastructure as Code using security best practices to secure the users, data, applications, and other business assets. The benefits of good governance deployment can have a positive reinforcement in the deployment of corporate needed checks and balances and business policies and provide insight into the enforcement.

Microsoft Azure provides many cloud-native automation tools for the deployment of any customized or predefined policies that support the governance needs of the business. The cloud operations and cloud security teams can support the business executive requirement decisions to efficiently deploy and report on needed policies. This is done at cloud scale to support the governance architecture; refer to Figure 7-1 to gain a visualization of how the governance services and support relate to the Azure resources.

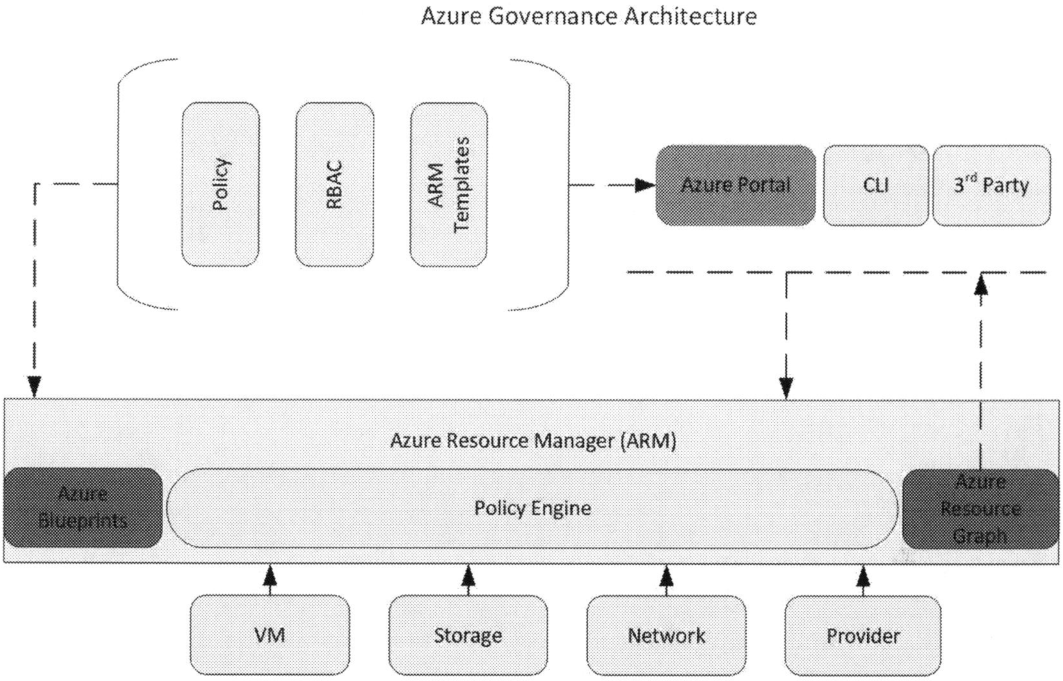

Azure Governance Architecture

Figure 7-1. *Azure governance architecture*

The best practices can be enabled and allow reporting of compliance and the overall cost of cloud resources. The governance can be applied efficiently based on the needed governance services. The cost of creating, updating, and deploying Azure governance is an employee resource price because there is no licensing fee associated with Azure governance with policy deployment.

Note   Microsoft updates the Cybersecurity Reference Architecture regulary, and the poster can be found at `https://gallery.technet.microsoft.com/ Cybersecurity-Reference-883fb54c`.

Microsoft has provided you an updated Cloud Adoption Framework to use and rely on for not only designing and deploying resources, but it includes governance guidance to support your cloud journey. The tools and guidance found in Azure cloud adoption tools and templates are a great guidance to create an Azure Center of Excellence architecture team.

Note   The Cloud Adoption Framework includes many tools that help with planning, governance, and managing Azure resources. It can be found at `https://docs.`
`microsoft.com/en-us/azure/cloud-adoption-framework/reference/`
`tools-templates`.

Management Groups

The Management Groups support security as your company continues to expand the Azure cloud tenant footprint with additional subscriptions. Also, as companies undergo mergers and acquisitions, the individual subscriptions need to be migrated from one Azure tenant to another and have the management group governance applied. Governance can be applied at the management group level as shown in Figure 7-2.

Azure Management Group

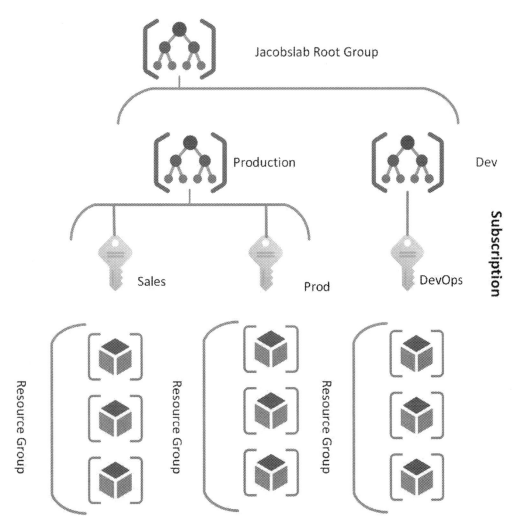

Figure 7-2. *Azure Management Group used for governance above the subscription level*

The first management group created in the Azure tenant is labeled the Tenant Root Group. The use of management groups helps to manage bot access, policy, and governance applied to each subscription. Additional management groups created after the first are labeled child management groups.

CREATE AN AZURE MANAGEMENT GROUP

The management group provides an additional governance control at a higher level than the individual Azure subscription level.

1. Open the Azure portal and search for management group. Select the option to start using management groups.

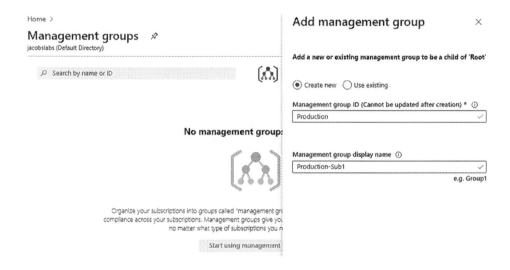

2. Enter the management group ID; it becomes a unique identifier inside your Azure tenant (note this cannot be edited later). Enter the management group name that will be displayed.

3. Click SAVE in the lower-left side of the Add management group screen. (Note, in a new subscription, this takes less than 60 seconds, more in highly leveraged subscriptions.)

4. The new management group is presented in the management group pane.

Tenant Root Group

🔍 Search by name or ID			

Using management groups helps you manage access. policy, and compliance by grouping multiple subscriptions together. Learn more.

Tenant Root Group (details)

Name	ID	Type	My Role	
Production-Sub1	Production	Management Group	Owner	⌄
Azure subscription 1	cb54a82d-65d0-46e0-b9f6-00042c650b69	Subscription	Owner	⌄

You can use the management group you created to follow the exercise to create a custom blueprint.

After creating your first Azure Management Group, you have the option to create a "child" management group, as referenced in Figure 7-3. A child management group supports the need to apply business governance across all resources, while business-specific governance may apply different controls across different subscriptions like production, test-dev, and sales resources.

Add management group   ✕

Add a new or existing management group to be a child of 'Production-Sub1'

⦿ Create new   ◯ Use existing

Management group ID (Cannot be updated after creation) * ⓘ

Management group display name ⓘ

e.g. Group1

Figure 7-3. *Child management group screen view*

The best practice is to keep the groups in a flat hierarchy, so their resources are not forced to focus on nested management groups. You need to be aware of some of the service limitations of Azure Management Groups. When using one management group per subscription, some additional design considerations include

- Only one root management group per directory.

- Each management group can have only one parent.

- Each management group can have many children (less is better).

- Management group tree cannot exceed six levels.

Azure Policy

You can automate the access control with enforcement with Azure policy and custom policy assignment. You can use Azure Policy for enforcing constraints but also supporting the use of standard practices like naming conventions and Azure tagging. A policy is applied when creating or updating resources. A policy can deny support of the governance controls.

Compliance reports are used to identify resources that are out of compliance and in some instances provide remediation methods. This is because policy definitions support parameters. Policies are created by the individual definitions and then assigned to Azure resources, and then the compliance reports are populated based on the results. Learning Azure policies is much like learning cyber security; they both have terminology you must learn, which is summarized in Table 7-1.

Table 7-1. *Azure Policy definitions and maximum count*

Terminology	Description	Maximum Count
Policy	Enforcement or auditing of business rules and standards	512 nested rules
Initiative	Grouping of more than one policy supporting multiple individual policy applications	1000 policies 100 parameters
Scope	Assignment of initiative or policy, management group, subscription, or resource group	500 definitions 200 initiatives
Assignment	Targeting an initiative or policy based on the scope	2500 tenant definitions
Exclusion	Deny assignment of the policy, at a scope level	400
Location	Store the policy definition	NA

Policies are not applied when resources move to objects between subscriptions or tenants. If you are moving a resource, then create another policy in the new subscription to support the overall compliance. A best practice is to review the noncompliance reports if resources are moved and no longer have the original policy assignment.

Businesses should consider using policy deployment to enforce unanticipated financial costs each month with example restrictions on research projects using Azure resources like

- Naming standards
- Azure tag requirements
- Storage tiers
- VM images
- VM disk size
- Resource types
- Instance size
- Geographical deployment

Azure Policy is a governance, which in turn is a security control, for all users that is applied to the Azure resource and not the individual user. Microsoft Azure provides policy deployment through the Azure Policy page and Azure Security Center. Azure policy definitions are defined using JSON as shown in Listing 7-1.

Listing 7-1. JSON code of policy definitions used to enforce monitoring of a VM

```
{
    "properties": {
        "displayName": "Enable Azure Monitor for VMs",
        "policyType": "BuiltIn",
        "description": "Enable Azure Monitor for the virtual machines (VMs)
        in the specified scope (management group, subscription or resource
        group). Takes Log Analytics workspace as parameter.",
        "metadata": {
            "version": "2.0.0",
            "category": "Monitoring"
        },
```

Azure Policy is implemented using definition parameters, the policy rules that are assigned and the scope to deploy. A policy is deployed using an assignment. However, the Azure Policy can be enforced or only used for reporting on compliance if the policy was enforced. A policy can be assigned but not enforced and remove any disruption if the policy is configured to "enforced" later.

Note   Presenting the compliance report to executive leadership gains support for policy adoption if the policy report was assigned but not enforced.

You should review the **Policy Definitions** from the menu to identify any built-in policies you may want to assign but not enforce. Please refer to Figure 7-4 to gain insight on Azure Policy that is a default out-of-the-box policies and review the drop-down to filter on monitoring policies. You can review the policies for your business by going to the Azure portal, selecting the Policy page, and then selecting definitions from the left menu.

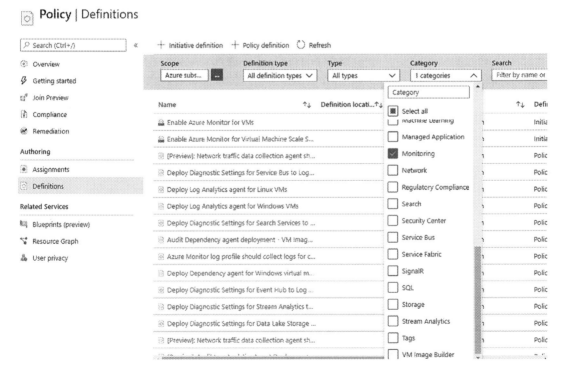

Figure 7-4. *Azure policy definitions view of built-in monitoring policies*

Once you identify the policy or create a custom policy based on the definitions, you can return to the Azure policy page as shown in Figure 7-5. From the Policy page, the default view is the overall compliance with menus to assign policies from in a single pane. This view is used for validating compliance, in this example for monitoring enabled. The policy assignment might be used to enforce business requirements to enable metrics and logs for Azure Monitor and Azure Sentinel.

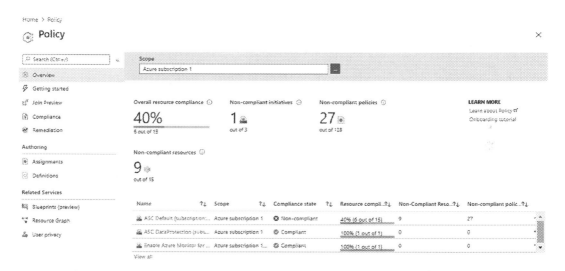

Figure 7-5. *Azure Policy page view providing a compliance report*

You may see in the Policy Definitions view the Azure Security Center rules, as shown in Figure 7-6. Security Center allows the security team to focus on security requirements based on the sensitivity of the data for each Azure subscription or resource. The policies deployed through the Security Center console could help to limit the scope of data using Role-Based Access Control (RBAC). You may choose an RBAC setting that allows enabling the security policy compliance to only the Azure security operations team (which you define) and their manager. You should plan the use of Azure RBAC to enforce least privileges inside the company as well as to partners outside the company.

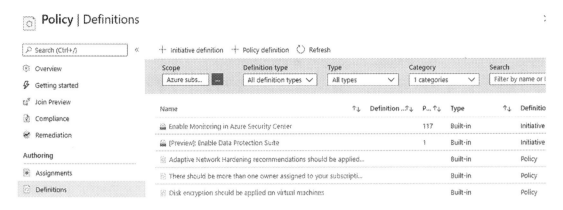

Figure 7-6. *Policy view for security policies used with Azure Security Center*

The policies that are deployed from Azure policy or from Azure Security Center use the definitions in the policy to prevent actions. Azure Active Directory is used to prevent unauthorized access to resources and data. You need to prioritize the processes to enable **Active Rules** in Azure Sentinel **Rule Templates** to identify Incidents of Compromise (IOC). The machine learning and artificial intelligence in the analysis of Sentinel ingested data can identify anomalies of data access and data copies that are excessive compared to normal baseline activities. These detected activities could be related to compromised user credentials or from authorized user credentials, Authentication and Key Agreement (AKA) (this is also known as an insider threat).

INSIDER THREAT

Cloud security takes on additional challenges from on-premises security including identifying outside and inside security threats. Traditional on-premises security used the edge firewall as an identification; threats inside are anyone, contractors, maintenance, custodians, and employees. Insider threats could compromise business integrity and even cause irreparable harm in Azure, so the use of public cloud requires new security controls and detection. Policy violations can be the result of carelessness or accident, so automation using Infrastructure as Code (IaC) is not only efficient but another security control.

Insider threat motivations range from disgruntled employees to financial gain, but the challenge is how to identify the cloud insider threat. The Department of Homeland Security recommends "novel methods to detect insider threats through disk-level storage behavior and how an individual's behavior diverges from prior behavior and/or that of their organizational peers."

Azure Sentinel has many template rules you can enable to be alerted on and to create an automated and appropriate defensive security response. The template examples, based on the data connectors, may include

- Time series anomaly for data size transferred to the public Internet

- Unusual data access attempts and custom alerts based on data

- Mass secret retrieval

Azure Sentinel data connectors support ingesting data from other Microsoft products like System Center Operations Manager and System Center Configuration Manager in addition to third-party solutions like Cisco, Palo Alto, Barracuda, Fortinet, and more. Additional data connectors supporting Azure Sentinel information provide the ability to remove false positive alerts.

Compliance Reporting

The Azure Security Center **regulatory compliance** dashboard provides the status of any compliance controls that are assigned to Azure resources for any security policies needed by the business. If you review the information in Figure 7-7, you can receive up-to-date compliance to policies like

- Azure CIS

- PCI DSS

- ISO 27001

- SOC TSP

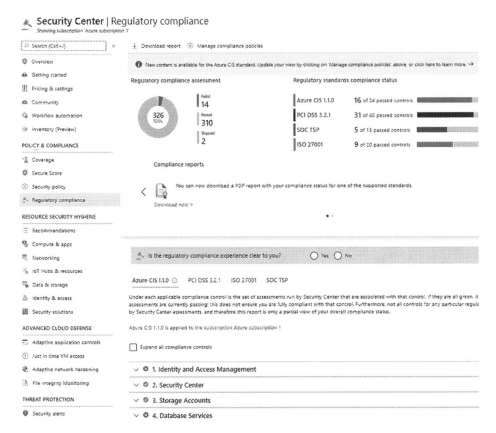

Figure 7-7. *Security Center Regulatory compliance dashboard for reporting*

Note   Use custom policy definitions to create your company defaults on GitHub:
`https://github.com/azure/azure-policy`.

Assignments

All policies, custom or default, must be assigned and can take up to 30 minutes to take
effect, unlike RBAC which is updated almost instantly. Creating the assignment supports
many flexible options based on the use case.

You begin the wizard by choosing a policy definition file from one of the templates
and provide a name and a description. You should create a written guidance that
supports a detailed description, and it should include a version number, creation date,

and creator of the policy. Options include enforcement and assigning the scope of the policy to the entire subscription or just to a resource group level. If this policy is assigned to a resource group level, you have the flexibility to exclude a resource group.

AZURE POLICY ASSIGNMENT

Assignment supports the policy to support the necessary governance to maintain compliance to business requirements.

1. Open the Azure portal and search for policy. Click the policy icon and go to the Policy page.

2. On the left-hand side of the menu, select the Getting started menu item.

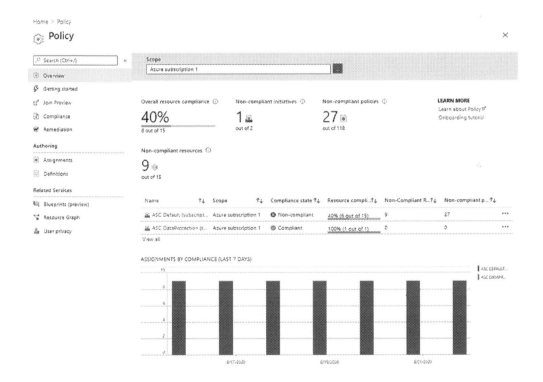

3. From the Getting started page, notice you can assign policies, assess compliance, or author definitions to create custom policies. Select the recommended policy, Enable Azure Monitor for VMs.

4. Select the ellipsis (…) options of the scope to select the Azure subscription and resource group to apply this policy. In our example, we want all systems in the security VM resource group to be included.

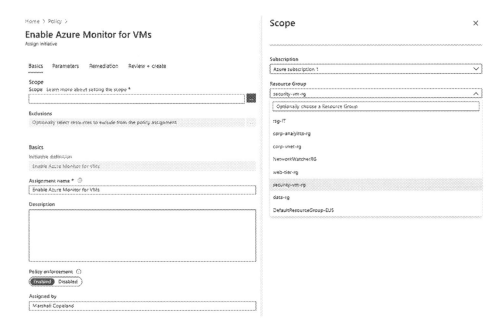

5. Click the Select button on the bottom left and enter the description and notice it identified the user that is assigning the policy. Click NEXT to go to the Parameters page.

6. Select the Log Analytics workspace (created in Chapter 4); for this example, we show the CorpAnalyticsWorkspace1. For this example, there are no optional VM images to add to the scope. Click NEXT to go to the Remediation page.

7. Select the check box to create a remediation task, and the policy to remediate option selected is to Deploy Log Analytics agent for Windows VMs. (If the VMs do not have the agent installed, complete that task.) Click Review and create.

8. Click Create and review the policy in the Assignments view of the Azure Policy page.

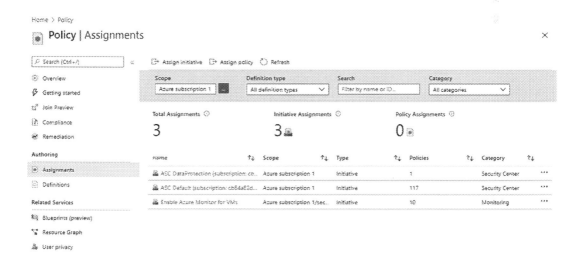

The new policy is displayed, and notice it is a Monitoring category and not a Security Center Policy.

Blueprints

Deploy and maintain the cloud efficiently with the support needed for the many business projects using Azure Blueprints. Azure Blueprints are different from Azure Resource Manager (ARM) templates and Azure policies. Infrastructure as Code (IaC) can be built using ARM templates and Terraform providers; these are two tools used in infrastructure deployment for building, changing, and managing infrastructure in a secure process. While ARM is designed to deploy resources to Microsoft Azure, the Terraform tools are platform agnostic; they can be used to deploy to Azure, AWS, GCP, Alibaba Cloud, and other private clouds like VMware. The deployment tools support an idempotent cloud infrastructure using a declarative model for known configuration.

Deployment of infrastructure using ARM or Terraform resources is to deploy a "day 1" model of the resource (i.e., VM) so it is idempotent, and change that happens after the initial deployment is referred to as "day 2." The term day 2 is referring to the change of a known deployment as it drifts out of compliancy. Azure Blueprints support the compliance needs of the governance model higher than the individual Azure resource.

Azure Blueprints are also declarative for a day 1 deployment; however, the blueprint goal is to deploy the entire resource environment at the Azure subscription level. Azure Blueprints are supported by the individual artifact types used in the creation of a blueprint model. It is these artifacts that include an ARM template that includes a resource group, VNet, NSG, and virtual machines. In addition, they include role assignment, Azure policy, ARM template, and the ability to "lock" the blueprint at the subscription level, preventing change.

Azure Artifacts are the definitions that create the resources for the Azure Blueprints. There are some Azure resources that are allowed to be used as a Blueprint artifact. They include

- Policy assignment

- Role assignment

- Azure resource group

- ARM template

You should be very aware that Blueprint locks are not the same as Resource Manager locks (Microsoft.Authorization/locks). The enforcement of locks is assigned with RBAC control during the creation of the Blueprint. Lock assignment can have three modes:

- Don't lock

- Do Not Delete

- Read only

The default setting is "don't lock" and allows the individual artifacts in the deployment of Blueprint to be edited unrestricted. Do Not Delete the projects can modify the artifacts but cannot delete them. The read-only mode allows the environment to be deployed, but it cannot be modified or deleted. You can and should plan to deploy additional resources into the resource groups that have a read-only assignment. The governance framework is to allow new resources to have the same policies assigned to other resources in the same blueprint assignment. The only way to change a blueprint is to have the assigned owner update the blueprint with a version control change.

Blueprints support version control, like ARM templates; however, the deployment of a blueprint is tracked and reported. This allows the cloud operations team to quickly understand what version of a blueprint was deployed and where in the Azure tenant was it deployed. This tracking of version-controlled deployment supports the life cycle management of the solution in support of the business governance.

Custom Azure Blueprints you create should focus on supporting a necessary business governance goal. First, create a draft and then create new versions of the blueprints and deploy into a subscription. Azure allows only one draft of each blueprint, so the only way to add another blueprint with different artifacts is to edit the draft and update the version as part of the definition.

The governance goal for the custom blueprint exercise is to limit the deployment of a network blueprint by only users that are assigned the network contributor role.

Note   The only prerequisite is to have at least one management group deployed. You can follow the exercise in this chapter and then return.

CREATE A CUSTOM AZURE BLUEPRINT

Create a custom Azure Blueprint using a sample and modify to support the governance scope.

1. Open the Azure portal; from the search bar, type blueprint. Click the Create button to start the journey to create.

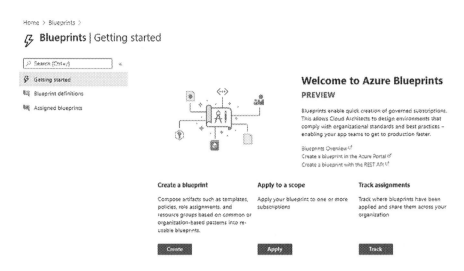

2. You should scroll through the blueprints to gain an insight of the number of samples available. In this exercise, you start from a blank blueprint.

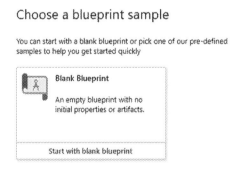

3. Provide a name for the blueprint, description, and the management group to determine the scope of the blueprint.

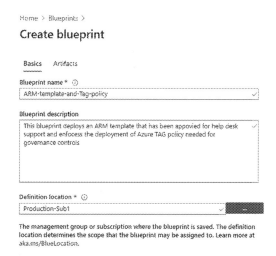

4. Select Next: Artifacts to add the resource group and tag based on the governance policy as part of the blueprint. It is optional to add a resource group tag (i.e., the life cycle of the RG is 365 days). Click Save.

5. Select the + Add artifact and select the ARM template; in this example, a resource group is selected. Click Add artifact.

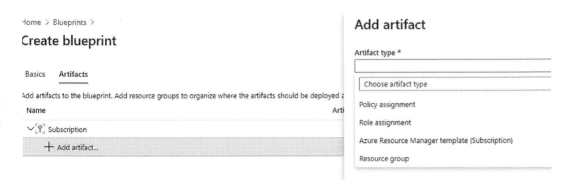

6.   Select the Resource Group artifact.

7.   Select the Save Draft option at the bottom left of the screen.

8.   You can now publish the Blueprint.

ARM-template-and-TAG-policy
Blueprints

⬆ Publish blueprint   ✎ Edit blueprint   🗑 Delete blueprint

⌃ Essentials

Name   : ARM-template-and-TAG-policy
Definition location   : Production-Sub1
Definition location ID   : Production
Version   : Draft

Latest artifacts

Artifact name

∨ 🔑 Assigned subscription

      ▨ Lifecycle-RG-365

This exercise demonstrates the Azure solution to combine a governance policy with an ARM template that enforces a corporate Azure tag requirement.

Role-Based Access Control

Role-Based Access Control (RBAC) supports very fine-grained control to resources in your Azure subscriptions. Azure Active Directory (AAD) provides the foundation for identity access management to support the enforcement of least-privileged access and remediation for companies that require security compliance.

Role assignment has three related components:

- Security principle

- Role definition

- Scope

With Role-Based Access Control enabled, it would allow or deny authorization to perform work the security principle is attempting to complete. The use of Azure RBAC is an effective security control. You can use Azure events and alerting for monitoring with Azure Sentinel. But the Role-Based Access as a control only applies to the user action; it attempts to perform on specific Azure resources or changes. It applies to actions such as

- Delete

- Read

- Update

- Start/stop VM

You need to realize that the title security principle includes users, groups, service principals, and managed identities. The user has an Azure Active Directory (AAD) profile. Roles are assigned to users or to the group that many users are a member of. A service principal is a security identity (like a user) that is assigned to applications or services in Azure. A managed identity is exactly that, an identity that is managed automatically by AAD. The credentials of a managed identity are used when developing Azure resource applications. A system can assign the managed identity, or the user can assign a managed identity as a stand-alone resource. The Managed Identity Resource Provider (MSRP) issues a certificate that is associated with that specific identity. Managed identities are locked and only used with Azure resources. When managed identities are deleted, the service principal is deleted also.

The Azure role is often more than one "authorization" on a single Azure resource. Operations like write, read, and delete can be included in a role definition. The definition starts with Actions allowed and explicitly denied with Not Actions for specific read, write, and delete authorizations. There are many built-in roles that you do not have to modify; just start assigning roles to specific users. And the best practice is to create an AAD group, add users to the group, and assign roles to the group.

When roles are assigned, they can be assigned for a specific Azure scope like the entire Azure subscription, resource group, or individual Azure resource. Granting access at the parent resource like the subscription allows any child resource to inherit the privileges from the parent object. Security teams should be aware that multiple role assignment does not result in least privilege, as in Windows network or NTFS permissions. As an example, if a user is assigned contributor role at the Azure subscription level, and a different role like Reader at the resource group level, then the user's effective permissions is the contributor role. The only way to prevent inherited permissions from a parent scope is to use a deny assignment.

Note   Deny assignments block actions to users, groups, service principal, and managed identities at the scope level.

Azure Cost Management

Azure services have a cost, and an inclusive cost is the virtual core (vCore) or virtual CPU. PaaS services run on multiple cores; they scale up and down and are based on a pricing tier. Azure serverless functions run on a shared VM in Azure data centers, as do Azure Sentinel and Security Center run on cores behind the portal view. Creating business IaaS and PaaS services is more easily calculated, but you need to stay on budget.

You can set budget alerts and optimize cost management with many of the costing automation in place to maintain project resource solutions. Tracking cloud spending and usage costs across Azure subscriptions becomes easier once you realize the information is available. Before you start setting alerts for budgeted projects, there are a few services to become familiar with:

- Azure pricing calculator

- Azure Advisor

- Cost budgets

Using the Azure pricing calculator is the first step to understand the cost of creating Azure infrastructures, both IaaS and PaaS services. The pricing calculator can be found at https://azure.microsoft.com/en-us/pricing/calculator/, and if you review Figure 7-8, you see all the main headings for over 200 Azure services.

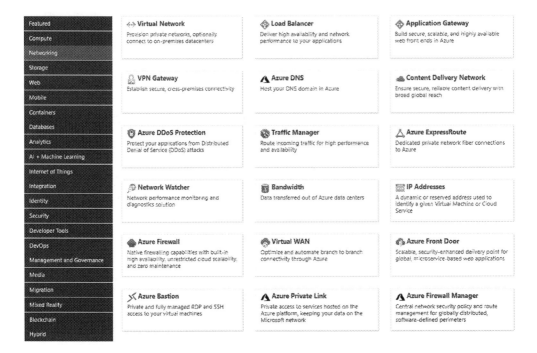

Figure 7-8. *Azure product estimation calculator, networking view*

The use of the calculator is intuitive, simply selecting the services that are needed for a business deployment, like virtual machines, virtual networks, VPN Gateway, load balancers, Azure Firewalls, and Azure Active Directory. As the services are grouped on the left-hand side, selecting individual items keeps a running total. Select the option to view the different pricing with a total and individual item. In some larger price point items, like the SQL Server example chosen (refer to Figure 7-9), cost savings options are presented using reserve pricing.

Azure SQL Database

REGION:
East US

TYPE:
Single Database

SERVICE TIER:
General Purpose

COMPUTE TIER:
Provisioned

Savings Options

Save up to 73% on pay as you go prices with 1 year or 3 year reserved options.

Compute

● Pay as you go
○ 1 year reserved
○ 3 year reserved

$888.95
Average per month
($0.00 charged upfront)

SQL License

● Pay as you go
○ Azure Hybrid Benefit

$583.80
Average per month
($0.00 charged upfront)

1   ×   730   Hours ⌄ ⊙
Instances

Figure 7-9. *Azure calculator with savings options for services, SQL example*

Once you have created infrastructure services in Azure, you can identify cost savings with Advisor and Budget alerts. Advisor reviews the current deployment and provides recommendations to reduce cost. The recommendations include more than cost savings (refer to Figure 7-10) like security, but look at the cost savings view.

Figure 7-10. *Advisor view to reduce cost impact recommendation*

Note   There is a second Azure calculator for Total Cost of Ownership (TCO) at
`https://azure.microsoft.com/en-us/pricing/tco/calculator/`.

The Azure portal includes the Cost analysis view. for critical components starting from the subscription all the way down to the individual resource group. As an example, in Figure 7-11, the cost of a small project is provided with a breakdown. The cost of an Azure bastion host is provided in the view and should help you realize that the VM the host runs is not under your control to reduce cost. You cannot turn the VM off; the cost savings options are limited, and to reduce the cost, you would delete the bastion host.

Figure 7-11. *Cost management view of the analysis of a bastion host*

You should take the time to set budgeting alerts for projects and services running in the Azure subscription. This enables you to be alerted at different spending price points, so the cost of the project is not a surprise at the end of each month.

CREATE A BUDGET ALERT

1. Open the Azure portal, search for subscriptions, select the subscription, and from the left-hand menu, select budget.

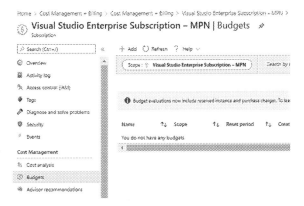

2. Select the + Add option at the top menu above the scope. This selection lets you create a budget.

3. Leave the scope at subscription. Enter the name of the budget, use the default reset period to monthly (notice quarterly and yearly options), and enter the suggested budget forecast. (This example is $275.00.)

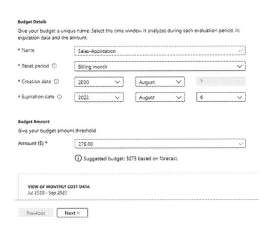

4. Click the Next button. Set the alert condition to 50% and enter the email address of the Azure budget owners for notification. (You could add a second alert at 75% also before creating the alert.) Click the Create button to complete the alert creation.

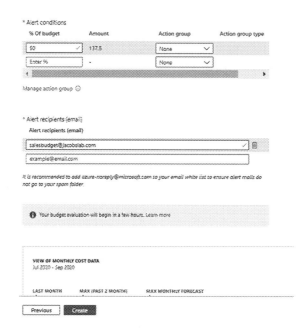

Once the budget is validated, the budget appears in the pane, and you have the option to add additional budgets for projects simply by changing the scope.

Azure has introduced a cost management feature usage integration to monitor cost controls in Amazon Web Services (AWS). You can set up a data connector, much like you did with Azure Sentinel, and the usage reports are stored in an S3 bucket in AWS. You can then create a cost usage report and enable the download of a CSV file.

Note   Cost management for Azure is available at no additional cost. Azure Cost Management for AWS is charged at 1% of the total AWS managed spend at general availability. Find out more at `https://azure.microsoft.com/en-us/pricing/details/cost-management/`.

Data Governance

You started this chapter with an introduction to the Cloud Adoption Framework, and some of the topics are included when considering data management in Microsoft Azure. The framework includes a combination of cloud tools and innovation within Azure titled the "Alignment to the methodology." You can review some of the articles that demonstrate the many different tools in the toolset to help with the methodology best practices at `https://docs.microsoft.com/en-us/azure/cloud-adoption-framework/innovate/best-practices/`.

You are responsible for classifying Azure data and maintain the privacy of the data stored in your Azure subscription. Microsoft creates a secure cloud infrastructure with many security features that you enable to support the level of security required for each of the business data classifications. Classification follows the cyber security framework requirements for supporting any compliance requirements.

Classification

The need for a classification of data you store in Microsoft Azure is implemented using a traditional Deming cycle or Deming model; refer to Figure 7-12. You can adopt this process as you organize what data is stored in Azure and what security controls needed to be implemented. Governance for your data, classified as secret or public, becomes the principles (written policies for people) and technical practices (Azure policy + RBAC + ARM) that ensure integrity through the complete life cycle of business data, in Azure or on-premises.

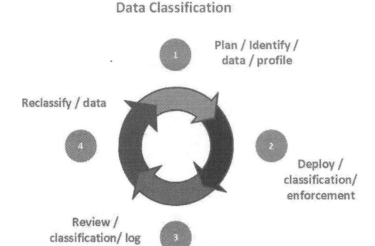

Figure 7-12. *Azure Deming model for data classification*

You begin with a plan to identify the data assets that are expected to be migrated to your Azure tenant. Once the classification is started and policies are written, you may want to review creating a custom Azure policy that helps support the confidential data. The checks include the validation for reporting from policies, Azure log audits, and access to data. Finally, you modify data classification or move data that should be reclassified based on the cyber security risks.

You may be asking how to classify data, and a simple example can be reviewed in Table 7-2.

Table 7-2. *Data sensitivity with two different classification labeling*

Sensitive Level	Classification Example 1	Classification Example 2
High	Confidential	Restricted
Medium	Internal use (not for public use)	Sensitive
Low	Public use approved	Unrestricted

One area that is sometimes overlooked is the ownership roles of the data and of the custodians. Data on-premises and data that is migrated to the cloud should have clearly identified owners. In addition, there you should have custodians identified in both roles and groups because the custodians are often in charge of data edits or relocation. As an Azure administrator, you do not fall into either the owner or custodian automatically; the separation of services applies to everyone when it comes to data. If an Azure user is an administrator and a custodian, they should be required to use a separate account to complete custodial work for auditing purposes. Your governance framework must support data in Azure and require separation of duties and clear processes and procedures to support through the entire life cycle of the data.

Refer to Table 7-3 for roles and rights to data.

Table 7-3. *Sample representation of data users' roles*

Role	Create	Edit/Modify	Delegate	Read	Backup/Restore
Owner	X	X	X	X	X
Custodian			X		
Administrator					X
User		X		X	

Users are often allowed to input data, edit data, and update data based on their work for the business. However, the information they can see may be restricted based on classifications of the data, users, or both. Questions that need to be answered about the type of data you are saving include

- Intellectual Property (IP)

- Personally Identifiable Information (PII)

- Financial data

- Government regulatory compliance

Data classification is your responsibility. However, Microsoft provides some help with identifying data classification using the Azure portal or automatically with Azure Policy. Additionally, Azure SQL Databases support data classification automatically. You should be aware of each of these solutions.

Azure Resource Manager (ARM) tags should be used to provide metadata information about the storage. The tags are a name-value pair that can be appended to the data. Classification tags would be used to apply based on how you classify data in Azure and allow the management of resources through Azure Policy. You should consider logically organizing the tags in business categories based on the department and data value to identify ownership for billing in reports.

Azure supports the use of policy to automatically apply when the resources or data are deployed. You can test the policy in an Azure development subscription and then include the data classification policy in a Blueprint version. There are characteristics of Azure tags to be aware of:

- 50 tags to resources (i.e., resource group).

- 512 characters for names.

- 256 characters for value.

- Names cannot contain special characters (<>/\&!).

Note   Azure Active Directory P1 includes Azure Information Protection which scans business documents based on defined criteria and in real time suggests a classification directly in email to applying labels confidential.

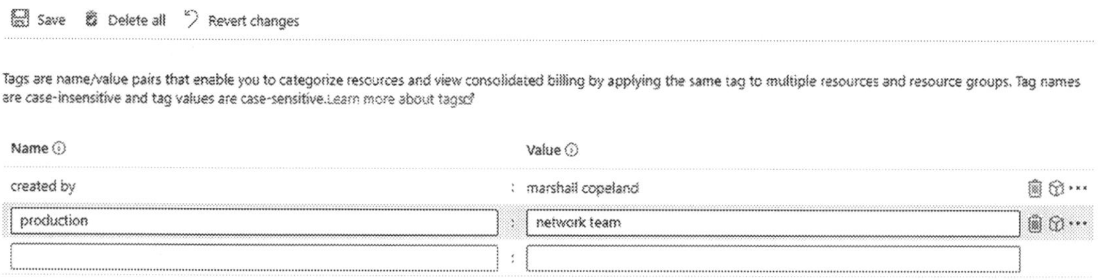

Figure 7-13. *Azure tag editing portal view*

You can use the portal to apply tags to resources as shown in Figure 7-13. Once the Azure resources have a tag applied, the searching and protection of data can be supported.

You can also use Azure Policy to enforce a tag when cloud administrators create the resources. The JSON language is created; default values should be used and additional restrictions mandated. The example code in Listing 7-2 shows the default value of customer data, owned by the sales team.

Listing 7-2. JSON tag value–name pair example for Azure policy templates

```
{
    "$schema": "https://schema.management.azure.com/schemas/2019-04-01/
deploymentTemplate.json#",
    "contentVersion": "1.0.0.0",
    "parameters": {
        "tagName": {
            "type": "string",
            "defaultValue": "CustomerData"
        },
        "tagValue": {
            "type": "string",
            "defaultValue": "SalesTeam"
        }
    },
    "variables": {},
    "resources": [
        {
            "type": "Microsoft.Resources/tags",
            "name": "default",
            "apiVersion": "2019-10-01",
            "dependsOn": [],
            "properties": {
                "tags": {
                    "[parameters('tagName')]": "[parameters('tagValue')]"
                }
            }
        }
    ]
}
```

Data discovery and classification are supportive of sensitive data. Azure SQL Databases support a method to discover, classify, label, and protect sensitive data inside the Azure SQL Database. As part of the Advanced Data Security offering, PII data like healthcare, financial, and business-related data can be discovered, labeled, and protected. You can use the Azure portal to apply the discovery and classification with a greater detail provided in the exercise.

ENABLE SQL ADVANCED DATA SECURITY

---

1.   From the Azure portal, connect to the SQLDB1 database created in exercises from Chapter 3. Select the database overview and then select the Advanced data security menu.

2. You can keep the default setting for the storage account to write the data for ADS. Enter a valid email address for reports and alerts. Select Save at the top menu.

3. Select the database, then select the db1 overview view, and scroll down the menu to review the Advanced data security discovery. Select the Data Discovery & Classification dashboard.

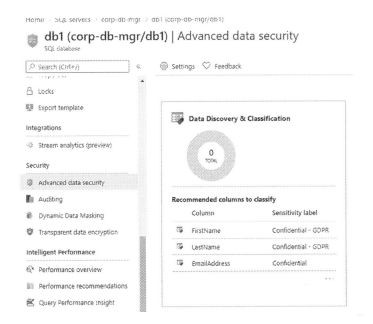

4. It is important to review the recommendations first, and then you can change sensitive labels. Select the (i) We have found 15 columns with classification recommendations ➤ to review the discovery items.

5. This sample database view provides the tables, columns, and sensitivity label applied during the discovery process. Take time to scroll through the results.

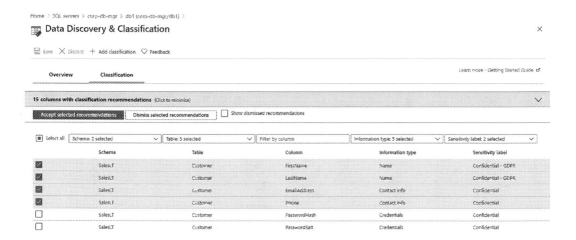

6. Select the first four recommendations to enable the option to save the labeling provided by the discovery process. Select the Accept selected recommendations, which are now highlighted.

7. The classification can be modified if your business has different PII data requirements. Use the drop-down arrows to change the information type or sensitivity label. Click Save in the top-left icon.

8. Return to the Database overview and select the Advanced data security menu to validate the four information types are displayed.

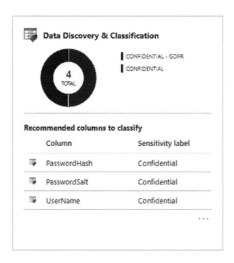

9. Advanced data security does provide a vulnerability assessment against the database. To enable, select the database, then select the db1 overview view, and scroll down the menu to review the Advanced data security discovery. Select the Vulnerability Assessment and click Scan at the top-left icon.

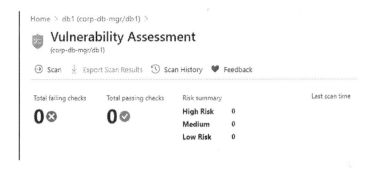

10. This sample database is small and only takes a few moments to scan with results provided. Return to the portal view for SQL servers, and select the server name and the db1 overview. Notice the Vulnerability Assessment ranking of high, medium, and low risks.

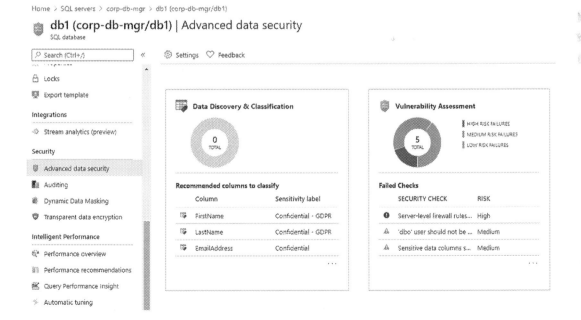

11. Select the Vulnerability Assessment dashboard to reveal the details of scanning.

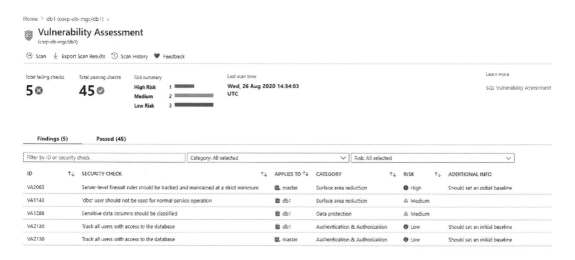

You are provided with priority details of the database with red as a high risk. If this were a production database, the security team can use this data to perform security remediation, working with the data owners and data custodians. You can export the scan results to be included in an executive report.

You can review the ADS vulnerability scans from inside the database server settings. You can choose to select all the Advanced Threat Protection types (refer to Figure 7-14) or options for SQL injection only.

Home > db1 (corp-db-mgr/db1) > Database settings > Server settings >

Advanced Threat Protection types

☑ All
☑ SQL injection ⓘ
☑ SQL injection vulnerability ⓘ
☑ Data exfiltration ⓘ
☑ Unsafe action ⓘ
☑ Brute Force ⓘ
☑ Anomalous client login ⓘ

Figure 7-14. *Cyber security threat protection types from ADS*

Azure Security Center, configured in Chapter 5, provides the overview of your tenant and subscription. From the Azure portal, search for Security Center and review the overview page as provided in Figure 7-15.

Figure 7-15. *Security Center's resource security hygiene recommendations*

From the Security Center overview, when you select the resource item it is displayed using a severity view priority. The same type of priority view is also automatic when viewing the data and storage resources; the information provides the needed guidance details to bring the security risk for the Azure object into compliance. This is another example of how Azure Security Center is providing integrated security to identify, alert, and recommend security remediation steps to improve the overall business security profile. Security provides prioritized guidance and remediation steps as shown in Figure 7-16.

Security Checks

Findings   Passed

Benchmarks: All

Search to filter items...

ID	Security Check	Category	Applies To	Benchmark	Severity
VA2065	Server-level firewall rules should be tracked and maintained at a strict minimum	Surface Area Reduction	1 of 1 databases		High
VA1143	'dbo' user should not be used for normal service operation	Surface Area Reduction	1 of 1 databases	FedRAMP	Medium
VA1288	Sensitive data columns should be classified	Data Protection	1 of 1 databases		Medium
VA2130	Track all users with access to the database	Authentication And Authorization	2 of 2 databases	SOX	Low

Figure 7-16. *Security Center remediation steps and severity view*

AZURE TENANT, SUBSCRIPTION, AND RESOURCE DATA

The first step is to create an Azure Tenant; then you can create the first Azure subscription. You then use the Azure subscription to start enabling resources for your business infrastructure, and data about how the solutions perform and other metadata is created.

The metadata generated by the Microsoft Azure Subscription and all the resources within, is used to provide a better cloud experience. There are types of data that you should be aware of as they are part of the data you own. Microsoft Azure creates data about your business using the Azure services, and Microsoft uses that data to improve Azure services. First is customer data; all data, including text, sound, video, and images, are customer data. Diagnostic data, discussed in Chapter 4, is collected or obtained from software locally installed in connection to the Azure Enterprise. Service-generated data is data derived from Azure online services, used by Microsoft as performance, security, and scaling Azure services.

Additionally, there is a professional services data, processed by Azure upon authorization and through professional services engagements.

Data Retention

You have started to move Azure policies in place, creating projects to support Azure Blueprints, and have helped data owners classify data. Now you need to reduce business risks by deleting old content to save cost in Azure and create a retention policy that supports your compliance needs. Data retention in Azure Sentinel's Log Analytics workspace is 2 years and 720 days in Microsoft Azure metrics.

Retention policies can be divided into four main areas for the Log Analytics workspace:

- SQL database (backups)

- Virtual machine (backups)

- Azure Monitor Logs/Metrics

- Azure Blob storage

Azure services are correlated in resource groups to help maintain the business life cycle of individual services that create an application of business applications. The same is true for data retention.

SQL database backups require an understanding of the settings for business to support the retention policy – backups using SQL Server technology, not a separate Azure service. A "typical" backup policy may look like this: full backup of the database every week, differential backups every 12 hours, and transaction logs every 10 minutes.

The backups are stored in read-access geo-redundant storage (RA-GRS) blobs that are replicated. There are two types of backup to consider for your retention policy, "point-in-time" and "long-term retention."

Point-in-time retention takes a database backup automatically every 7 days, so you never have 8 days in this backup life cycle. These backups are automatically deleted.

Long-term backup retention is configured for each customer and supports a retention period of up to 10 years.

Azure VM Backup retention uses the Azure Backup service for all VMs. The VM disks are copied into the Azure Backup vault. Azure recovery points are the same reference as a VM snapshot, and there are many recovery points that may be created per VM, up to 9999. The backup policy is flexible to create a retention period. Figure 7-17 shows the Azure portal to configure VM backup settings. The default setting is to retain the backup for 180 days.

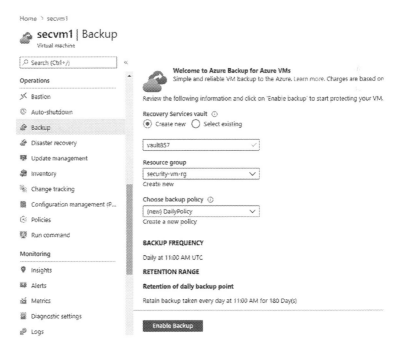

Figure 7-17. *Azure Backup page to configure a backup retention policy*

Azure Monitor Logs include logs (refer to Chapter 4) and performance data when the insight metrics option is selected. The operating system data is collected, and Azure host data is collected. Also, the Log Analytics data collection includes data from Azure tenant services such as Azure Active Directory.

Activity logs written to Log Analytics cannot be modified or deleted for reporting and auditing purposes. The logs are stored event data for 90 days; however, you can set a retention (refer to Figure 7-18) for 30 days up to 2 years.

One of the best practices is to set a retention policy to keep data available for up to 30 days and stream the data into an Azure Event Hub at the same time you write to the Log Analytics workspace. The Event Hub could have a longer retention time and is configured in the same way Monitor Logs are saved into the Log Analytics workspace. Figure 7-18 shows the Data Retention slider from the Usage and estimated cost menu of Log Analytics.

Figure 7-18. *Log Analytics retention slider, 31 days to 720 days*

The Blob storage management life cycle includes multiple tiers – Hot, Cool, and Archive. During the life cycle, it includes immutable storage which allows you to store the business-critical data in write once, read many (WORM). Data can be read but not modified or deleted. The service is available for general-purpose V2 Blob storage in Azure regions. It is normally used to protect critical data, that is, prevent ransomware from modification or deletion. Azure administrators do not have privileges to edit the data.

Blob is immutable storage, and it supports holding data based on two use cases for business. The first use case is "time based" which allows data to be read but not modified or deleted until the retention time expires. The second use case is "legal based" which, without an interval, allows the data to remain read only until the legal hold is cleared. Refer to Figure 7-19.

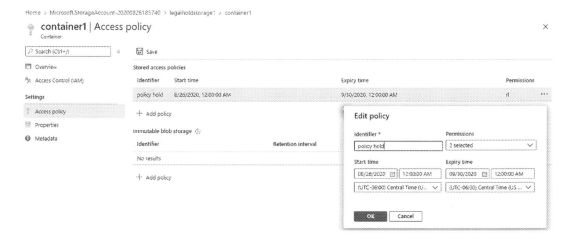

Figure 7-19. *Azure container storage with storage access policy*

Blobs in one or both holding classifications require you to understand a few Azure features. At the end of the holding time or legal hold, data is moved into the WROM state in less than 60 seconds. Blob stays in an immutable state until all legal holds are cleared. Refer to Figure 7-20 for legal holds or time-based hold settings.

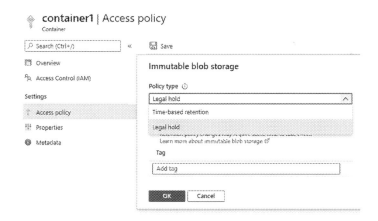

Figure 7-20. *Immutable Blob storage retention options, time-based and legal hold*

Legal holds can remain effective even after the time-based has expired. And if the time-based hold has expired but still has a legal hold in effect, data cannot be deleted.

> **Note**   You can download the Microsoft Cybersecurity Policy Framework at `www.microsoft.com/en-us/cybersecurity/content-hub/Cybersecurity-Policy-Framework`.

Summary

In this chapter, you were introduced to the Azure governance framework model to support your real-world management of an Azure tenant and subscriptions. The use of management groups to support your governance requirements was shared and how it provides a layer above subscriptions and policies.

You learned about Azure policies, built-in and custom, and how you apply them to subscriptions and resources. You learned that Azure policies are from both the Policy page and Security Center. The compliance reports are presented in the Azure Security Center portal and support in improving your Azure security score.

Next was Azure Blueprints, where you learned to combine the Azure policies, the ARM templates, and version control to enable faster and more secure deployment of the infrastructure. Finally, you learned how to set up budget alerts to help projects stay under budget and how Azure data governance is achieved for Azure storage resources.

Index

A

Access Control Lists (ACLs), 24
Active Directory Domain Service
    (AD DS), 213
Active Directory Federation Services
    (ADFS), 13, 14, 16
Advanced Data Security (ADS), 98
    auditing, 101
    authentication, 100
    Azure Security Center, 267
    best practices, 99
    cyber security, 266
    enable, 262–266
    guidance/remediation, 267
    login, 100
    masking policies, 99
Allow/Deny rules, 53
Amazon Web Services (AWS), 256
API security, 6
Application programming
    interface (API), 6, 86
Application Security Group, 60
    TCP/IP, 61–63
    TCP/IP port vulnerability, 65, 66
    web tier, 61
Authentication and Key Attack (AKA), 238
Azure Active Directory (AAD), 3, 8, 16, 85,
    160, 213, 249, 250
    federation, 16, 17
    groups, 9

    non-federation, 17, 18
    users, 8
Azure bastion host, 79, 80
Azure Blueprints, 97
Azure Container Registry (ACR), 217
Azure cost management
    Advisor view, 253
    Azure pricing calculator, 251–253
    budgeting alerts, 251, 254–256
    business deployment, 252
    Cost analysis view, 254
    vCore, 251
Azure data platform
    categories, 113, 114
    logs, 116, 117
    metrics, 118, 119
    services, 113
Azure deployment, 97
Azure Front Door service, 66–69, 71–73
Azure governance
    architecture, 228, 229
    benefits, 228
    Cloud Adoption Framework, 230
    cost, 229
    management groups, 230, 231
        child management group, 233
        creation, 232, 233
        design, 233, 234
        Tenant Root Group, 231
    security team, 228

Printed in the United States
By Bookmasters